GOOD ENOUGH PARENTS

DR. HILI KOHAVI

D1541739

Producer & International Distributor
eBookPro Publishing
www.ebook-pro.com

Good Enough Parents
Dr. Hili Kohavi

Translation: Adi Cafri

Contact: hili.kohavi@013net.net
ISBN 9798848928884

For my parents, with love

GOOD ENOUGH PARENTS

A Practical and Theoretical Guide for Parents of Children of all Ages

DR. HILI KOHAVI

1 PART I
WHERE ARE YOU GOING?
THE GOALS OF PARENTING

Emotional Management

To be "Themselves"

Abilities and Motivation

Raising Human Beings

PART II
2 ENJOYING THE WAY
PLACING OURSELVES AT THE CENTER (TOO)

Being Parents

It Takes a Village

Parental Awareness

3 PART III
MANY DIFFERENT WAYS
PARENTING DURING LIFE'S
SPECIAL CIRCUMSTANCES

4

PART IV
GO SLOW
ADDITIONAL THOUGHTS ON PARENTS & PARENTING

A FEW WORDS BEFORE WE BEGIN—
HOW THIS BOOK CAME TO BE

In the same way children are sometimes "born" before their parents even conceive—through either will or vision—this book came into being long before it was written.

It was "born" on the day I first read the sentence coined by the wonderful British psychiatrist and psychoanalyst John Bowlby: **"Successful parenting is a principle key to the mental health of the next generation."** This quote, which I believe wholeheartedly to be true, sowed the seeds for the writing of this book.

It's been many years that parenting is in the center of most aspects of my life: as a psychologist working therapeutically with parents—in a private clinic and in the public sector; as an academic researcher, studying and teaching the quintessence of parenting; and also, perhaps more than anything else, being a mother of four exceptional children. These past years I have been exposed to many different avenues of knowledge regarding parenting—knowledge based on deep psychological theories, on current research findings, and knowledge that came from practical application through working with parents and teaching parenting in the academia.

This book was created to highlight the parents' part in creating our children's character, in building the person they become. It's true that parenting isn't the be all and end all, and there are many aspects out of our control, but it is still clear that we have a key, irreplaceable role: to raise "human beings." If we adopt Bowlby's way of thinking, parenting is, in fact, an important and valuable role—not only for *our* children, but in many ways, for the well-being of the next generation as a whole.

This book was written out of a deep faith in the power parents hold, in their positive influence, their good intentions, and their willingness to do all that is necessary for their children's ultimate well-being and fundamental functioning in their environments. My professional and personal experience has taught me that parents will do much more for their children than they would do for themselves. That said, however, it's best not to go too far with this. Nowadays, we are aware of the dangers of "over-parenting" and the harm it can cause our children; thus, good parenting should aspire for balance—not too much and not too little. Also, in our endeavor to be good parents, we have to manage to treat ourselves, too. It is important to understand why parenting is so complicated and jarring, and it's no less important to look at our "parental identity" with kind, accepting eyes.

This book is divided into four sections:

PART I **deals with our goals as parents—the goals we have for our children.** In what ways can we help develop our child's self-worth? How can we help them experience our world as a safe place? How can we assist them in being happy, with a solid self-identity and positive social skills? How can we raise children with confidence in their capabilities, ones who possess inner-motivation and positive values? How can we assist them in becoming empathetic to others? Who wouldn't want to raise children like *that*? As I've stated, it's not all up to us, but there are qualities and parental characteristics that can help guide children in these important directions.

PART II **deals with us—the parents.** It deals with the complexities that come with parenting, the fascinating connections found between parenting and happiness (spoiler alert: it's not what you think…) and focuses, too, on the qualities of Mindfulness and self-compassion in parenting. It handles the issue of our ability of being in the "here and now," and how we can be friendlier to ourselves. In addition, there are chapters that deal with those who share the burden with us, since, as per the African proverb: "It takes a village to raise a child," such as the involvement of fathers in their children's upbringing; the place of romance and being a couple; and the relationship between parents and their children's school system. The end of this section concerns the fascinating phenomenon of "intergenerational transmission" and the way in which our childhood experiences may affect our parenting.

PART III

concerns special parenting conditions, such as being parents to adolescents, being divorced parents, parenting in "New Families," and being parents to children with special needs. It's true that each one of these topics can fill their own book, and yet, I hope you will manage to find principles and guidelines that may be of assistance to you. You are welcome to read the chapters or sections relevant to your family, and you are welcome, of course, to read the other chapters in this section, as well. Surprisingly, you may find in these chapters some principles that may be relevant to your family, even if you don't fall under the exact category of the chapter.

PART IV

is intended to broaden our horizons, to look at parenting through a wide-eyed lens. Here you will be able to read about the attributes of parenting in the wild, (surprisingly, we were *not* the first species to "invent" parenting). Another chapter is devoted to the historical development of the concept "parenting" (could you have guessed it was a relatively new concept? You'd be surprised at how looking back historically at questions of parenting can be interesting and relevant to our lives as parents today). In conclusion, I will share my own thoughts and insights regarding children's psychotherapy, and the reason for working therapeutically with parents. These aspects were key elements in the creation of this book.

The book addresses parents—mothers and fathers—of children of any age—toddlers, school-aged children, and adolescents, as well. It's incredible to find how, in many cases, the principles are the same for all ages, and only the handling of them needs to change as per the age group in question.

It is important to state that written insights could never fully encompass the complexities of a singular, unique family. So, I invite you all to read this with a sense of curiosity, openness, and interest, but to still combine it with a healthy amount of parental intuition (which is, as ever, irreplaceable). I hope you all take the ideas, principles, values, and thoughts, in a way that will fit the person you are and develop your own, unique form of parenting. I also invite you all to write to me, to respond, share ideas, thoughts, and ways of action. I promise to update the contents of the book from time to time, so that it aligns with the fascinating occurrences of our world, and the invaluable feedback I will receive from you, the readers.

Sincerely,
Hili Kohavi

1

PART I
WHERE ARE YOU GOING?
THE GOALS OF PARENTING

WHERE ARE YOU GOING?
A PREFACE TO PART I

"May he be exactly like me"

"May she be my exact opposite"

"As long as he is his own man"

"May she be happy"

"May he have good friends"

"May he be a good friend"

"May she honor her parents, and remember who raised her"

"May he become a good parent"

"May she hold solid values, and give back to the community"

"May she possess self-confidence"

"Most importantly, may he feel loved"

When we get into the car, we do not start driving until we know our destination. "Where are you going?" our GPS asks and we reply, set a specific destination, and only then do we begin the journey. That is how we know we're on the right path.

And what about parenting? Have you ever asked yourselves what your goals are as parents? What is, in fact, your role? What would you consider an ultimate success?

Only if we know our destination, can we reach it; can we know that we're headed the right way.

It is true that parenting is more than a mere path, it's a way of life—in many respects, it is the most important and significant path in our life. We are not used to thinking of it in terms of "destinations." However, it is advised to stop and consider for a moment, perhaps even take a pen and paper and write—actually write down—what your goals are as parents. "Where would you like to go?"

To raise "human beings"

If we put aside the question of keeping our children safe and healthy (which are, without a doubt, some of the most important parental goals), it seems that one of our main jobs as parents is raising "human beings."

Picture a newborn baby. In merely a matter of years, that baby will become a person: a person we envision with a positive self-image; one who is capable of feeling a wide range of emotions, and is still emotionally balanced and capable; someone who has a set of core values, who contributes to society, is empathic to others, has social skills and is capable of cooperating with their peers; someone who can have significant relationships; a creative person who thinks, plans, succeeds, and actualizes their talents and capabilities... and what else?

This list can be completed according to your own core values.

Naturally, the values and their given order of importance will differ from parent to parent. Oftentimes we may see values subvert each other, forcing us to adapt or choose, to "recalculate our route." (We are convinced our son will be happy if he goes to a youth group, however, he adamantly refuses; you are avid meat-eaters, but your daughter is hoping to become a vegan. There is no end of possible examples.) Either way, the question arises: how do we do it? How do we raise "human beings?"

A person is created through a multitude of different causes: characteristics we were born with, social influences, people who influenced us through the school system, and additional aspects that are a question of luck and chance. And yet still, you, the parents, have a central and invaluable part of developing your child's person. The process is not instantaneous. A baby cannot become a "person" without mature parental figures who love, nurture, and pass on key principles to them.

How can we assist our children in becoming "human beings?"

Many people in our day and age believe that everything is co-dependent: dependent on context, dependent on relationships, dependent on people. Many people also think there is no "right" or "wrong" in psychology—that everything is relative and ambiguous.

Well, psychology has much to say regarding these subjects—and it says so clearly, loudly, and unapologetically. Today, more than ever before, we know what is considered good parenting.

Good parents love their children and make them feel loved. It has been scientifically proven: love is an essential component.

Good parents look at their children with kind, enthralled, and admiring eyes. This is how we contribute to their own self-worth. The child capable of believing: "I am of worth," receives an excellent and fundamental starting point to life.

Good parents give their children the feeling that our world is a "safe place." That feeling of safety, which children acquire during their earlier years, will continue to positively influence them throughout their entire lives. In an amazing and fascinating way, it is parenting that gives that certain basis for the child's future relationships.

Good parents assist their children by allowing them to grow up in a happy and positive environment, something which highly affects their personal happiness.

Good parents allow their children to be themselves, thus helping them have healthier mental states, and ultimately more contented lives.

Good parents treat their children as individuals with separate wants, thoughts, and feelings. They hold a sincere interest in getting to know who their child truly is. Such treatment is a boon for life, and will, one day, allow your children to become even better parents themselves.

Good parents encourage their children to experience a myriad of experiences and challenges, as befitting their age group, abilities, and interests, and avoid over-protecting them. They set their children realistic goals—not too high, and not too low.

Good parents allow their children to aspire and dream. By so doing, they help the children develop a hope for a bright future, and the ability to aspire and eventually reach their goals and self-potential.

Good parents assist their children in embracing worthy and good values, thus helping them become positive contributors for their surroundings.

The chapters in the first section deal with these key qualities: **love, self-worth, safety, joy, a sense of "true self," self-awareness, empathy, inner motivation, ambitions, social values**, and more. We hold the ability to promote all these attributes, and we wouldn't want to give up on such a chance.

Does it sound stressful? Obligating? Well, this is the place to say that most parents do their parental duties naturally and intuitively, even without reading about such things in books. Furthermore, let's not forget that there isn't a parent who is perfect—**but nor do our children** need **perfect parents**. They need *real* parents, who are, at times, overworked, tired, or can't find the patience to listen to their children even for a minute. We're all like that, and that's okay—it's reasonable and, most importantly, human.

So, please, don't be alarmed, and don't overload yourselves with needless guilt. Guilt never helps anyone. Curiosity and openness, on the other hand, are highly valuable, so reading and giving parenting and our children extra thought, can most certainly be beneficial in helping us navigate our family in the directions we care to. In addition, thinking and reading about our parenting can help strengthen our intuitions that guide us throughout our daily lives, and give our parenting skills some additional support.

But before we set our parental goals and begin on our "journey"—let's remember that we are also allowed to have fun. Parenting is a lifetime job; it is complicated and comprehensive. There are times that with the sheer number of responsibilities and chores, we forget that it's also meant to be one of the most rewarding and fun jobs in the world. One of the goals in this book is to help us put ourselves in the limelight and remember that we deserve to enjoy the journey; to enjoy parenting, our children, and the key role we play in their lives.

So, where are you heading?

Let's get on the road.

CHAPTER 1

LOVE IS THE BASIS
On the immense importance of parental love

> *"A baby can be fed without love, but loveless or impersonal management cannot succeed in producing a new autonomous human child."*
>
> —D. W. Winnicott

Europe, 1945. The Hungarian researcher **René Spitz** takes upon himself a thoroughly ambitious task. Over numerous years, he follows the development of dozens of babies orphaned due to the Second World War. These orphaned babies lived in relatively good conditions at their set institutions—they had shelter, a clean bed, medical care in reasonably hygienic settings, and, of course, proper food and drink. They were only missing one thing: they didn't receive *love*. The babies didn't have a single, constant adult who was in charge of their care. Their treatment, instead, was passed on from one person to another, one matron, to the next. All personnel were dedicated to their work, but there was no consistency, there were no personal attachments; there was no love.

Spitz's research findings are depicted in heart-wrenching video footage he filmed by himself (▸ available on YouTube: Rene Spitz, Hospitalism). The discoveries were dramatic: not even one of the orphan babies succeeded to thrive. The lack in parental care brought on *irreversible* developmental deficiencies. One third of the babies died before they reached their second birthday, while the others showed a startling decline regarding developmental milestones. Numerous babies were physically stunted, while others had various disabilities; some became blind, others couldn't walk or talk—but not one of them grew to be a healthy, functioning child.

There was only one scenario where the baby reverted back to a healthy development pattern, and that was when the baby's mother returned to their life in between three and five months; otherwise the damages to the children became permanent and irreversible.

Spitz's research was among the first evidential-based findings that proved that parental love is essential for children's development. For our mere existence—during the formative infancy years, and for much longer after—we need at least one figure in our lives who loves us: an older, stable, parental figure, whose presence is consistent and long-lasting; someone who will watch us with awe and give us proper care.

Today, there is no doubt about it: parental love is not a privilege. Parental love supplies the emotional fuel for babies to become whole, healthy human beings.

The secret of parental love

Spitz's research vastly changed the treatment policy regarding infants staying in institutions. However, besides the extreme and difficult conditions such as the ones depicted in Spitz's research, his work also poses the ultimate question—*what happens in normal, healthy, natural situations?* What is the secret ingredient that parents supply their children with, that allows them to develop, and to eventually grow from helpless babies to wonderful little humans? What are the crucial elements of parental love?

The answers to these fundamental questions will be explained in the following chapters. Nowadays, we know so much about the qualities of parental love; knowledge which is truly accessible and easy to implement.

In the beginning of their lives, we supply our children with "glasses," through which they experience the world. We assist them with regulating their emotions, create order in the overwhelming chaos that surrounds them, and help them process sensory experiences: *"It's hot!"*, *"That tastes good!"*, "You're tired…", "Are you in *pain?*"

As their life progresses, we have an on-going key role: we supply the building stones for the development of our children's self-perception; we help them attribute themselves in a positive, bettering light. We also assist them in creating a healthy self-image with which they go out into the world, allowing them to cope successfully with life's challenges. At the same time, our parenting is what shapes our children's perceptions regarding interpersonal relations: are relationships with others a safe, enjoyable experience, or is it a source of anxiety and insecurity?

As I've previously stated, most of the time we do these parental tasks naturally, and without specifically naming them. Still, a deeper understanding of these different aspects and terms can allow us to be more conscious of our actions and to give them the right amount of balance (not too little and not too much).

So, yes, it is true that parenting is not everything, but in those first formative years, and in the many years after, we, the parents, have a central role in assisting our children to become happy, well-balanced, social, and mentally-sound individuals. There is no greater mission than that. After all, the children of today are the adults of tomorrow; or, in the words of the British poet William of Wordsworth: "*The child is father of the man.*" The effort we put forth for our children, is the foundation and fuel they receive for their adulthood; it is what influences their future adult selves.

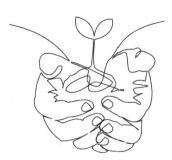

THE BOTTOM LINE

The grim reality forged in Europe in the wake of the Second World War allowed researcher Rene Spitz to follow the development of orphaned children. Those babies, despite having all basic physical needs met, didn't have a stable, permanent, and loving adult presence in their lives. The research proved that not one of those babies grew to be a healthy, functioning child.

Spitz's breakthrough research was the first to attempt a deeper understanding regarding the components of the normal, healthy, and natural parental love. Today it is clear that parental love allows for an essential basis for children's development. That same parental love allows for them to grow into healthy adults—ones who are healthy both in mind and body.

CHAPTER 2

I CAN SEE IT IN YOUR EYES
The importance of parental enthusiasm for children's self-worth

> "*Every day, Adam's mother tells him he is the best-looking, smartest boy in the world. But at pre-school, he finds out that other children do some things better than him.*"
>
> An excerpt from "*Mama's Best Boy*," by **Zeruya Shalev**

Who's Mommy's little genius?

In the book, "*Mama's Best Boy*" quoted above, the author touches on a question that bothers many parents: "*Is it right to tell our child that they are the* best?" The smartest, the most beautiful, the most wonderful, the most talented? Sooner or later, they will go out into the world, and find it all to be mostly inaccurate. After all, there will always be another child who is smarter, more beautiful, more talented. So, what should we do?

Adam's mother has no qualms or hesitations regarding her answer. In the book, Adam tells her that she probably needs glasses, because she obviously can't see well. She gives him all these compliments and doesn't seem to notice that there are children who are more handsome, smarter, and stronger than he is. She, in response, says, "*Each child is the most beautiful child in the world, and also the most talented, and the best at everything else—in their mothers' eyes.*"

I agree with her and base my agreement on one of the most salient theories in the psychology of parenting: *Self Psychology*, as was coined by the psychoanalyst **Heinz Kohut.**

Healthy narcissism—wrap it up to go, please

We've all come to think of narcissism as a disorder. We all feel resistance when meeting someone who is inherently in love with themselves; someone who is constantly busy with embellishing their accomplishments and incredible qualities.

The roots of the *narcissistic personality disorder* come from Greek mythology. The young, handsome Narcissus broke the hearts of all the women who met him, while treating them all with arrogance and disrespect. The Goddess Nemesis, as punishment for Narcissus's actions, cursed him with boundless self-love. When Narcissus was thirsty and bent to the river to drink, he caught his reflection and fell so deeply in love with his image, that from that moment on, did nothing but stare at himself. Eventually, he died of thirst and hunger.

It's no wonder people who are highly narcissistic tend to create a mixture of disgust and pity within us. Therefore, Kohut's idea of there being a *healthy* dose of narcissism was inherently novel. To understand the concept of healthy narcissism, and the reason we need and want to develop it in our children, we must first go back to infancy.

Mirror-mirror on the wall, tell me: who am I? What is my value?

When we want to know what we look like—we turn to a mirror. How simple. Some mirrors are flattering, while others distort our image—familiar with the occurrence?

When a baby is born, we, the parents, are their mirror. Through our eyes, our children discover themselves: Are they good and wonderful? Are they the children we dreamed of having? Or are they a disappointment? Do they worry us and make us sad? The way we look at them turns into the way they eventually look and think about themselves. And how does that happen?

Infants and younger children still lack a coherent sense of self. They derive information from the outside world in order to understand their very being. Parents are the main source through which the child learns about themselves: who am I? What am I worth? In Kohut's terminology, the parents serve as the babies' *selfobjects* (yes, written as one word). These *selfobjects* are in between area of "Other," and "Myself." Those same inner-outer characters help children feel their self-worthiness; they are who create their self-value.

Thus, when we look at our children with excitement and enthusiasm, they can see it in our eyes. Just like with a flattering mirror image, they learn about themselves through our eyes, and know that they are good and wonderful. However, when parents look at their children with disappointment, when their expressions are full of worry, the child learns that they are a source of worry, of disappointment, perhaps even unworthy of love.

Such a situation may arise when a child is born with special needs or with an atypical appearance; conditions that no one had hoped or planned for (▶ see Chapter 28). It can even happen with families who had a boy rather than the hoped-for girl, or vice versa. And what about children who display characteristics the parents don't necessarily like? Such as children who are exceptionally active, or perhaps too quiet? Or possibly that parental disappointment may come because our children have qualities that remind us too much of unwanted parts of ourselves? And still, worry-filled eyes or expressions of disappointment can vastly harm our children's developing sense of self. You should make the upmost effort to make sure this does not happen. Allow me to explain.

You're a wonder! There's no one else like you in the whole world!

> *"Behind each child who believes in himself, there is a parent who believed in him first."*
>
> **—Matthew Jacobson**

The way we look at our children begins to affect their self-worth as early as their first months of life, and, in many ways, this process never stops. In each of life's stages, children learn their value by looking in their parents' eyes. It's true that as we grow, some people, other than our parents, may serve as our *selfobjects* (people such as teachers, friends, and our life partners); yet still, our parents' position remains crucial. This is why it's so important to be aware of the way we look at our children. When we reflect awe and kindness, we help contribute to their own belief that they are good, wonderful, and worthy. This is the *healthy narcissism*, and it's one of the most important qualities we hold.

As opposed to the narcissistic *disorder* mentioned earlier in this chapter, it's the *healthy* narcissism that helps people believe in themselves: to believe in their talents and capabilities. The healthy narcissism helps us be on good terms with ourselves rather than constantly at inner war with ourselves (► see Chapter 20, concerning self-compassion). Today, we know that people whose parents looked at them with awe and admiration in their formative years, tend to develop healthy narcissism; as such, these people need and look for less outside affirmation. Their self-worthiness is well-established and consistent.

However, it's important to say that every person has a certain need for outside affirmation. It's a natural and normal process of life. Yet still, parental love helps create positive self-worthiness in children and adolescents, thus giving them one of life's most significant gifts: the belief in their own abilities, and healthy self-love.

Our children need our parental perspective: the importance of parents' emotional expressiveness

The importance of positive parental glances for children's development isn't a mere theoretical idea—it's scientifically proven. In a series of fascinating research, the American psychologist **Edward Tronick** proved the essential role of parents' emotional expressiveness. Tronick filmed one-on-one interactions between parents and their babies. In each interaction, the parent, naturally, expresses a wealth of emotion toward their baby, to which the baby, in turn, reacts with much joy. At some point, the parent is asked to turn their head for a moment, and then look back at their child with a "frozen," expressionless look on their face. The video footage caught the babies' reaction to the shift in the parental expressiveness.

It's fascinating to see: the babies, whose parents' faces remain expressionless, react with shock, which quickly deteriorates to severe agitation. They try to catch the parent's attention, to "bring back" the missing emotional expression, and once they don't succeed, they all begin to cry (▶ watch this yourself, search for "Still Face" on YouTube). At the final stage of the experiment (which only lasts for a short few minutes) the parent returns to a normal, natural emotional expression. The babies quickly calm once the parents return to normal, and fast "recover" from the situation.

If you ask how research such as this can be relevant to our own daily lives with our children—take note of the following experiment. An American researcher named **Patricia K. Kuhl** conducted a variation on Tronick's classic experiment. In her research, the parental "freeze expression" was achieved through the parents' focusing on their cell phones—something which happens often during our daily lives. Kuhl checked the babies' neurological reactions to such "disconnected" communication. The results showed the babies' clear discomfort and agitation, due to the unexpected "disappearance" of the parent.

Now, at this point, it's important to state that as long as these "disconnections" are short-lived—there is no expected damage. "Disappearances" such as those are normal and an inseparable part of our daily routine. Yet still, Tronick's and Kuhl's research proves how important our **emotional presence** is in our children's lives. Most of us are emotionally present—naturally and intuitively. However, there are certain situations in which children may suffer from a continual lack of parental emotional expression. This can happen, for instance, if one of the parents suffers from depression—whether it's postpartum depression, or a different kind all together. Situations like these can be harmful, even if the children are incapable of saying exactly where the deficiency lies. If you are suffering from such a condition, do not hesitate to seek professional help. And as an additional note, it's best to make sure that the screens don't take up too much of our attention, especially not while we're with our children. We'd best learn to put the screens aside once in a while; to put the cell phones on silent mode and allow ourselves to be fully present with our children.

Regarding children, tokens, and Phillip's screwdrivers

You may read these lines and end up asking yourselves: *and what if my child has genuine difficulties? All her classmates may already be reading, and she still can't recognize all the letters; all the boys are already dating, and he's not even beginning to look interested; her friends have all started working as babysitters, yet she's still afraid of being home alone.* Should we be in "awe" of them during such times, too? What exactly should we be doing when we are in such awe? What kind of distorted messaging are we giving our children…?

Well, let's start by saying that even with children who struggle, they, too, need their parents' admiration. They probably need it even more than the children for whom things are easy. These children especially need to be "filled" with their parents' pride, sense of capability, and self-value.

The American educator **Richard Lavoie** made a movie which is truly inspiring: "When the Chips are Down" (find it on YouTube). The movie specifically addresses the issue of children with learning disabilities, but its teachings can be attributed to any difficulty or disorder children may experience. Lavoie assumes that all children function with the perception that they either may "win game tokens" or have them taken away. It's similar to grown ups' bank accounts: deposits and expenses; gains and losses. It's the reason children for whom everything is "easy," can afford answering a difficult question a teacher posed. The worst outcome would be that they get the answer wrong, and even so, they still have plenty of game tokens. "Nothing happened"— such children have a surplus of confidence that allows them to make mistakes. Conversely, a child who suffers from significant difficulties (learning disabilities, social exclusion, or any other problems) may start the day with a diminished amount of game tokens. Such a child wouldn't "risk" answering a teacher's tough question, since if they are wrong—if they get laughed at, mocked—they would lose their *precious few* tokens. The risk is simply too high.

Here is our job as parents: we must boost the amount of our children's game tokens. We must allow them to leave the house every morning, with as many tokens as they can possibly have.

The approbation we feel toward our children, the positive reinforcements we give them, are what replenish their game tokens. But be aware: in order to supply them with their stock of tokens, your admiration must be genuine. So, if our child suffers from marked disabilities, we must help find their strong point—those good qualities and talents—and praise their commitment and efforts. It's there we must give them an abundance of positive reinforcements. Moreover, as parents, we have the ability to "summon" events for our children that will create reason for enthusiasm and awe. We have the ability to put them in situations where they can demonstrate their capabilities. "If your child has a talent for using a Phillip's screwdriver," Lavoie says. "Loosen all the screws in your house and give your child the opportunity to tighten them." Meaning, create opportunities for your child to demonstrate their talents, and be suitably impressed by them. It's the best way to increase our child's self-esteem. (▶ see Chapter 15, regarding dealing with children who have difficulties).

I love you simply for being you—and not because you're perfect

If we return to Shalev's story, the protagonist, Adam, cannot understand how it's possible that his mother thinks he's the tallest, most handsome, and smartest, while there are clearly other children who are taller, more handsome, and smarter than him. And so, the truth of the matter is that parental wonderment is a sensitive task, it is both complicated and elusive.

Moreover, our main job is to look positively at our children for their wondrous beings, and not because they're perfect or follow certain criteria. In other words, we must try to view our children "as they are," all their characteristics included—good ones and not quite as good. However, looking at them favorably does not merely mean complimenting our children's certain talents or passing on a message of them being "perfect." (*"You're such a talented painter;" "You're the smartest boy in your class;" "My child is a-l-w-a-y-s good,"* etc.). When we peg our children with a specific label—even if it's a positive one—we might end up creating anxiety regarding our expectations ("What if I don't win the school's painting competition?", "What if I'm not picked for student council?", "What if I can't get a high enough grade on my final?"). Yet still, when we see our children "as they are" and look at them with kind, impressed eyes that are filled with wonderment, we promote the growing basis for a positive self-image—one that isn't dependent on outside achievements or fulfilling certain conditions (*"Sadly, I lost the election for the children's council, but I know my parents are proud of me for* trying *and the effort I put into it.* I'll try again next year."*).

In order to help our children believe that we truly don't expect them to be "perfect," it's important for us to show them our own weaknesses and imperfections ("What kind of mother am I—I have no idea how to make meatballs...", "I had such an awful day at work today—nothing went according to plan. Never mind, tomorrow is a new day."). Taking our own weaknesses with a dose of humor, in a way that shows both self-compassion and camaraderie, allows for us to show our children that we are *good* parents—but not near perfect ones.

And when they inevitably disappoint us?

Let's be honest: it's impossible to raise children with constant enthusiasm. They can be extraordinarily annoying at times. And we're human, too. There are times when they cross that proverbial red line, and it's impossible *not* to get angry with them, perhaps even punish them. It's all true. But we must make sure we're doing it with respect to the child, and not out of disregard. We cannot come from a position that expresses despair, disappointment, or cutting criticism (*"This boy—he's such a failure... where did we go wrong?"*). Alternatively, we must try to discipline them through a position that expresses our appreciation and true willingness to educate our child, and to give them the values we see as most important.

Assume, for example, that you found out that your beloved child stole a pack of gum from the local corner store, or perhaps that they were in a violent altercation at school. And yet, even in such complicated situations, it's better to address the problematic occurrence as an opportunity to educate and pass along our messages and values, and not as a "severe tear" in our relationship with our child—or worse: with our child's personality ("We've raised a criminal," or "juvenile delinquent"). In other words, even when your child disappoints you and acts out, treat them with respect and do not insult them. These reactions will allow your child to eventually learn from their mistake, apologize, and move on, without irreparably harming their own self-image. Such actions will also allow you to *gain* from these unpleasant situations, and also raises the possibility of positive lesson-learning abilities later in life (▶ see too Chapter 7, that deals with regulating emotions and Chapter 16, which deals with setting boundaries).

The way we think of them becomes the way they think about themselves

Our children grow up and slowly develop their own behavioral characteristics and attributes. It often occurs that parents have certain criticisms regarding personality traits they find in their children (*"She's lazy;" "He's fat—he constantly neglects his body and health;" "She's self-centered—she doesn't care about anyone other than herself;" "He is dreadfully lacking in any form of curiosity about the world;" "She's stingy and possessive—how is it that her friends can forgive her?"*).

It seems that just as we can be our own worst critics, so, too, can we become our children's. After all, you would never dream of allowing *someone else* to talk about them similarly (*"Lazy," "Fat," "Egotistical," "Cheap."*).

However, just as parental *positive* veneration can help children grow and develop, harsh criticism serves a destructive force. It's important for us to be aware that the thoughts we have regarding our children, over time, become the way they think about themselves. Do you really want to raise children who think themselves to be "lazy," "self-centered," "lacking in curiosity," or "fat and neglectful of their own body?"

Instead, when you find characteristics in your child that you disapprove of or find behavioral patterns that will eventually do them no good, take it as a parental task: soften those characteristics and guide them to a more helpful direction. But do it with the upmost respect for your child and avoid hurting them. You can encourage your child to be more physically active, more curious, get them more interested in the people who surround them, be more generous and flexible with their thoughts—all such things are worthy goals. However, it's best to try and achieve such attributes without hurting your children's feelings, insulting them, or labeling them in negative ways. So, rather than criticizing the negative *characteristic*, it's best to encourage positive *behavior*—emphasize and "label" them when they pop up.

In order to succeed in doing this, try to look for an opportunity: a moment during which your child, who usually tends to be rather self-centered, shows interest in others; a moment when your stubborn daughter shows some flexibility and willingness to concede; a moment when your son, who is extremely possessive, is generous with his baby sister. When you spot such moments, label them, call them out (*"What a wonderfully generous thing you just did!"*, *"Well done on being so flexible and giving in!"*). Show your appreciation for such positive behaviors, even if they are minor. Your enthusiasm is what will create more positive moments and set the direction you aim for.

THE BOTTOM LINE

Children learn much about themselves through the ways their parents treat them. Your thoughts about them and the way you treat your children are central sources of information for them; through which they eventually build their own self-worth. There is nothing more important for children than possessing a positive self-worth. That positive image is what they later take with them once they go out into the world. This is true for every child, and it has special importance regarding children and adolescents who suffer from difficulties.

Give your children the clear message that they are loved simply for being "themselves," and not for following specific conditions. Even if it's inescapable and you must get angry with your children and discipline them, it is still essential to keep their positive outlook. Only in such a manner will you manage to transfer the important messages you wish to impart.

Remember that our thoughts regarding our children are the cornerstones for their own self-image. As parents, we hold a huge amount of power—we should use it in kind and beneficial ways.

CHAPTER 3

A PLACE IN THE WORLD
Raising children who believe the world is a secure place

Safety, trust, peace of mind, calm, the joy of intimacy, good companionship, the ability to receive help and to lean on others, the ability to function independently—who wouldn't want to raise children with these qualities? Who doesn't want to be such an adult?

Apparently, these qualities are achieved, largely, through the relationship between children and their parents. The relationship we develop with our children, quite amazingly, is the model upon which they build their conceptions regarding key matters, such as: trust, security, relationships, and intimacy. This fundamental model is likely to continue to be a part of their lives for many more years, perhaps even a lifetime.

The secret magic of parenting

Today we know that our parenting is what plants the seeds regarding our children's main perceptions of the world. The quality of the relationship parents form with their children influences children's perceptions regarding topics such as: how good and secure the world is; whether interpersonal relationships are a source of pleasure and joy, or alternatively a source of anxiety and fear; how safe it is to develop a sense of independence and try new experiences, and when they do pull away—will they have a place to return to.

This process is well explained through the **Attachment Theory**, which is considered today as the most highly researched and evidence-based theory in psychology (► for additional information, see framed text on page 57). This theory has much to say regarding our children's emotional needs, and how we can assist them to perceive the world as a good and safe place.

Our children need "emotional refueling"

Can you remember a point when your cell phone died and you didn't have a charger at hand? What did that make you feel? Stressed, irritated, restless…? And what about when the fuel light blinked on in your car, forcing you to drive long minutes on fumes, all while telling yourself that next time you'll make sure to refuel well before, so you wouldn't find yourself in such a situation again?

When our phone's battery is low, or when the fuel light is on—we feel limited, we feel constrained. Alternatively, when our phone's battery is at 100 percent or when the car fuel tank is full, we feel as though the whole world is at our fingertips. We can do anything we please.

The Attachment Theory refers to our powerful need for a **secure base**, or "*refueling station*:" emotional refueling that would supply energy for all our actions and activities. Parents are the ones who supply their children with that same secure base. We are the fueling station. We are the charger.

Life, as we all know, is full of things we have to handle: our children wake up each morning to a world full of challenges. They deal with numerous fronts at once: social, academic, emotional; countless happenings on a daily basis. Through our safe, empowering presence, and by merely loving them, we supply our children with energy to deal with all their life tasks. Just as the cell phone charger allows us to function a whole day without hassle, so does the emotional refueling we supply our children with: it lets them go out into the world, prepared to take life's challenges head on.

Our children need that secure base. The better we refuel them emotionally, the freer and more confident in themselves they will feel. Nurturing, supportive, and stable parenting allows for children to be more curious, to try new things, to learn, and to have fun. It's true for the toddler who enters daycare for the first time, and it's also true for that nineteen-year-olds who'd just left home to study at a far-away college. The principles are the same—only the distance changes.

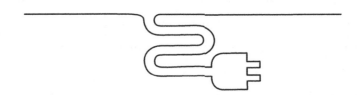

Our children also need us as a "safe haven"

Once we have moved away—it's crucial for us to have somewhere to return to. If you look at a baby who has just started crawling, you'll probably notice how eagerly they leave their parents' sides, drunk on the sheer joy at their new ability—their newly-found freedom; but they still only go so far. At some point they will notice their parents at a distance, and then quickly crawl back to them. They'll cuddle up for a moment, receive the needed confidence, then will go right back to crawling.

Similarly to the crawling baby, our children—no matter their age—need us as a **safe haven**, or a *docking station*; they need somewhere they can return to after they've drawn away, a place they can pause, rest, refill, and get that needed security and confidence, before they go back out into the world anew.

It seems as though there is no age that's considered as "too old" to need that parental hug. As with the "secure base" that allows the children to distance themselves from their parents, our being a "*safe haven*" permits them to return when they need emotional refueling. Such back and forth—leaving the parental "secure base" toward the outside world, and the returning to the parental "safe haven"—allows for the creation of "*the circle of security*" (▶ see image). The "secure base" gives our children the opportunity to distance themselves, and learn and experience new things, while the "safe haven" is what allows them to return and feel that we're always "there" for them.

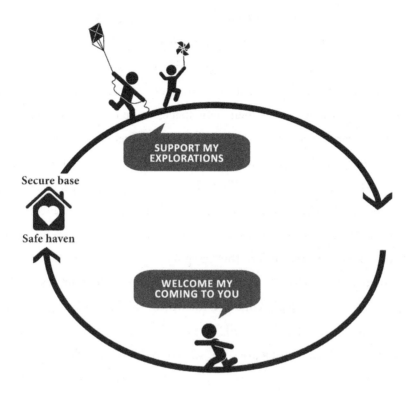

Per: © Cooper, Hoffman & Powell, 2019. Circle of Security International

The "glasses" through which children see the world

And why is attachment between parents and their children so important?

Beyond the cohesive "emotional fueling" we supply our children, it's apparent that the way we treat them during their formative childhood years is what highly affects their "glasses." Those "glasses" continue to be the tool through which they see the world. In professional jargon, it refers to the *attachment pattern* the children develop: *secure* attachment, versus *insecure* attachments.

"If I'm crying—is there someone to come and comfort me?", "If I'm afraid—is

there anyone to keep me safe and ease my worries?" and *"Is it safe to go a little farther away from Mom or Dad and discover new things?"*

The answers to these questions highly affect the attachment pattern our children eventually develop. Parents who are regularly well-tuned to their children—encourage them to find their own space, while comforting them when needed. These parents help their children to develop a secure attachment toward them. It is those children who believe that the world is a good and safe place. They tend to be happy and independent; they are open for trying a wide array of new experiences; they're curious about the world around them, and still capable of leaning on their parents when they encounter difficulties or are in distress. Fortunately, most children fit into this category.

This process is essential, since the secure attachment pattern acts as a self-fulfilling prophecy. The child goes out into the world with "optimistic glasses," and that positive world view they received from home usually proves itself in all their relationships "outside." Thus, a positive, self-strengthening cycle is built.

On the other hand, there are sometimes parents who are distant and disconnected from their children—physically and emotionally; parents who routinely evoke feelings of terror and fear within their children; or alternatively parents who can't stand any form of separation from their children and tend not to see them as individuals. In such cases, the children are susceptible to developing a pattern of *insecure attachment*. These children may go out into the world wearing "tough" or "pessimistic glasses," ones that will prove to them, over and over again, that the world is a cruel, unfair, dangerous place. This negative starting point—built in the household—may also act as a self-fulfilling prophecy, thus creating a vicious circle which escalates and worsens the situation "outside."

Research findings confirm that the initial attachment patterns developed toward one's parents tend to consistently characterize the children later in their lives. These patterns can predict much from child behaviors—while in daycare, at school, and even as adults. Sounds obligating? Well, it is. Psychology, in this instance, leaves no room for doubt: one of our life's missions is to raise children who believe that the world is a good, safe place. But how do we do it?

The ability to "be with"—the value of being present

Many psychological theories deal with the question of how to raise confident children, ones who believe that the world is good and safe, and who see relationships with others as a source of joy and pleasure. Surprisingly, the answer is rather simple. According to the American psychologist **Daniel Stern**, this process happens mainly due to the parents' ability *"to be with their children."* In other words: it is our daily parental presence in our children's lives which positively affects their feeling of safety and security.

But what is such presence? The American psychiatrist, **Daniel Siegel** expands on Stern's ideas, claiming that such parental presence is achieved through our ability to turn our full attention "to the present moment" when we're with our child: to listen to them, take an interest in them, to calm them when needed, to play with them sometimes, and to treat them with interest and care. Siegel states that parents can help their children grow into calm, confident people thanks to these four *"S Qualities:"*

- **Safe**—the child's ability to feel safe.
- **Seen**—the child's sense of feeling important, that there are those who see them as they truly are.
- **Soothed**—the child's knowledge that there are those who comfort and calm them when needed.
- **Secure**—the child's sense of the world being a safe place, somewhere where they can "feel at home." This feeling is achieved through a combination of all three other "S Qualities."

However, be aware that we are not supposed to be present in our children's life in every situation. Alternatively, when we *are* staying with them, it's important we attempt to be *emotionally* present, too: through listening to them attentively, and calming them when they need it. And if we failed in being present—for whatever reason—we'd better try to correct our failing (*"I'm sorry, I wasn't quite here for a moment. My thoughts drifted me away. Tell me again what happened at school,"* or: *"I'm sorry I yelled at you, I didn't mean to. I was worried about something else"*).

And yet, another important note to stress here is that when dealing with "parental presence," it's important not to overdo it. Being *emotionally* present doesn't mean over-involvement or overdone parental interfering. See ahead.

"Helicopter parenting" and "snowplow" parents—and all the good intentions therein

Psychological theories sometimes have a life of their own. It happens when an important and central psychological theory gets a misleading or incorrect analysis—analyses that can lead to wrong parental behaviors. And it's all done with good intentions. It seems that a misunderstanding of the Attachment Theory brought on the common phenomenon of "**helicopter parenting**."

The term *helicopter parenting* was coined by the American journalist **Hara Estroff Marano,** and it depicts a trend where parents constantly hover around their children—closely, like a rescue helicopter—simply waiting for the time when their child might need assistance or suffer some kind of hardship. That moment can pop up when our son is at the playground and another boy refuses to play with him; or when the teacher gives our daughter a low grade on her test; or even when our college-age child has a problem with their college roommate. When these "helicopter parents" notice such a moment—they are instantly poised to help, to save their child from the situation, to *fix* it all.

Lately, another term was added, describing an even more extreme parenting style—the "**snowplow**" parents. While the helicopter parents hover from above, poised and ready for any issue that may arise, the "*snowplow*" parents walk *ahead* of their child, diverting any conflict or problem that may pop up—well before they happen.

However, both parental patterns *weaken* our children, rather than strengthen them. They harm the children because they interfere with the child's ability to build independence. Research has actually shown that there is a connection between such parenting methods and higher levels of depression and anxiety in children. It's very well possible that your daughter's teacher made a mistake while marking her test, or that their roommate did indeed behave badly. Things like that happen, though. That's life. Children grow and develop when given the chance to handle the challenges life hands them—on their own. So, unless we truly feel like a red line has been crossed (for example, when it's a matter of safety, or when the child, objectively, cannot defend themselves), we must do our best to allow our children to handle the different hurdles by themselves. That independence will only benefit them. Sometimes they will manage to fix their problems by themselves—but not always—and that's all right, too.

"Dependency" isn't a bad word— Bowlby's fascinating social perspective

The Attachment Theory was first formulated by the British psychiatrist and psychoanalyst **John Bowlby**. The theory is based on the assumption that we are born with an innate need to form emotional bonds with our parents. The emotional availability of parents toward their children, and the relationship built between them, plant the seeds of the feelings of security the children develop in the world. It is our parents who teach us the benefit of relationships with others, and that is an important and fascinating process. It's not only humans who are disposed to building emotional connections with their parents. Many animal species—including birds and mammals—are equipped with this same internal system that connects offspring with their parents.

In an incredible and especially interesting manner, John Bowlby's personal life story was imbued with many attachment issues and separation from parental figures. Bowlby was born and raised in London. His father was a surgeon at the royal court, and thus was absent more often than not. Bowlby's mother believed, as many women of her age and social class did, that parental love and coddling can lead to dangerous spoiling of children, and so she met her children for no longer than an hour a day "during teatime." Bowlby received plenty of love and affection from his governess, who raised him and took excellent care of him during his infancy. However, once he reached the age of four, the governess had to leave the family, and Bowlby took the separation hard. When he was seven, he and his older brother were sent to a boarding school, a difficult milestone that affected his life harshly. When Bowlby was seventeen, his parents believed he was destined to be a mariner, but he wrote to them that he planned on finding work that will positively influence the whole of humanity. Today it's clear that he indeed succeeded in that mission.

In his later writings, Bowlby gave his clear and decisive opinion regarding the society we live in. It's an utterly fascinating read. He references the negative connotation our society has toward the word "dependency." According to him, we've become a society that values *independence* above all else: independence, individualism, the ability to cope on your own, to stand on your own two feet. We attribute "dependency" and "coddling" as problems that have to be treated and solved. However, dependency, needing someone, and emotional closeness—are all things that create the emotional foundation for the rest of our lives. When it comes down to it, it is actually the dependency, the need for others, and the ability we have to lean on them, which will allow a healthy mental development; it will allow us to grow, and eventually also find independence.

Fortunately, unlike the norms generally accepted during Bowlby's time, parents in our day and age are no longer fearful of loving their children. Yet still, Bowlby's social critique is very much relevant in today's day and age, perhaps even more than ever before. As a society, we have a lot to learn from his words: about the importance of parenting, and regarding the emotional bonds between children and their parents.

It's not always easy to establish a secure attachment

I've put much emphasis on the parental characteristics that can help develop a secure attachment pattern with our children: emotional presence, stability, the ability to "be with" them. In addition to these important *parental* qualities, the *child's characteristics* also have an impact on the pattern of attachment the child develops. If you have more than one child, you probably know that children can be fundamentally different one from another. There are children who are harder to handle: children who cry a lot, children whose emotions are hard to regulate, ones who are difficult to calm, or others who are extremely shy. Any of these traits sound familiar? Highly sensitive or "complicated" children can pose challenges for any parent: affect our parental enjoyment and impair our sense of parental efficacy. It's not easy being parents to "difficult children." These children, due to their challenging characters, sometimes experience less attentiveness, and less presence from their parents.

A similar experience can arise when a child with special needs is born, or perhaps when the parents themselves are suffering a rough patch due to their own personal reasons—grief in the family, financial troubles, social isolation, postpartum depression, or difficulties which are related to the parent's own tough childhood experiences (▶ see Chapter 24, regarding intergenerational transmissions).

If you feel like *being with your children* is difficult for you—for any reason—don't merely accept the situation at hand. Try and find the right sources to assist and support you: take advice, understand from where the difficulty stemmed, try and handle it satisfactorily. Parents who manage to be emotionally present in their children's daily lives—those who listen to their children, hold them, understand their disappointments, give comfort, and show awe at their being—these parents up the possibility of giving their children the gift of secure attachments.

Even if it's not always easy—most of the time it is possible.

At this point, I'd like to add a few more calming words: it's true that it's advised and encouraged to do everything possible to help raise securely attached children. However, if you feel as if your child has developed something different to that, it is not the "end of the world." If you're fully aware of the situation, if you can pick apart the components of your parenting that may have contributed to it, it's highly possible you can improve their attachment patterns. For example, you can be more physically and emotionally present in your children's lives (▶ see too the practical list of advice in the latter part of this chapter). When parents change the way they deal with their children, when they become more attentive and calm in their presence—the children can change and improve their own attachment patterns toward their parents, allowing them to develop a basic trust in their parents and the world around them.

So, practically, what can we do?

- **Remember that our main job as parents is "to be there" for our children, and to supply them with a secure base**—a "fueling station" from which they can leave, and a "safe harbor" where they can return and receive additional protection and security.

- To achieve this, **play with your children, laugh with them, listen and take an interest in their lives, allow them to take interest in your own lives, and do fun activities with them**. The ability of "being with" your children is one of the most important foundations for raising children with secure attachment capabilities. However, this must be done naturally, in a measured and non-exaggerated manner.

- Occasionally, **insecure attachment patterns of the parents themselves, created during their own childhoods, infiltrate to the relationships they**

develop with their children. It happens, for example, when a parent asks their child for incessant affirmations of love. This is unhealthy, and it's advised to avoid such a situation. It's true that every parent wishes for their children to love them. Assuming you are "good enough parents," you can be assured that your children do, indeed, love you. They aren't required to prove their love and calm your insecurities, if they exist, in this matter.

- **Another problematic pattern arises with parents who "cut themselves off" from their children.** There is no doubt that boundaries are essential in raising children, and it's allowed to get angry with them when needed, but there is no point with completely "cutting off" your children when tempers are raised (*"If you don't stop screaming—I'm leaving home / I won't talk to you for the whole day."*). Such parental behaviors can be harmful. If you tend to do so, try and figure out from where it stems. This may be a behavioral pattern you experienced *yourself* as a child. Either way, it's best to try and change this pattern, and avoid repeating it. In no instance, and under no circumstances, should a parent threaten to "cut off" their child.

- If you're parents to infants, remember that this isn't the time to take a long trip without them. **It's during the beginning of your children's lives that there is a serious importance for continual, consistent parental presence.**

- During your child's life, and the older they get, **we have to find the balance between their need for closeness, of warmth and security, and their need for independence.** This is no easy task, since the balance point constantly changes. It can seem as though we've finally reached the right point, and in a blink, our children grow, and their need for independence changes and evolves. *It was only yesterday when we taught him how to cross the road on his own, and now he wants to take the bus with his friends to the beach.* Is that reasonable? Logical? Age appropriate? It's not always clear. However, we cannot escape it: we have to learn to let go, to trust them, to believe in their abilities and encourage their growing independence. At the same time, we still have to "be there" for them, to create an open dialogue, and refuel them emotionally when needed.

- **If you're parents to older children, don't be helicopter parents, or "snowplow" parents.** Your children do not need you to occupy such roles. Allow your children to handle their own tasks and challenges—as per their age and abilities, of course.

- In fact, **as our children grow, we have to become a "waiting station."** Just as with the fueling station or the cell phone charger analogy, we are not supposed to run after them, we aren't supposed to refill them when their battery is already full. We shouldn't preserve their dependency on us, but neither should we push them to independence that doesn't fit their age, abilities, or circumstances. Rather, we should simply be present—a stable, loving, attentive presence, that is ready for the moment when they need us.

- In addition to all that was previously said, it's best not to get confused: **children of all ages need our awe-filled eyes, our love, and our emotional support.** The love for our children, the safety, and stability we give them—those are the most important gifts we can pass on, both when they are young, and when they are grown up.

THE BOTTOM LINE

As parents, we supply our children with two basic needs which are similar and complimentary: we provide a "secure base" for them, a place from where they can go out and experience the world, and we also serve as a "safe harbor"—a stable place which welcomes them and allows them their needed emotional refueling. Our physical and emotional availability toward our children plants the seeds for their basic trust regarding the world around them. This basic trust continues to be a part of them throughout their lives, influencing their relationships. Thus, possessing secure attachment capabilities is truly one of the most important gifts parents can give their children.

That secure attachment pattern develops mainly due to our ability to "be with" our children, to be present in their lives, as per their needs: not too little, not too much.

CHAPTER 4

CREATING CHILDHOOD MEMORIES
The importance of a positive atmosphere while raising children

"People will forget your words, will forget your actions, but people will never forget the way you made them feel."

—Maya Angelo

Allow me to open with two memories from my own childhood:

I was probably a child of about seven, staying at my grandmother's house. There was a program on television that taught children arts and crafts. The intro was of a fast-forwarded masterpiece: a simple piece of paper that transformed through quick, sharp origami folds into a beautiful crane. My grandmother was incredibly talented when it came to arts and crafts. I asked her to make me a crane like the one on the TV, but she said she couldn't, that she had no idea how to. I was furious at her. I must have kicked the living room table, for, a split second later, a priceless crystal vase that had been set on it fell and smashed into smithereens. My grandmother was struck speechless. There were no bounds for the feelings of guilt and shame that rushed through me.

In another image locked into my memory—a year or two after the fact—while playing with one of my friends, a new television remote fell, broke, and stopped working. At the time, remote controls were considered a wonder—rare and costly wonders. Again, I was consumed by guilt. My mother suggested we put a Band-Aid on the remote. She went to the medicine cabinet and pulled out a few Band-Aids, then together we stuck them on the remote, and—wonder of wonders—it worked once more. I distinctly remember the feeling of relief and the sincere gratitude toward my mother.

Here I should point out that, generally, I wasn't a destructive child. Still, or, perhaps because of that fact, those two events are etched into my mind. They are small scenes from everyday life. These two seemingly minor, insignificant occurrences remain a part of me—most likely due to the heightened *emotional turmoil* that came with them.

…and what do *you* remember from your childhood?

What will your *children* remember in twenty or thirty years?

Fascinatingly and rather incomprehensibly, it's our daily lives with our children—our emotional responses toward them and the atmosphere present at home—that is the key element in creating their future memories. However, living our lives while constantly thinking about what and how our children will remember things, is impossible. But still, it's good to reflect on it from time to time.

Emotional climate—because the atmosphere is what counts

Imagine yourselves taking a trip to the other side of the planet—or perhaps to the nearest park. It's likely that what will determine your enjoyment will largely fall on the weather conditions. Not for nothing the first thing we ask when talking to a friend who is travelling is "How is the weather?" We all know that having pleasant, warm weather can, oftentimes, hold a lot more significance to the outcome of a trip than the actual destination.

Outside weather determines the general atmosphere—in trips and, so too, at home when regarding our parenting. Children are highly affected by the "weather;" from their emotional surroundings, perhaps even more so than anything else. Positive experiences in their youth create steady building blocks for a stable, optimistic, and calm personality when they grow older. Who doesn't want to raise such children? Though it is true that no child grows up in a completely stress-free environment that lacks in any strife, arguments, or upheavals, it's still one of our parental responsibilities to ensure that the positive feelings and experiences outweigh the anger, arguments, and contention.

Emotions are contagious and immortalized

Feelings tend to be contagious. Such a statement is usually referred to when talking about "negative" emotions. When a loved one is angry at us, we instantly "catch" the anger, and send it right back. It's not easy to stay calm when someone criticizes us or shows their disappointment in us, and it's just as hard not to send such feelings back at them. However, such "catching" tendencies should also be used for *positive* aspects. If we can create a happy, pleasant, and playful environment, a safe place where one can express oneself freely, find humor, and be creative—it's highly likely that our children will "catch" such feelings.

In order to do so, try and find the things that create a joyful and positive atmosphere in your home. Music, for example, creates a happy and calming environment. Think how easy it could be to add music into your daily routine: while cleaning up, making dinner, during bath time… so, rather than berate your children for not cleaning up their room or not taking a shower when asked, try and have them clean the room—or shower, for that matter—while listening to a song they like. Challenge them to finish the chore by the end of the song. Make the chore a fun game (▶ see Chapter 13, regarding the "Tom Sawyer effect").

A positive and happy environment may also be created by eating together around one table, while eliminating all screen / technological distractions. While sharing a meal, it's advised to have a conversation as each family member in turn shares a positive, fun experience from their day. *What did I enjoy today?* Such a conversation holds much value, from many different angles. First, it helps you remain up-to-date regarding each family member's day and activities, (it is vital for our children to realize that we do, indeed, have a life apart from being their parents). Secondly, such conversations allow for your children to develop better listening skills and a higher sense of empathy toward others' experiences. And, above all else, when we share positive experiences from our day, we let such events take up a more significant space in our consciousness, something which helps elevate our mood. Furthermore, positive reflection regarding the day's occurrences helps us create and "tag" such events in the future (▶ reference Chapter 8, regarding the key element of "being thankful").

Each of these points has a neurological explanation, too. When we laugh, or when we are calm and happy—our brains release endorphins. When we have positive interactions with people we love, our brains release the "love hormone," oxytocin. Both the oxytocin and the endorphins contribute significantly to our feelings of enjoyment, of our *joie de vivre*, and our wanting to spend more time with the people we love. Thus, a certain positive circuitous is created, strengthening itself: good experiences create more good experiences. As I stated beforehand—feelings are "catching." Moreover, it is apparent that feelings tend to imprint themselves, so the positive feelings in the present lead to positive feelings in the future. Joy, love, and curiosity today increase the chances of joy, love, and curiosity tomorrow and for the rest of your life.

The brain's negativity bias

Recalling positive experiences from of our daily life can sometimes be a challenging task, and we have to put effort toward it. The reason for this difficulty is related to a profound survival mechanism named *the negativity bias of the brain*. This neurological mechanism amplifies and directs us to recall *negative* and *unpleasant events*, rather than those positive ones. Evolutionarily speaking, negative experiences have a greater weight for our survival. If there is a tiger in the woods—it is imperative for us to remember it and be on constant alert, so we can better protect ourselves. Millions of years of evolution targeted the point of us remembering the tiger rather than the pretty birds and butterflies.

However, today, we are aware of how crucial those same "birds" and "butterflies" are for our mental health and well-being. And so, in order to overcome our negativity bias, encourage your children to retell the positive—the good—aspects of their days; train their brains to pay more attention to them and enjoy their existence. Similarly, you should do the same for yourselves. Pay more notice to the positive experiences throughout the day, then share them with your family. You all can only benefit from doing so.

The magic in the simple moments

One of the most complicated challenges of parenting is related to a lack of *time*, a lack of joint time between parents and their children. It is most likely the constant stress and time deficiency that brought on the term "quality time"—as though we can compensate for the lack of time with our children, by spending *quality* time with them. I disagree with this presumption. Firstly, let's remember that "time" is measured by "quantity" and not by "quality." Secondly, I'm sure that you'll agree that the term "quality time" brings a certain weightiness to it; it attracts feelings of parental guilt such as, "*I wish I was more like that mother, who constantly takes her children to the movies and sporting events...*"

However, when researching the question of the most significant time spent between parents and their children, it's discovered that such moments happen during the everyday life—in the simple daily moments. It appears as though these small moments, the ones that consist of daily routines, may in fact hold the most significant value to our children and the bond we share with them. This can manifest through an easy conversation while folding the laundry, while shopping together at the supermarket, and even while taking a short drive together. Such moments can be priceless if we merely let them occur, and then explicitly put weight to them and catalogue them: "*I loved our conversation from this afternoon. I was so happy you shared what was going on at school and with your friends.*"

In addition, rather than sink into fierce guilt over not managing to create "quality time" with our children, the simplest way to spend that coveted time with them, is to have them join in activities we enjoy doing ourselves. If you enjoy taking walks in nature—take your children out for trips; if you enjoy baking—have them join in; if you like playing football—play it with them; and if you decided to stay home and watch a football game on TV—invite them to watch with you. When we truly enjoy ourselves, rather than force ourselves to do that "quality" time and activities with our children, they can feel our joy and interest, "catch it" from us, so everyone wins in the end.

In other words, *shared time* with our children is essential; children indeed need our consistent presence. However, if we truly think about our best moments with them, we'll probably find that the "quality" of these moments isn't determined by the act itself or the effort we put into bringing it about. Instead, it's our *emotional presence* that matters: the conversation, the act of listening, and the ultimate connection forged between us and our children. As I said before—the magic of the simple moments.

The special value of one-on-one experiences

When we check what people remember from their childhood, we find that many of us remember moments of one-on-one with our parents—without our siblings nearby. This is a key distinction. And why is this so?

In our daily lives, oftentimes when children spend time with their siblings, they are put into certain categories that don't necessarily reflect their true selves (or who they wish to be): "the stubborn one," "the competitive child," and even "the easy one." However, when we spend time one-on-one with our children, we allow them to be nothing other than themselves, free of whatever role they'd been pushed into. That is a very significant experience.

It's true that following this advice isn't easy. Our lives are exceptionally busy, so there is nothing more natural than doing activities together with the whole family (a normal occurrence, and a perfectly acceptable one, too). Yet still, there are times when our daily circumstances create possibilities that allow us to be alone with one of our children (for example, when other children are invited over for play dates, or when they go to after-school activities). At times we can *create* such opportunities (*"Who wants to come with me to run some errands?"*, *"Who wants to go for a short walk around the neighborhood?"*). In this context, too, it is less about *what* you do with your child, but rather the importance lies with merely being together.

When such occurrences present themselves, it's worth pointing out the significance of them—both to ourselves and to our children. "*I had so much fun being only with you for that short time,*" "*I loved spending time with you today—you're such a wonderful, curious child.*" Additionally, with the importance of one-on-one time, it's also central to have activities with only some of the family: "Boys only," "girls only," "the older ones," "those who love basketball"). Each different grouping allows for additional types of dynamics and experiences—experiences that allow them to find changeable niches within the family unit, which is a wonderful thing.

One-thousand children give advice for good parenting

And what more should be meaningful from our children's point of view?

Erin Kurt, a teacher and family coach from Canada, conducted a very interesting project. Every year, around the time of Mother's Day, Kurt would ask her students to write a list of advice on "how to be a good mother." She specifically asked them what they enjoyed doing with their parents. The project itself continued for seventeen years, and included the five different countries where she taught, thus eventually she accumulated "advice" from over 1000 school-students.

Interestingly, though the children were of different backgrounds, ethnicities, and cultures, many of them shared similar experiences and advice. Apart from that one-on-one time I've mentioned, the children mainly listed small, everyday moments: "*I like when my mother reads me a bedtime story,*" "*I like it when my dad tucks me in,*" "*I love listening to funny stories from when my parents were young,*" "*I like being able to snuggle with my mom and dad and watch television together,*" "*I love having Mom and Dad talk to me and take an interest in me.*" Additionally, the children mentioned how much they enjoy being able to play— "just because"—and lastly, you might be surprised to hear, that the children like it when parents make sure they eat healthy food, and they're glad about having boundaries. So, yes, even if in that one specific moment they seem annoyed at not being able to eat that extra bit of candy, or your teenager complains about an early curfew, in the end, children know to appreciate such things. They also remember it fondly.

THE BOTTOM LINE

Just as with the weather outside, a positive emotional home environment creates a *favorable emotional climate* which benefits the children's development, and their positive childhood memories. Though raising children without anger or stress is quite impossible, we should still try to make sure the positive aspects and experiences outweigh the unpleasant ones. We can create such positive experiences in our day-to-day lives with our children, through routine activities we enjoy doing, those one-on-one moments, and by giving room for creativity and playfulness. When we enjoy the time spent with our kids, they feel the same way, and a positive cycle of emotions is formed—a process which strengthens itself, thus ensuring everyone enjoys the benefits it creates.

CHAPTER 5

IT'S CHILD'S PLAY!
Playing and having fun as an integral part of parenting and child development

> "*We don't stop playing because we grow old, we grow old because we stop playing.*"
>
> **—George Bernard Shaw**

Has reading up to this point given you the impression that parenting is a *serious* deal?

All right, then, forget about that! Well, not entirely... but a little... still... smile... roll on the floor laughing... have a pillow fight with your children... jump on the bed with them... horse around on the playground together... splash them in the bathtub... (or at the very least—don't interrupt while they do all these things on their own).

Let's admit it—most of the time we want our children to be proficient: to get organized, to hurry up, to study, and do what they "have to." However, among all such important, necessary daily tasks, it's essential for us to remember that playing and having fun contribute monumentally to our children's emotional, mental, and social development. And yes, you are reading that correctly: playing, laughing, and experiencing a happy home environment—are all more important for our children's development than many other skillsets and areas of knowledge.

And if you're supposing that this chapter that deals with playing and having fun is aimed primarily at parents of *younger* children, then, once again, you are mistaken. This chapter is for *everyone*: for parents of school children, for parents of teenagers, and even for us, adults—since with regard to playing, humans are forever "young at heart." We can enjoy and benefit from playing throughout our whole life.

So, let's take a peek into this fascinating, magical world, and find out what exactly are the special qualities of playing that make it so essential and significant for us all.

A special space between reality and imagination

Watch your children while they play. Notice how seriously they take it; how devoted they are to playing; look at the pleasure they get from it.

Playing, in its nature, happens in a special space—a space fitted between reality and imagination, between our inner world and the "normal" outside world. Differently from our daily, routine tasks, which necessitate us to be on point, efficient, and driven, playing has rules of its own. While we play, we suspend, at least for a little while, the rules of reality, and walk into a special kind of atmosphere: one which promotes enjoyment, creativity, and fun.

Playing also generates the feeling of being able to create our own worlds; nothing is impossible. Playing can take many forms, fitting into the children's age group, personality, and personal preferences: imaginative playing, board games, or sports—all manners of playing hold their own different qualities.

Imaginative play: experiencing new identities

When your child finds a broomstick and starts riding it, in a split second, they become whoever they want to be (or perhaps the character they are most afraid of). Imaginative playing allows children to explore different identities, adopt characteristics and traits that are far from their own, invent new usages for the objects around them, and create—for that little while—a completely *fictional reality*. All these qualities nurture creativity and curiosity and promote humor and enjoyment. The imaginative free-playing allows children to process the concepts they are most concerned about: the things that scare them, wonderings, fantasies, or their wishes. When the imaginative play is shared with others (friends, siblings, or even with you, the parents), it allows for an excellent training ground for interpersonal relationships. It provides a space where we can look at situations from different points of view, establish empathy, closeness, and friendship, and also deal with feelings of jealousy and competitiveness.

So, even when your children's imaginative playing creates a huge amount of noise and mess in your home, try to take a deep breath before you think about stopping them (and sending them to cool off in front of the television). Remember that creativity and playfulness are some of the most important and most magical elements for your children's emotional and social development.

Board games: sometimes you win, sometimes you lose

"Monopoly," "Scrabble," "Battleship," "Connect Four," and so many more. In addition to symbolic, fantasy, and imaginative playing, your children can benefit much from playing board and card games, as well. These games, being more structured, contribute greatly to the child's ability to follow rules, wait their turn, delay gratification, win, and also—lose (!).

Here it's important to note: there are children, and parents, who do *everything* to avoid playing games where there are clear winners and losers. These children feel as though they "have to always win," and thus, tend to avoid situations that can culminate in losing. This phenomenon seems to have been exacerbated these past few years. However, *losing* is an essential and inseparable part of playing (and of life itself). Children who refuse to lose, are most often in a state of avoidance and anxiety over new experiences. It's so incredibly important for children to learn to deal with states of failure. Moreover, the winner-loser games allow us to view situations from different perspectives: *when I win, someone else loses,* and vice versa. This is a key lesson to learn.

Sport games: all the benefits in one place

"To grow up healthy, children need to sit less and play more," so states an up-to-date report of the World Health Organization.

Soccer, basketball, tennis, table tennis, bowling, dodgeball, catch, and so many more—the possibilities are plentiful, and so each child can find the kind of sport games or movement activities that suit them best. The most important thing is not to give up on sports as being a part of the child's routine.

Similarly to board games, sport games also train us in how to win, lose, and play by the rules. To all this, though, there is the added value of physical activity, and all the benefits that come with it. Nowadays, there is no doubt regarding the great contribution physical activities and sports have on our health—both physical and mental. In addition, competitive sport games help establish a positive self-image for the child. It helps develop their social skills, their sense of belonging within a team, and evokes a sense of joy and fun. Moreover, when we immerse ourselves in a heated sport game, the whole world can seem to "fall away." This creates a fantastic mental break. And so, sports truly have all the benefits in one "basket."

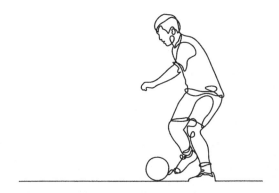

Computer games—and here the party ends...

If you've read the chapter up until now, and thought with a relieved sigh—"*Well, that's wonderful, because my child doesn't stop* playing *on the computer or the phone,*" I'm sorry to disappoint you. Differently from all the other sorts of playing and games, most of the "screen games" (on the computer, phone, tablet, or other) aren't truly playful at all. Many of these games are fast-paced, with a very high stimulation rate, and also include violent and aggressive content.

Research-based evidence indicates that the parts of the brain most active while children play computer games, are the parts responsible for survival: *fight, flight,* or *freeze,* certainly *not* the areas responsible for playing, imagination, and creativity. Some computer games even cause a heightened production of cortisol, the hormone released while under stress and pressure. When this hormone is released for a long period of time, it can harm the brain's development. Additionally, we also know that computer games include elements that can cause actual addiction. This makes them highly problematic, and even dangerous.

One of the basic characteristics of addiction is the need of upping the stimulus in order for the person to get that desired feeling. So it happens that children whose main reality is a "virtual reality" find it harder to enjoy and to be satisfied and interested in the "normal," regular reality.

In other words, the problems that lie in computer games are twofold: not only are they lacking the qualities of playfulness, but they also tend to overtake the child's free time, thus, harming the children's natural playing abilities. Moreover, differently from actual games that naturally *better* the children's moods, recent research states that many of the "screen games" are linked to negative moods in children. And so, if we want our children to be able to truly play, we have to *lessen* their screen time, and *not* view computer games as true games (▶ for additional information, see the next chapter that deals with screens).

It is never too late, nor are you ever too old, to play

"It is in playing and only in playing that the individual child or adult is able to be creative and to use the whole personality, and it is only in being creative that the individual discovers the self."

—D. W. Winnicott.

These wonderful words were said by the great psychoanalyst **D. W. Winnicott**. He was the one to illustrate the magnitude of importance playing has for our mental development—for both children and adults. Winnicott treats the aspect of playing and playfulness in a broad way, and includes within it the worlds of creativity and creative activities. Anything a person does for the sake of pleasure—meaning not for a set, outside goal (painting, sculpting, playing a musical instrument, listening to music, watching movies, playing a sport, baking, etc.)—can be deemed playful and creative. And creativity is, in fact, the true meaning of being human, and the ultimate source of happiness.

Winnicott emphasizes that there is no "finishing line" for playing and creativity—there is no age when it is considered "too late" or inappropriate to keep doing so. Thus, it's important to develop playing and creativity at any age, as an inseparable part of our lives. While *children* play with different objects and games, *adults* "play" around, most often, with ideas and thoughts: we invent, create, we imagine. Even when we allow ourselves to be immersed in a particularly good book, or when we watch a thrilling movie, when we play an instrument, listen to music, or create something—we are in the element of "playing;" an "in between" area, where the lines of imaginary and reality are blurred. In other words, any artistic expression holds the element of playing and creativity, and it greatly contributes to our mental health, no matter our age. It's never too late.

How can we support our children's playing experience?

First and foremost—do not interrupt them

Children, by nature, want to play, and do so at almost every opportunity. We don't have to teach them how to play; there's no need to guide them or instruct them; we don't need to buy any special instruments, or even put aside special time for it. Very simply—if we don't *disturb* them, children will play. By the way, new findings from the neuroscience division, found "playing systems" which are implemented in us, neurologically and genetically. We are born with an inner need to play, and there are certain tracks in our brains that guide us in that direction. It's no wonder that many animal species play, too. Additionally, we also know that while playing, our brain secretes certain chemical materials—endorphins and dopamine, specifically—that are natural pleasure-inducers. They protect us from pain, contribute to our overall joy, and even help boost our immune system.

When this magic comes to pass, when children dive into the realms of play, we should try and hold back any kind of judgment ("*It's a shame you're not using your time well,*" or "*A ten-year-old girl shouldn't still be playing with dolls*"—which, incidentally, you'd be surprised to hear that is entirely incorrect…). Additionally, try not to be too stressed about the noise and mess the playing creates—after all, there's no better sound than children playing and enjoying themselves.

Create a safe space for them and allow them some free time

For children to play, they have to feel safe and protected. A child who feels threatened, cannot play. They simply don't have the availability for it. If your home is unsafe—it will be a place they find difficult to play in; if the atmosphere in the house is severely tense—children will find it hard to create playtime; so too, if your child will be "swamped" with different demands (*"I told you to tidy up your room!"*)—they won't manage to be immersed in play.

Children who "rush" from one activity to another—aren't available for playing

After-school classes and activities have many advantages. They expose the children to new hobbies and interests; sometimes they also allow children to bond with more children outside of their familiar social circles—and that's great. However, it's important not to overdo it. Children who don't have free time because they go from one after-school activity to another, lose out on the value of playing—the spontaneous play and ability to simply "be" without any clear goal.

"In every adult, a child remains:" play with them!

It's not only children who enjoy playing. We love playing, too. After all, the child we once were still remains a part of us, no matter our age. It's true that we don't always have the time, and it's true, too, that our children will also play without us. But the benefits of parents and their children playing together is indescribable—no matter the child's age (or the parents'). Joint playtime creates a special bond between parents and their children. It allows for a different form of communication, shared pleasure, and the pricelessness of simply being together while being truly present. By the way—*grandparents* can also be excellent partners in play with their children-grandkids.

In order to achieve this, find the kinds of games that are right for you—ones which you enjoy playing, too, and play together with your children from time to time. This can be any kind of sport, it can be a board game (one which you enjoyed when you yourself were a child), and it can be, quite simply, doing funny faces in front of the mirror. Play with your children as if you were one, too—suspend reality for a while, put aside your cell phone (!), dive into the realm of special games together with your child: a realm full of imagination, laughter, fun, and sometimes battles and competitions, wins and losses. All this has a tremendous value for you, for your children, and for the connection between you both, as well.

Give your child the chance to... ~~win~~ lose!

Have you gotten used to playing with your children and always letting them *beat* you (*"Because that is what adults are supposed to do"*)? Well, starting from a certain age (usually the age of six or seven), there is great value in allowing your child the chance to *lose* every once in a while. Children fear the mere notion of losing—sometimes to the point where they avoid playing all together. This, however, is a mistake. Games with a winner or loser create an excellent opportunity to express the pleasure of simply playing together, and the fact that the final outcome is not the most important part. Sometimes you win, and sometimes you lose. That's simply the way it is, and the way it's supposed to be.

This principle, by the way, is also relevant to the times when children and teenagers consider applying for a position in the students' council, in a youth group, or in a high-school delegation; even while "gambling" whether or not to ask out that girl who's in their math class. It's only those children who are willing to take that risk of losing (or getting a negative answer)—who will actually try. Remember there is a value to any and all such experiences, even if the *outcome* isn't the one hoped for. The *way* is sometimes more important than the end result.

Incorporate playful atmosphere in your daily lives with your children

In the previous chapter, I stated that the atmosphere in the house is what counts. An American psychologist and researcher named **Barbara Fredrickson** claims that there is a special value to positive experiences while raising children, at a ratio of at least one to three; meaning, for every negative interaction in the house (i.e., anger, stress, fights), it's important to have at least *three* positive interactions (laughter, fun, hugs, compliments, astoundment, positive reinforcements, and moments of fun). Although the research findings are divided in regard to the exact ratio of 1 to 3, everyone still agrees that plenty of positive experiences and a good atmosphere in the house promotes good mental health and happiness in children, and greatly contributes to the foundation of their self-worth.

All these good outcomes are essentially in your hands. To promote them, combine playful atmospheres in your everyday lives. Almost each routine, dull action (a shower, tidying up the room, putting the dishes away, a long drive) can become fun and enjoyable if we simply treat it as such. Differently from mutual structural games, playfulness doesn't require us to put special time aside. If we simply direct ourselves to do so, we can combine playfulness in our routine lives with our children, and thus make our lives happier and better.

THE BOTTOM LINE

Playing, playfulness, and creativity are among the key activities for our children's mental health, but so is true for teenagers and adults, too. It's never "too late" to play. Playing allows for the creation of a special link between reality and imagination—a space where new worlds can be created, and joyfulness and vitality can be promoted.

Children benefit greatly from imaginative play, board games, and sports. However, most all computer games do not necessarily promote playfulness and creativity, and may, in actual fact, be dangerous due to their violent and harmful content. Such games also hold an element of addiction, and tend to eat up all the children's free time.

As parents, it's essential we don't disturb our children's playtime. We can also benefit much from playing together with our children, and from creating a playful, enjoyable atmosphere in our daily lives with them.

CHAPTER 6

BRING ME BACK MY CHILD!
Raising happy children in the age of screens

> *"We shape our tools, and thereafter our tools shape us."*
>
> —**Marshall McLuhan**

Raising happy children during the age of screens? What are the connections between children's happiness and screens?

Well, you may be surprised to hear—there is most definitely a connection, and it's an *inverse* connection. Evidence-based research findings prove that screens *harm* our children's happiness. The more screen time—the less happy the child.

To be honest, it might have been better to write this chapter in invisible ink, one that disappears and allows for you to rewrite everything again; to change it all, update it, delete some, fix other bits. Otherwise how can you write about parenting in the age of screens? Each attempt to focus on current technological processes, might, in the blink of an eye, read as outdated. There's no way to see the future; what seems today as nothing but "science fiction," can fast become the near future—and then soon become the present. It all happens so fast.

And still, I will try. I'll attempt to focus on parenting in the age of screens, be-cause not everything is changing so incredibly fast. Indeed, technology evolves in dizzying speeds, but what doesn't change so fast are the fundamental human principles that stand as a basis for all humanity. Child development and the evolvement of parenting are achievements humans have cultivated throughout millions of years of evolution. So, does screen technology *support* these evolu-tionary achievements, or may it instead *threaten* them? And what will be the long-term consequences of the screens interfering in our lives? As of today, it's hard to say.

The screen technology is still young, and so we are still lacking research find-ings regarding its long-term effects. However, one thing is certain, and that will act as our starting point: the screens are here, and they're here to stay. Moreover, there's no doubt that the screen technology has countless advantages: unlimited knowledge at a mere touch of our fingertip, being exposed to wonderful cultural assets (such as every song and poem ever written), accessible connections with people from all over the world, being able to stay in contact with childhood friends, the fantastic and incredible solutions the screens give to people with disabilities, and much more. And if anyone somehow still had doubts regard-ing their necessity, the COVID-19 pandemic and subsequent worldwide lock-downs—forcing us to stay home and social distance—emphasized and magni-fied the screens' doubtful importance. It's through the screens that we managed to keep continual communication with our loved ones; through the screens we managed to keep a semblance of normality—all without leaving the house. But, with the many and varied positive attributes, there are still quite a few disadvan-tages to screens that we should definitely be aware of. In this chapter I will draw on some principles that will help us—the parents—adequately use the screens, enjoy their advantages, and minimize the damage they can cause.

Some proportions

"The children now love luxury; they have bad manners, contempt for authority; they show disrespect for elders, and love chatter in place of exercise. Children are now tyrants, not the servants of their households. They no longer rise when elders enter the room. They contradict their parents, chatter before company, gobble up dainties at the table, cross their legs, and tyrannize their teachers."

Can you guess who wrote these words, and when they were written?

Well, these words were written by Socrates, in the year 450 BC (!).

So, yes, some proportions wouldn't hurt. It seems like every generation is convinced that the newer one is headed toward "ruination" and going down "dangerous paths." But should the proportions exonerate us from dealing with the influence screens have on our children? Surely not. As I've stated, life in the age of screens has numerous characteristics that should disturb us—or at the very least, aspects we should be well aware exist.

When do they start, and what does it substitute

According to the American Internet Association, more than a third of babies in the United States have a "smart device"—before they can even walk or talk! Today, it is hardly rare to see babies sit and eat while watching YouTube videos (*"Because they eat so much better this way"*); infants who have yet to gain their balance while walking, toddle along with a screen in their hands (*"God forbid they get bored at some point"*); families have family dinners while they watch funny videos on their phones (*"Because it keeps the peace and prevents fighting"*). The screens are all around us, all the time, and everywhere. *All the time. Everywhere.*

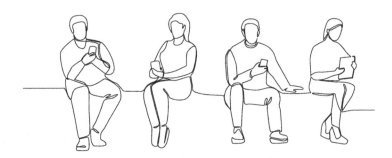

And why is this so problematic?

Because a family dinner is a wonderful opportunity to better our children's communication and social skills: sharing the experiences from our day, listening to others talk, showing interest, knowing what the other family members do throughout their day. And if it "costs" us having to listen to fights over our pasta plates... well, remember that the good outweighs the bad, and that a family quarrel is also an important form of communication through which children learn a lot.

And what about children who eat in front of the screen? This situation causes them to lose their feeling of hunger and fullness; it cancels out the experience of tastes and smells that accompany eating. Their attention is elsewhere—and they don't even realize what they're eating. Babies and toddlers who sit and eat in front of a screen lose the important chance of pleasant, fun human interaction with those who are feeding them or eating with them. "Is it good, darling?", "Do you want some more?" And in the case of older children, eating in front of the screen is terribly unhealthy and can lead, among other things, to obesity.

These subjects are relevant to everyone—even to us, the adults—though, that said, they could have special and particular meaning for our children. Our children have been born into the age of screen technology, and have never known a reality different and apart from it. I've stated before that it is difficult to tell what long-lasting influences these processes will have on their communication skills, their happiness levels, and their brain development. However, most professionals tend to agree that it's best to *postpone* the age that children are exposed to screens—at least as much as possible. Simultaneously, it's key not to give up on exposing the children to the *real world* and its many wonders: the physical ones (*"It's so much fun to walk on the beach barefoot!"*), the humane ones, and the social ones. What a wonderful world we live in.

Can we be bored for a while, please?

In the past years, the concept of boredom being an enemy infiltrated our lives and our children's lives (*"Mommy, I'm bo-o-ored!"*). Once upon a time we could have sat in a café, waiting for a friend to arrive, all while looking around us, staring into space, daydreaming, and... being bored. Today, being bored is no longer possible. That small screen we always have on hand is willing and capable of filling our time with any such content. Every minute is used to its fullest. There is no break. However, it's important to note that boredom may lead to magnificent outcomes.

The psychoanalyst **D. W. Winnicott** attributed the "**ability of being alone**" as one of the most important qualities for keeping a healthy mental state. Recent research in neuroscience proves how right Winnicott was. Nowadays we know that when we are alone, resting, bored, "doing nothing at all," our brain activates a nervous system named the "*default mode network.*" This system is responsible for the brain's "maintenance" through daydreaming, our imagination, our ability to ponder and reflect. This brain activity is involved in creative discoveries, and it is, in fact, one of the signs for good mental health.

And this is exactly the explanation for why boredom and "doing nothing" are such wonderful, irreplaceable inner resources of creativity and imagination. The screens threaten to take these precious moments away from us—and away from our children, too. So, next time your children yell out, *"Mom, Dad, I'm bored!"* tell yourselves—*"Excellent, let them be bored for a while... only good things can come from that..."* and don't be tempted to find a quick solution to magic the boredom away.

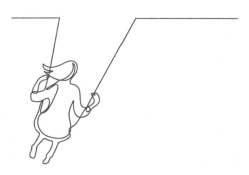

More screens—less parents

Let's admit it, one of the greatest problems regarding parents' handling of their children's screen time, is related to the fact that the screens pose an available and easy solution for us: they give us some quiet and are excellent "babysitters" for our kids. With very little effort, they can become "substitute parents" for our children, whether it's when we return tired and late from work, if we're busy with something around the house, if we're waiting to see the doctor, or if we simply need a break. But what are the consequences of doing this? In many disturbing and fundamental ways, it seems as if the screens compete with our parental resources and weaken them, too.

For example, it's easier to sit a child down in front of a pre-recorded story on the tablet than to read them an actual book. The electronic story is more available, more convenient, saves us time, and can spare us the arguments that sometimes come with reading an actual book (*"Daddy, only one more, ple-e-ease!"*). On the whole, it seems as though it's exactly the same story, and *"What could it possibly matter?"* But it's apparent that these are two very different activities, and there's no doubt which one is best. Listening to a *real* book contributes greatly to the child's development—their linguistic skills, their comprehension, their imaginative and emotional development, and even their emotional regulation. On the other hand, listing to an *electronic* story doesn't necessarily hold any of these advantages (▶ for additional information, see the framed text, on the next page).

And what about when it's regarding older children—ones who no longer remember that once upon a time you used to read them bedtime stories? Many of these children have become, in recent years, heavy screen users. If they aren't limited, their screen time can reach up to five or six hours a day—perhaps even more. And what problem does this pose?

Think of all the activities you do with your children on a daily basis: you listen to them, hug them, get mad at them, comfort them, make them meals, play with them, make sure they are ready for the next school day, even remind them to take the dog out for a walk. However, when our child is in front of the screen for so many hours of the day—they get much less of that. In other words: children who spend hours each day in front of the screen, receive fewer parental resources. Additionally, they also do less sports, hang out less with friends, and their inter-personal communication lessens. This isn't good. Not at all.

INTERESTING TO NOTE

Real books versus electronic stories—what happens in our children's brains?

Findings from brain imaging research (fMRIs) show that while children are listening to a storybook read to them by their parents, the children's brains activate many different nervous systems: systems in charge of understanding language, systems that show the use of imagination, systems connected with understanding emotional situations, and many more. These nervous systems all act simultaneously, and with complete synchronicity—like an orchestra playing a wonderful musical piece in perfect harmony. This brain activity contributes to the executive functions of the child, which is one of the most important resources for the regulation and proper functioning in our daily lives.

However, watching electronic stories through screens stimulates the children's brain in a completely different way. It activates areas in the brain that are in charge of simple, immediate attention. All the neural activity previously mentioned isn't active at all, or active in only minor ways and without synchronicity. That same wondrous "orchestra" described earlier doesn't play in the same way when our children watch a tablet. The researchers who conducted this experiment warn on the danger of harming these essential executive functions of our children, when substituting electronic media over *real* stories and books presented to them through parental, human interaction.

In a separate research series, it was found that the level of under-standing and brain processing of a text is far higher when reading it from a printed book than when we read the same text from a screen. It seems apt that even in today's day and age, there is still no true substitution for "real" books, and, without a doubt—no substitute for the human connection that occurs when parents and children read stories together.

The screens harm our happiness

In 2018, the American researcher **Jean Twenge** published a remarkable and comprehensive research. Along forty years, Twenge investigated the question of teenagers' happiness and emotional welfare. Throughout the years 1976-2016, she gathered questionnaires from over 11 million (!) teenagers living in the United States. The research findings are shocking (▶ watch her TED talk; search for iGEN and Twenge).

Firstly, Twenge discovered that from the year 2012, a rather dramatic thing happened to the well-being of children and teenagers: their moods deteriorated drastically, the rates of depression spiked, and the cases of suicide of children aged 12-14 doubled. It seems as though the explanation for these disturbing facts has to do with the increasing use of "smart" devices, which became mainstream at the time.

Secondly, Twenge found fascinating and disturbing connections between the type of activities children and teenagers do during their free time and their moods. This research found that sports, outdoor activities, and social gatherings were *positively* connected to children's happiness, while screen time was related to bad moods and depression. Astoundingly—and scientifically proven—the more hours the teens spent in front of a screen, the higher the rates of despondency and sadness they had (➤ see attached graph).

Twenge summarized the research with saying that we don't have to separate ourselves from our smartphones, but we should learn to use them rather than let the devices "use" us.

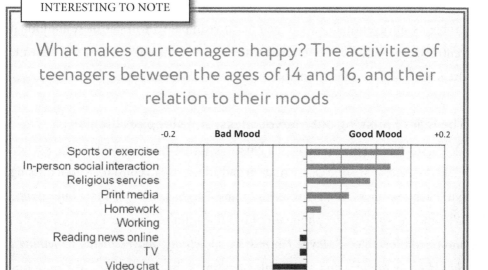

INTERESTING TO NOTE

What makes our teenagers happy? The activities of teenagers between the ages of 14 and 16, and their relation to their moods

Source: Twenge, J. M., Martin, G. N., & Campbell, W. K. (2018). Decreases in psychological well-being among American adolescents after 2012 and links to screen time during the rise of smartphone technology. *Emotion, 18*(6), 765–780.

Additional dangers it's important to be aware of

I opened by saying that the screen technology is already here, and that it's here to stay. So then, what is the use of discussing its flaws and dangers?

Fighter pilots tend to say: "The fighter plane you already noticed is not the one that will bring you down." Thus, the more we're aware of the downsides and dangers associated with screen usage, the better we'll be able to handle the problems and eventually lessen their negative impact. I will state here additional central dangers that are associated with screen technology; later I will also address ways of dealing with them.

The fear of missing out, nervousness, and sleep problems

One of the mental phenomena that have developed in the past few years is called FOMO—*Fear of Missing Out*. Children and adults live in constant fear of missing out. Each text message makes us jump up—*"perhaps it's something important."* When we're without our phone for only a few minutes, we start feeling nervous and uncomfortable—*"Maybe I'm missing something, maybe there's something I should know about going on."* Well, sometimes this is the case. At times, our smartphones are used to pass on important messages. But, honestly, most of the time the information can very easily be classified as "not important." At the same time, screen usage is linked with significant sleep issues, for both children and adults—specifically, it reduces the amount of sleeping hours, and impairs sleep quality.

The dangers of addiction

Nowadays there's no doubt that our screen use can become an actual, honest addiction. The extent of this worrying phenomena is expected to grow with each year. Many of the screen games and apps include highly sophisticated elements—all targeted at making us want to use them more and more often. Professionals and neuroscientists compare the effects screens may have on children to that of using hard drugs. The American psychiatrist **Victoria L. Dunckley**, in her book "*Reset your Child's Brain*," depicts a long list of actual *psychiatric* conditions and disorders that can arise in our children and teenagers due to extensive screen usage. In this context, it's important to note that children who suffer from

ADHD—Attention Deficit Hyperactivity Disorder, and children who cope with social difficulties, are at higher risk for such an addiction to screens.

The danger of harming interpersonal communications

Humans are social creatures. Our interpersonal communication skills develop quickly during our first years of our life. This process happens mainly due to our exposure to other people. Interpersonal interactions hold different aspects: facial expressions, eye contact, verbal and nonverbal communication, tonality, and many more. Screen time harms our opportunity to create such interactions—the genuine interpersonal relationships—and by doing so, it sabotages our developing communication skills. And let's not fool ourselves: "communicating" with others through the computer while playing games is nothing like true human interactions and face-to-face conversations, nor can it be a sufficient substitute.

The danger of being exposed to inappropriate content

With each generation, parents want to protect their children from content that they deem inappropriate for their age. The screens have made this an uphill battle, to say the least. Children who use smartphones, even without doing any active step from their side, are susceptible of being exposed to violent, harmful, or pornographic content. They will have no way of screening the content beforehand, of understanding its meaning, or protecting themselves from it.

The social dangers

Among the dangers listed above, the social dangers are probably the most harmful and disturbing of all. Children live their lives surrounded by others, and part of their learning curb is with them "trying out" a wide range of emotions and social situations, and learning to handle them properly. Being socially excluded by other children has always been one of the more violent and serious experiences a child can go through. The chat groups and the different social networks make these phenomena more common, more harmful, and much more dangerous than they had been in the past. Think about the terrible experience a child feels once they say something in a group chat, only to be removed from the group by a mere press of a button—and their shame is there, in front of everyone.

In the past, when a girl verbally abused another, she could see the effect her words had on that girl by noting her facial expression right away. The immediate feedback could have been enough to help push her toward apologizing, or at the very least being a little more aware of her bad actions. Now, when our children insult each other while hiding behind their screens, the emotional, human feedback is missing. It simply doesn't exist. Moreover, in many cases the children harm each other with the use of screens while dozens of other children witness the attack. This makes the vulnerability and social harm much greater and more extreme.

Additionally, in the not-so-distant past, these social problems used to happen mainly "outside" of the children's houses—most often at school. When the children returned home, they had some peace, they had a break from it all. Their home remained a safe haven. Nowadays, there is no moment of peace, nor do they get a break from it. Quite the contrary. The worst social attacks can and do happen when the children are home, behind their closed door. It all reaches them through their screens—the same screen you can't disconnect from and definitely can't do without.

And if that isn't enough, adolescence presents additional dangers. Imagine for a moment a teenage girl playing around with taking pictures of herself while wearing a bikini. She then sends the pictures to her best friend. The best friend's brother finds the photo, and in the blink of an eye, sends it along to all his friends. In a matter of minutes, the photo reaches hundreds of boys and girls. Some attach "funny" titles to the photo, but one might think photoshopping the picture so it looks like she is naked is good prank. After all, it makes the photo much more appealing. What are the chances of the girl arriving at school the next morning as if nothing had happened?

Unfortunately, this scenario and countless others like it aren't imaginary in the least. Things such as this can happen in every teenage group, even the best of them.

So, what can we do?

- If you're parents to younger children—**postpone as much as possible the point when the children are first exposed to screens**. Don't worry—your young ones won't miss out on anything by being denied screen exposure. Quite the contrary, in fact. The longer the delay, the more your children will have the opportunity to experience the "real" world, and especially enjoy the benefits of interpersonal communication—which is more important than words can say.

- From the moment your children are exposed to screens, **don't leave them alone in that virtual space**. Play their games, go into the applications together, make sure you're aware of the content they're being exposed to, and as much as possible—oversee the goings-on in their social networks. When a child starts riding a bike, they first use training wheels; we're at their side, to guard and protect them, until they slowly gain stability and no longer need our help. So too, should it be with screen exposure. We cannot let our children navigate this complicated world alone, they need us there with them.

- **Set ground rules for screen use and enforce them consistently.** Your child's cell phone carries on being *yours*, not "theirs," and you've got every right (even the obligation) to set the rules for using it. For example, there's no reason to take the child's phone out with you when you're going to a restaurant or leaving for family time at grandma's. Also, when their friends come over, you should make sure they put the screens aside and let them enjoy their time together: have them go out and play basketball, jump rope together, play card or board games, and simply have fun meeting "face-to-face."

- Furthermore, when your child first receives a "smart" device, it's highly suggested to have them **sign a form or contract that clarifies the usage terms.** To draft the contract, think about what is most important to you. For example, you can decide that the phone should mostly be used for communication, not games. You can also decide which applications your child can download, and any additional downloads would have to first get approved by you (there are special apps which are targeted specifically for this parental mission). (▶ For further examples and ideas, search Google: "phone agreement between parents and children.")

- In the first years during which your child uses their "smartphone," it's important that they know that you **check the device from time to time and are involved in what they do on it.** Children can accept any rule, as long as you're decisive and present it in a clear way.

- **Explain the possible dangers: what is allowed and** not allowed **to do.** Guide them in how to act when exposed to content that is not age appropriate; explain to them that under no circumstances are they allowed to send other children harmful messages they've received. Instead—encourage them to come to you and tell you about any problems they encounter in the virtual space.

- **Encourage your children to engage in fun activities—ones outside of the virtual space.** After all, the most effective way to reduce our children's screen time is to encourage them—the younger ones and teenagers alike—to incorporate other activities in their routine; activities that are not done in front of a screen. This could include youth groups, sports, after-school classes, playing an instrument, dancing, socializing, etc. In most cases, the screen is used as a default—a fallback for when the children have nothing else to do. Children and adolescents who have various fun activities incorporated in their daily lives are less drawn to screens.

- **Be aware of the model you yourselves set**. Let's admit it—we're all addicted. And our children see us—heavy screen users that we are—and learn from us. They see how the screens become inseparable parts of us; they see how we jump at every text message; they see us immersed too often in pointless games and social media. If we want our children to use screen time with a certain amount of wisdom, then we should give them the right model for screen usage: we'd better put the screens aside for a few hours, perhaps leave them at home every once in a while, and to be fully present with our children when we are talking or playing with them.

- **Take advantage of the technology—for your own benefit**. Alongside your awareness to your own model of behavior, it's just as important to know how to use the technology for your own parental needs. One of the greatest advantages of a WhatsApp group, for example, lies in the possibility of being in a direct line of communication with other parents—the parents of our children's and teen's friends. The direct line of communication allows for the most effective tool, when you hear the sentence, *"But e-e-everyone else is allowed to..."* (buy ice cream after class / come back from a party in the middle of the night / consume alcohol—each age group and its own special challenges). Technology enables parents to connect and also to coordinate such important points.

- **Do not allow screens to be your children's "substitute parent."** It's true that it is convenient and tempting, but it's important to remember that there is no adequate substitution for human interaction, face-to-face conversations, and, above all—there's no substitution for parenting. Children become "people" through their relationship with their parents—parents who are present in their lives, who guide them, communicate well with them, and remain attuned to them. These are parental qualities we are not allowed to give up on having. Remember, the children of today are the adults of tomorrow.

THE BOTTOM LINE

The screens have infiltrated our lives and are constantly around us—everywhere and all the time. It's true that they have countless advantages, and it's also true that fighting their existence is futile. However, it's still essential for us to be aware of the dangers they hold so that we can try and mitigate the damage brought on by their use.

When it comes to toddlers and young children—it's advised that we postpone their exposure to screens for as long as possible. Children, more than anything else, need the human connection with their adult caretakers. Screens can compete with these bonds, and even harm the vital interactions the children have with the outside, real world.

Older children need ongoing mediation in the virtual space. It's important to be there with them, to make sure they are not exposed to problematic content or experience negative social interactions through the screens. It's also vital not to allow the children to become addicted to the screens. At the end of the day, children whose screen time is used in smart, moderate ways, tend to be happier than children who are stuck in front of a screen most hours of the day.

CHAPTER 7

LIKE A BRIDGE OVER TROUBLED WATER
Parental coping in the matters of emotional regulation

Allow me to begin with a story that passes through word of mouth between different groups of parents:

While shopping at the supermarket, the child of one of the customers started having a tantrum, screaming, "Candy! I want candy." In reply, the mother said in a calm, quiet voice, "We'll be done in a minute, Mia. Only another few more minutes." "Candy!" the child continued. "Candy, buy me candy!" But the mother kept her cool. "Mia, we only need to buy a few groceries. In a couple of minutes we'll be at the cash register. We'll be done soon." At that point, the child simply "lost it." She kicked her feet and swung her arms about, sobbing hysterically. "Candy! Want candy! I want to go home!" "We'll be going to the car in a minute, Mia," the mother kept going in her soft tone. "We'll be there in a minute, and then have only a short drive until we get home." And, just as the mother said, she reached the cashier, paid for the groceries, left with her cart toward the car, and the child calmed down.

At that point, a young man who'd just left the supermarket too walked up to the mother. He'd witnessed the whole scene from before. "Hello, ma'am, I saw you in the supermarket a couple of minutes ago," he said. "And I couldn't help but marvel at the peaceful way you handled little Mia here. I was astounded by the way you spoke to her and calmed her." "Thank you," the mother replied with a smile. "It's nice to hear, but her name isn't Mia. The child is called Emma, I am Mia."

We're all familiar with situations such as these. It takes such energy, at times, to simply regulate our children's whirlwind emotions. Nowadays, there's a growing understanding that regulating our children's emotions is one of our most important parental tasks.

It starts in the child's very first weeks of life: infants are almost completely dependent on outside regulations that come from their parents. When they cry, we look for suitable ways to calm them. But the parental regulation doesn't end at infancy. At any age, we are "there" to assist our children in regulating their emotions; moderating their extreme behaviors; helping them calm down, move past their tantrum, and return to their needed balance. In certain life instances, emotional regulation can be especially vital and central to our daily lives. This is especially true, for example, during transitory periods: the transition from daycare to school, or from elementary school to junior high; when a new sibling is added to the family, or during the tumultuous years of adolescence.

And just as we saw with the story about the woman in the supermarket, it seems that these processes of parents regulating their children's emotions are very much dependent on our ability to regulate our own emotions, too.

The air conditioning metaphor

To fully grasp the parental task of emotional regulation, we can think of the way air conditioning works. The air conditioner's main function is to regulate the temperature in a room, regardless of the weather outside. No matter if outside there is a storm or a heatwave, inside, with the air conditioning, the temperature will remain just right. *24°C, if you please.*

In extreme weather conditions—either when it's terribly cold or unimaginably hot—the air conditioner has to work hard, spending much energy in regulating the temperature. An old, overrun unit might not do it as well. To succeed with the regulation, we need a strong air conditioner with much energy and power (sometimes even two units are needed...). However, when the outside weather is pleasant—not too cold and not too hot—then the task isn't as daunting, and any kind of air conditioner will manage to fulfil its purpose.

So too, happens with the relationship between parents and their children. There are children whose emotions are relatively easy to manage. These children tend to be, by nature, calm and content. When the children are mostly comfortable and calm, the parents don't need to expend too much of an effort into reaching a good atmosphere in the house, one which holds flow and calmness. It's true to say that every child "loses it" from time to time, but with easy-going children, such instances are few and far between, and do not destabilize the atmosphere at home.

However, there are children and adolescents who are especially tumultuous. Children who, at times, create "snowstorms" or "heatwaves." They get displeased, insulted, mad; they throw themselves on the floor in anger or slam doors... and the air conditioner—well, the air conditioner needs to work overtime, and expend much energy in trying to regulate the room's temperature. Sometimes it falls short. Sometimes *we* fall short.

And so it occurs that we give up or pull away, or get carried away with our own anger and "lose it" ourselves. It's then that we, too, need someone or something to help us regulate our emotions. When the matter at hand is tumultuous children or during hectic periods of time, then the parental challenge becomes particularly complicated. The simple act of recognition of there being a difficulty is a big step on the road for adequately dealing with it.

So, how do we handle tumultuous children and teenagers, or children who are going through a rough time? Here, I will offer some practical advice.

Did you fall again?—learning how to dig yourselves out of the hole

The first stage in dealing with children who have a tendency for tantrums or emotional tumultuousness, is to help ease them out of the storm and calm down—and to do so as soon as possible. For that to indeed happen, the children need us *at their side*—not standing opposed to them. Please note, the fundamental assumption here is that the children's tantrums are not entirely under their control. All children (and yes, the adolescents are included in this, too) want to behave properly. All children want us to be happy with them and their behaviors. Our children do not enjoy their own temper tantrums. And so, when such tantrums do happen, it's first and foremost important to try and end them in a quick and effective manner (▶ see too Chapter 15, regarding coping with children's difficulties).

To better understand this, imagine a child walking along a path filled with holes. From time to time, to the extensive frustration of all around, the child stumbles and falls (again) into a hole—meaning, they get caught up in an emotional outburst and have a tantrum. However, when your son or daughter is in the hole, they don't need you to preach from above; they don't need you yelling, *"You've fallen again? What are you doing? We're tired of your slip ups!"* Children who fall into a hole need one thing, and one thing only: they need a steady, strong hand—your hand—to help pull them out. There are children who calm with a hug, others who need to go wash their face, drink a glass of water, or even go out for a short walk. That said, most all of the children *do not* calm down when we tell them to go to their room and *"think about what they've done."* This method is usually completely ineffective, and it's best to use it as seldom as possible. When your child is inside the hole, when they experience a temper tantrum, more than anything else, they need your continual presence and willingness to help them come out of it. *"You've fallen in? Come, let me help you out. Hold my hand—come on, out we go."*

Moreover, when our child manages to pull themselves out of the tantrum and calm down, rather than keep holding onto the anger we felt (*"We cannot stand your tantrums anymore"*), it's better to tell them: *"Well done for calming down! Next time you'll manage to do it even faster."* It's in this way that we give our children positive reinforcement with calming and coming out of the "hole." It's true that no one is happy with the mere falling—but if we're there already, it's vital to know how to get out. It's important to know how to calm down. And then comes the next stage.

Every child needs a "fresh start"

This stage is one of the most important ones in dealing with highly emotional children. Right after the child or teenager calms down, we have to ask them to apologize for their reaction (and to make amends if needed), then we hug them, *accept* their apology, and *forgive* them. In other words, we allow them to start afresh. What does this actually mean, and how do we do it?

We start with apologies and making amends: If, during the tantrum, your child spilled their whole bowl of cornflakes on the floor—help them calm down, apologize, and clean up the mess they've made. In another example, if during a family meal, a fight arose with your teenage daughter and she ended up angrily leaving the table, muttering unflattering comments about your person, help her return to the dinner table, to take responsibility for her actions, and to apologize: *"I'm sorry I yelled so much, I know I didn't speak to you nicely."*

Then comes your key job: accepting their apology and forgiving them. Truly forgiving them and allowing them to start over. (*"I accept your apology and I'm not angry anymore; in my mind, we can simply forget what's just happened and start afresh"*). True, it's not an easy feat to manage, nor is it particularly intuitive. It's difficult since we find it especially hard at times to truly forgive. We get angry, we get upset—we're hurt—and we continue reminding the child that the same thing happened yesterday, and the day before, and the day before that. By doing so, we essentially stop ourselves, and them, from moving forward and getting over the uncomfortable situation. Additionally, parents who are introduced to the concept of "starting fresh," tend to oppose the idea, claiming that *"What could the child possibly learn from that? That they get to behave exactly as they like? That we will simply carry on forgiving any which behavior?"* But, here we once again forget our fundamental assumption, which is that all children want to behave properly. They gain nothing from their tantrums.

And why is it so important for our children to be able to start "a new page," so to speak?

It's vital because a child who constantly feels like their parents are angry at them—even after they'd apologized and calmed down—loses their motivation to go back to good behavioral patterns. A child such as this might say to themselves, "*They're angry at me regardless. It's pointless. Nothing I do will help, so there's no reason for me to try and behave nicely (even apologizing isn't worth it—what would I get from it?).*" And that thought process, naturally, is the opposite of what you wish your child to think. On the other hand, tumultuous children who learn they have the opportunity to apologize and start over—*truly* start over—begin using that option more and more, and over time, they manage to formulate self-regulating emotional control.

And what is the next step?

If the tempest was a "singular event," then you can put the whole thing behind you and move on. However, there are times when the storms are simply unignorable: especially bad ones, or such that occur time and time again. In these cases, it's important to talk things over and to fully figure them out. This, though, is best to do after a few hours or the day after.

Hit the iron—while it's... cold!

No, that's not a mistake. Assuming you aren't a blacksmith, but instead parents to children or teenagers—it's best to wait for the iron to cool. Children under the haze of a tantrum or an emotional storm aren't capable or available to properly listen; they cannot think, and cannot make any conclusions for the future. As I stated, when your child is tempestuous, your main job is to help them out of the storm and to calm down. The next day, after the event passed, you can find the right opportunity to tell them: "*You were really upset yesterday—let's try and understand what happened. Were you insulted? And even if you had been—was that the best way for you to handle it? What could have been done differently? What can be done differently in similar situations?*" A conversation such as this can only be effective when you, yourselves, are calm and are no longer angry or upset (the way you may have been during the event), and your child has had the chance to recover and calm down.

I'll stress this point yet again—no child enjoys emotional tantrums. No child enjoys having others angry at them or disappointed in them. All children want their parents to appreciate and praise them for their behavior. Tempestuous situations happen for any number of reasons, and we can never know them all: it can start over painful, real events ("*My boyfriend left me*"), or by reading the given circumstances incorrectly ("*Apparently, the girl he was hugging was his cousin—I only* thought *he was leaving me*"); sometimes the emotional outbursts are related to the child's temperament ("*My mother says that I've always been overly emotional*"), or evoked by attention deficit hyperactivity disorders, raging hormones, tiredness, hunger, stress, and many more reasons.

We shouldn't ignore the storms. There is much to learn from them:

We can learn and teach our children how not **to get caught in them.** For example, "*I should find out a few more facts before jumping to conclusions; I can* *take the dog out for a walk when I feel "it" coming on; We'd better make sure our child won't reach the stage of being so hungry again."*

We can learn to moderate the emotional response. Rather than exploding in a 0-60 manner—in the way most storms tend to happen—we can make a kind of scale, an emotional rating of anger. Then we can teach our children (as well as ourselves) how to react in certain situations at a rate of "a seven" instead of always "a ten." We can also explain this to our children by likening our emotions to that of an electric switch: Suggest changing the *on / off switch* ("all or nothing"), with a *dimmer* that allows us a wider range of emotions that fit into different life situations (*"That was really annoying, but it was annoying at a level of 5—not a 10"*).

And finally, we can also learn, and teach our children, **to escape the emotional storm faster**, at the next opportunity we're caught by it.

Either way, the learning stage will go down more efficiently if it's done the next day, when the iron is cold.

And when the parents are stormy too—what then?

The process of regulating emotions tends to be "contagious," and that presents the main difficulty. When one of our children is upset and loses control, we tend to "catch" their storm, thus trapping ourselves in a whirlwind of our own emotions, making us susceptible to "drowning" alongside our child. However, there is nothing more stressful for a tempestuous child than to see their parents—their strong, stable parents—lose control and become as stormy as them. During the storm, our children need us steady, calm, and in control of the situation. This, of course, is not always easy to achieve. In many cases, we are pulled alongside them into the storm. We love our children, we desperately want to help them, and it's difficult for us to watch them lose control of themselves. All this leads to us getting dragged down into a storm of our own. What can we do to prevent this?

Look at ourselves from the outside: Why is this happening to me?

In most cases, the mere awareness of our situation is the key for us to manage to avoid it or to end it fast. When we understand what is actually making us so upset, it's easier to figure out the ways to eliminate the storm. So, during a time of calm—not in the midst of a tempest—try and ask yourselves: "Why does this happen to me? When does it happen?" ("*Is it when we're particularly tired or hungry? After a long day of work? After a fight with our partner? In the evening after all our patience for the day has been used up?*"). Try and pay attention if one of your children disbalances you more than the others, and the possible reason for it (*maybe your boy reminds you of yourself? Perhaps you're particularly* worried *about your girl—and if that's the case, what can you do to help her?*). An external outlook allows for us to achieve a better, broader understanding of the given situation; it helps us act from a calmer and more curious mindset (▶ see too Chapter 11, that deals with the concept of mentalization).

We're angry due to caring—we're caring out of loving

If one of our children often tends to anger us, it's important that we ask ourselves as to the reason this happens. In most cases, if we examine the cause for such anger, we will see that beyond the anger, there is a very different emotion hiding away: If the anger is peeled away, similarly to the outside layer of an onion, we will usually find a layer of completely different emotions—a layer of worry. If we keep peeling away layers, we'll see another layer—one of monumental love. This discovery is important. It also holds a calming element to it. Our anger isn't without basis. We get angry because we care, and we care because we love them.

Yet still, it's more than possible that we get "too" angry. It's best to be aware and in control of this.

Oops... I was angry at my boss, but I yelled at my kids

At times, the anger directed at our children, in fact, stems from a completely different source. It can be due to our own inner turmoil, stressors from work or relationships, or simply life itself. These processes are known and are well familiar. They are called *spill-overs*: situations in which our emotions leave their original contexts, and transition over to other aspects. Note the moments when this happens to you. Our attention to these spill-over moments is the key to eliminating them.

I'm out of control—I'll be right back

Sometimes, our understanding of what can cause us to "catch" our children's emotional storms, may help us avoid our next eruption. This, however, doesn't always succeed. Arguing with our children can cause us at times to simply "lose it." (She once again won't go into the bath; he wrote awful things on his social media account; she was once again late coming home from a party—"*I've told you a thousand times!*") When you're angry and upset, often a simple "time out" can help: take a few deep breaths, take a moment to go out to the balcony, make yourself a cup of coffee. It's harder to lose control when you're holding a warm cup of coffee. And what else can we do to get out of the whirlwind emotional state—specifically when we're already in it?

Imagine you're theater actors, performing on stage

When you're in a confrontation with your children, and when they, in turn, lose control, try and think of yourselves as *actors on a stage*—theater actors playing the roles of parents. When we create that "space" between us and the stormy situation, when we manage to take a slight outside look, we can suddenly have the opportunity of reacting with a more measured and tempered manner—and not simply continue acting impulsively and automatically. Thinking of ourselves as theater actors can help us create this "space"—"*Okay, then I'm the mother in this uncomfortable situation—what would 'she' do now?*"

Get help from your partner

If your partner is with you, you can use them to help escape the situation and return to a state of composure—but it's important to do this correctly. Let's assume, for instance, that you got into an argument with your child over doing their homework. The argument escalated, making you both highly upset. In these situations, there's no point in having your partner come into the argument, placing themselves on "one side or the other's" ("Your mother is right! Do your homework—now!", or, alternatively, "Leave the kid, what do you want from him?"). This can only cause yet another escalation. Instead, it's best that the other parent come from a calmer, more measured, and level-headed place—one that would allow the angry parent to exit the situation, and by so doing, create a "break" or a pause (just as if you were resetting a computer). From this calm place, it'll be easier to find newer ways to solve the conflict.

Make amends—apologize to your children!

If we did "lose control," after recognizing that it happened, it's also important for us to apologize to our children (*"I'm sorry I got so angry, it seems like I really overreacted"*). This is a form of making amends, and that holds great significance—even if the incident in question was a while ago. This amendment doesn't leave us diminished in the eyes of our children, but quite the opposite—it's with our ability to apologize that we become their role model for how we wish they themselves will behave after "losing it." A child whose parents teach them that it's okay and even good to make amends, to apologize and start anew—will do so themselves, throughout their entire lives, and that's a wonderful ability to gift our children with.

What happens in our brains—the high road and the low road

The American psychiatrist **Daniel Siegel** created the method termed IPNB (Interpersonal Neurobiology). Siegel investigated the connections between different human behaviors—mainly the interpersonal processes relevant to parenting, and the neurological basis they hold. He notes that there are two main neural-processing routes that are activated when we are in a conflicted situation: the *"high road"* and the *"low road."* The high road is the route in which different parts of the brain activate simultaneously. Areas of the brain related to emotions, thought, and data processing are well connected. This can be analogous to an orchestra playing together, all instruments in perfect harmony. When we react to turbulent situations in our lives while leaning on the "high road," our reactions are, subsequently, regulated, calculated, seen through the lens of "the big picture," and allow us control over our emotional and behavioral elements. However, at times, we can "lose it" and react to situations through the "low road." This route is characterized with our reacting through "gut instincts," without control, management, oversight, or coordination between the different areas of our brain. It is during these situations when we erupt, lose our temper, yell, and so forth. There is no doubt that within the relationship we have with our children—and in life in general—we should aspire to react to different events through the path of the "high road," and *not* through the "low road." It's true that all parents have, at times, fallen into reacting with the "low route." It happens to us all when we're worried, tired, hungry, or simply lack energy. Yet still, there are parents who feel that they react through the "low road"—too often, with increasing severity, during long periods of time, or without managing to calm down and apologize. For these parents, it is highly recommended to find the reason behind their stormy behavior and to try and change their actions. It's important to state here that there are ways to get help; consulting a professional is a sure way to do so. Here, too, the key to change lies in being aware of the situation.

Do we always have to be happy...?

Before we conclude this section, it's important to keep our facts straight: emotional regulation doesn't mean that we and our children need to be happy all the time. The weather outside doesn't assure 365 days of warm sunshine, blue skies, and fluffy clouds. Moreover, a child's ability—and their parents'—to experience a wide range of emotions, that naturally include sadness, anger, disappointment, and so forth, shows a mental fortification and is evidence for a healthy psyche. When I refer to emotional regulation, I mainly reference the issues of the *emotional expression* of those same, so-called "negative" emotions. It's allowed and natural (!) to be angry or disappointed, but it's best not to yell and scream at your teacher over it; we're allowed to be sad, but it's best not to close ourselves in our bedroom all day without talking to anyone.

It seems that it's specifically our parental ability of identifying our children's emotions, giving them a name without shying away from them—"*I can see how disappointed you are over the school trip being canceled"*—that allows for our children to properly process their "negative" emotions rather than "fall to pieces" over them. When we don't scare easily over our children's emotions, we end up helping them understand that just like the weather outside, our emotions, too, are only temporary and transitional (▶ if you have yet to do so, don't miss out on the chance of watching the fantastic film "*Inside-Out*" with your children).

THE BOTTOM LINE

Regulating our children's emotions is one of the most important and complex parental tasks. It becomes especially difficult to do when regarding children who are particularly stormy, or while going through rough times. In many cases, tempestuous children cause their parents to "catch" their emotional storm, making them lose control of themselves, and fall out of regulation. There are ways that can help our children calm down and relax; for instance, allowing them to "start anew," and by working through the event only in hindsight, when the storm has run its course. At the same time, it's vital for us to be aware of the times we ourselves lose control, and for us to handle the instances efficiently: either by taking a "time out," getting help from our partners, reassessing the situation, and also apologizing to our children when needed.

Finally, remember that our children should and indeed do experience a wide range of emotions. Our task lies with helping them understand that "negative" emotions are something that passes, and to give them a hand with avoiding turning that "difficult" emotion into stormy, unregulated behaviors.

CHAPTER 8

I NEED IT! NOW!
The importance of teaching our children to delay gratification and to be grateful

Have you ever walked through a mall with your child, but once you arrived home, realized that you were unable to return without buying a new set of football cards, a SpongeBob helium balloon, or a useless plastic doll? Or perhaps you've heard your teenager explain to you how she simply must have those designer shoes from a brand you've never heard of, otherwise she wouldn't be able to show her face at school ever again. ("Just give me your card number, I'll order it online—it's on sale now!")

The phenomenon of "buy this!" and "I must have it!" is one of the more disturbing realities of our lives. Nowadays, when most everything is so cheap, available, and inviting, children never *stop* wanting, and we, the parents, oftentimes never stop fulfilling their wishes. If you, too, are in the cycle of "the children want—the parents give," you should probably rethink your actions. The wide range of temptations that surrounds our children, puts their ability to delay gratification and appreciate what they have at a high risk.

Perhaps you're telling yourselves: "*But why does that matter? When I was a child, I wanted that so badly—the new Lego, the bicycle, the computer games... my parents couldn't afford it all, but I've got the opportunity to indulge my kids, to make them happy and give them all the things I desperately wanted for myself but couldn't have.*" However, it's apparent that the ability to delay gratification holds a great value as for itself—without taking into account your own financial situation or the given price for whatever your child desires at the time.

One marshmallow now, or two later?

To understand why it's so important to delay gratification, I'll start with the *Marshmallow Test*. The Marshmallow Test is a classic study conducted in the 1960s, though its findings are still very much relevant for today. In the study, the brilliant American psychologist **Walter Mischel** posed a simple dilemma to four-year-old children. They were brought into a room separately, one by one; in the room stood a table with one marshmallow on it. The researcher said to the child: "I'm going to leave the room for a few minutes. Once I leave, you may eat the marshmallow here. But if you wait and *don't* eat it, in a few minutes when I return, I'll give you *two* marshmallows." At that point, the researcher indeed left the room, and the children's reaction was caught on camera. Two out of three children ate the one marshmallow the moment the experimenter left the room. All the rest made a herculean effort to wait for the researcher's return. The children's reactions to the test were fascinating and not a little entertaining (▸ find it on YouTube; search for "Marshmallow Test"). However, the interesting part of this study was the follow-up done fourteen years later, when the children were eighteen. Apparently, the children who kept themselves from eating the marshmallow when they were four, were all together better students, held better social skills, and even showed better handling of stressful and frustrating situations, when compared to the children who didn't resist temptation.

It is apparent that delaying gratification is one of the most important skills we can possess. We work hard now, so that we can be rewarded in the future. When parents are unaware of the value delaying gratifications holds, they may be tempted to buy their children everything they ask, to agree for them to have that extra treat, to allow them one more game on the tablet, and so forth. On the surface, it seems as though we are making our children happy, but on a deeper and more meaningful level, we could be doing them harm.

It's important to understand that **delaying gratification** and its twin—**self-control**—are things we need to work at, we have to put effort in this process, like a muscle. The muscle won't develop unless we hold it to specific training. Sometimes we may think: "*One more sweet, one more game... what difference does it make...*" Well, the answer is tied to the messages our children receive when faced with our too-quick agreement to everything they want. Children who get used to getting everything fast and now, may come to believe that the world at large works in the same way. These children can one day find it hard to put in effort to study for an important test; they can be frustrated over having to practice playing an instrument, dancing, or gymnastics ("*Ugh! I can't get it right!*"); moreover, they may find it difficult to handle arguments among friends or deal with any type of failure. Thus, there's no doubt that the ability to delay gratification is one of the most important skills we can give our children. It's vital for them to function well in the real world, for their future successes in different life matters, and their ultimate joy in what they do.

Delaying gratification—some principles we should acquire

Do they want EVERYTHING? Let them pick out one thing (or hold them to a budget)

You're going with your daughter to the supermarket and she wants every candy bar in sight… your teenage son goes into his favorite online shop, and in a matter of moments the "shopping cart" is filled with a double-digit number of desired items… one of the most effective ways of teaching children to delay gratification is to allow them a *choice*: they want it "all" and we will only agree to "one" (or allowing them a set budget). This also applies to when you say, *"one candy a day"* or *"no longer than half an hour on the tablet."* Giving our children the option to contemplate their wants, to weigh and choose, trains our children in delaying gratification, and even gives them a positive experience when accessing control over the decision process.

"Yes, we'll buy you the new computer game (in a month—for Christmas)"

There are, of course, certain games, musical instruments, pets, bicycles, or any other large gift that you decided to buy your children, that you fully believe they will benefit from greatly. Excellent—buy it for them, but try to do so around their birthdays, or around a significant holiday; a time that your child can wait for patiently. In other words, there is a value to this "space" that passes through the child's wanting and you satisfying their wishes.

"No need, Grandma will buy it for me"

You may be trying very hard to teach your children to delay gratification, but then the grandparents come along, or the cool uncle who loves spoiling your children, and they overtake the situation: they buy your children whatever they want—in your place. Well, I'm afraid there's no choice but to ask them not to do it. It's not always easy. There are grandmothers who feel as though they simply *cannot* come over without bringing some form of present to your children. So, yes, it's true that grandparents, aunts, uncles, and family friends are all on a different level from the parents. At times they are allowed to "spoil" your children without it being considered a bad thing. But it's still important not to overdo it. Explain to grandma and grandpa—who are, as always, full of good intentions—that large, often-given presents eventually end up harming the children, rather than contributing to their upbringing. Stress that the children are happy to merely see them and truly don't need so many presents.

Don't use presents and sweets as a means for compensating parental guilt

If you tend to buy too many presents for your children—ask yourself where this tendency stems from. At times it's our way of overcoming the feelings of parental guilt. If this is the matter—don't simply accept it. Check within yourselves what could be the cause for your guilt: are you returning too late from work? Do you not have the patience to listen to your children and to be with them when you're at home? Whatever you discover, find the ways to lessen and minimize your parental guilt in effective and *relevant* ways, and not by giving them multiple presents.

Don't put your children in impossible situations

It's true that delaying gratification means the ability to stand up to temptation, but let's not overdo it; let's try not to have our children face too many complex challenges. If the local toy store drives your children mad—there's no point in taking them there each time you have to pick up a present for a birthday party; and if your children love sweets, don't fill up your pantry with countless brands of candy which they're not allowed to have.

Pay attention to the model you yourselves provide

As with each topic concerning parenting and raising children, we have no other choice but to also look at ourselves. So, honestly, let's ask ourselves how is our own ability of delaying gratification? Can we go out for errands without buying "something small" for ourselves? Do we spend hours on online stores, counting the days until the packages arrive? Remember, it's hard to teach our children to delay gratification when we ourselves do quite the opposite.

"Thank you for buying this for me"—the importance of gratitude

Okay, let's be realistic and not push this too far. It's definitely important to teach our children to delay gratification, but that doesn't mean we have to abstain from shopping and consuming products. There are things our children do, indeed, *need*, and there are things that we, quite simply, *want* to buy them. When you buy your children a present of some sort, even if it is something they need—teach them to appreciate what they received and give honest thanks for it. It's important for children and adolescents not to treat gifts and items they receive for granted. It is apparent that gratitude is one of the more valuable traits we have for our overall mental health.

Research has shown that people who show gratitude, tend to be happier, more vital, and hold a higher ability for empathy. Gratitude creates a positive feeling—both with the person giving it, and the one receiving it. Thus, it generates a self-strengthening cycle of positive feelings.

Additionally, when we know to be thankful for a gift, we also protect ourselves from the problematic phenomenon of "adjusting" too quickly to material objects we have, and lessening their value. By the way, this problematic tendency of getting used to things we have too quickly (even when it's regarding something we dearly wanted) is one of the reasons for the research findings which consistently show that positive *experiences* contribute to our happiness levels—more so than mere material objects.

If we return to the issue of thankfulness, it's important to note that, differently from optimism, for example, which holds a strong *genetic* basis, gratitude is considered an acquired skill—one which we can *teach* our children, and train them to use.

How do we do this?

We train our *children to say thank you for everything they receive ("Thank you for buying me the football cards.", "Thank you for buying me new sneakers"); we teach them, also, to be thankful for positive experiences they have, and not take them for granted ("Mom, thank you for taking me to the park.", "Dad, it was so fun to go to a movie with you!")*. We should also get our children to pay more attention to the positive experiences they had throughout the day. When we turn our focus to positive things in our lives, and when we are thankful for them, the "space" they take up grows, and subsequently, our happiness levels rise. It's not complicated to do. As I've mentioned before, a family conversation around the dinner table, during which each one of you shares something you'd enjoyed from your day, is an excellent way to train our children—and ourselves—to note the good aspects of our lives. Additionally, writing birthdays cards and little "thank you notes" to family members, such as *"Mom, thank you for the sandwich today, it was great!"* can greatly up our sense of gratitude—both ours and our children's. Positive psychology research points to the value in children's and adults' abilities of being thankful for the good in their lives—for the small and simple things, and for the big and meaningful ones, too (▶ see frame in this chapter, and Chapter 4, page 70).

INTERESTING TO NOTE

The immense value of gratitude for our mental and physical health

The duo of psychologists **Robert Emons** and **Michael McCullough** conducted a series of studies, in which they examined the effects of practicing gratitude. Each evening their research participants were requested to write down a gratitude list: five good things they were grateful for in their lives. The list could include small, simple things, such as "the first coffee of the morning," or "having listened to good music throughout the day," and it could also include large, significant things, such as, "I'm so thankful for having a roof over my head and being healthy." The writing task didn't take longer than five minutes a day. After a few weeks, the participants in the research group were compared to participants in a control group that were requested to complete a *neutral* task which had nothing to do with gratitude. The differences between the groups were dramatic. The people in the research group who completed the thankfulness lists, were happier, more invigorated, friendlier, more generous, and even more physically healthy when compared to the people in the control group. These differences between the groups remained for a long period of time after the research was ended. How is it possible that a mere handful of minutes of writing in a notebook could make such a significant difference? Emons and McCullough explain that gratitude inserts positive feelings into our lives, ones which act as self-strengthening cycles. Warm, positive emotions bring us closer to the people we love, and they, in turn, reflect positive emotions back at us. It's a situation where everyone wins—in many different avenues of life. Think about it: how easy is it to include gratefulness over our daily experiences in our daily lives with our children? So very easy, and so very rewarding.

THE BOTTOM LINE

We live in a culture that encourages never-ending consumption. When faced with a wide range of temptations, it's important to teach ourselves and our children to delay gratification. Children who get what they want right away are, in no way, happier than children who learn to wait patiently until they receive what they ask for. Quite the contrary, in fact: it's the effort, the perseverance, and the ability to delay gratification that prepares us and our children to better deal with life's challenges. They also contribute to our emotional well-being, thanks to our ability to appreciate what we have, and our individual achievements, as well.

When our children get something, small or big, it's vital to teach them to be thankful for what they received. Gratitude—for material things, experiences, and the good we have in our lives—is one of the main contributors to our overall mental and physical well-being. This skill is something we can develop and encourage our children to develop over time.

CHAPTER 9

LIKE FATHER, LIKE SON
The importance regarding similarities between children and their parents

We are all familiar with this. The moment our children are born into this world—though some would say even while they are still in the womb—a race to identify similarities between us and them begins: "Look, he looks just like his father when he was a baby;" "She has her mother's smile... her grandmother's dimples... and her energy levels are straight from my husband's side."

It seems that the endless search for similarities between us and our children is tied to a basic evolutionary need—the need to be certain they are, indeed, *ours*, to know that we *did it*: we ensured the continuation of our genes and our growing legacy.

However, emphasizing those similarities between us and our children also answers a key psychological element: it serves as an essential part in the process of formulating our children's sense of identity. Sounds unclear? Let me explain.

"The most important thing is for you to be yourself" (But first—be like me)

We all agree that one of our main roles as parents lies with helping our children establish their own unique sense of identity. We want to help them find their personality traits, to nurture their special skills and heart's desires, to get to know their fascinating inner world, and for them to grow up to be "who they truly are" (and not who we'd *like* them to be). However, parenting is never one-dimensional or simple. It seems that one of the central aspects regarding the formulation of our child's *unique* individuality passes through highlighting the *similarities* between us and them.

Think for a moment about a close friend of yours; picture them in your mind. How similar do you believe the two of you are? It's likely that although the two of you are fundamentally different people, you hold quite a few aspects that are very similar. It feels wonderful to have someone close to us, who, in many ways, is also similar: someone who shares the same traits and hobbies, someone who is in a similar situation as we are in life.

Well, it seems as though our children feel the need to be like us, as well. They need it as a basis for their sense of self. The similarities to their parents give children the feeling of safety and assist them in familiarizing and cementing their own growing individuality.

The first to have written about this was the psychoanalyst, **Heinz Kohut**. Kohut calls it a need for a sense of "**twinship**." The similarities between children and their parents can be through the aspect of physical looks—"*We both have a mole next to our eye*"—but, more importantly, the need for "twinship" lies with the deeper more meaningful aspects of personality traits, thinking patterns, hobbies, interests, and so forth.

When children recognize a character trait in themselves that is similar to their parents', they feel a connection, they feel a sense of belonging. These feelings greatly contribute to the children's mental welfare. The feelings of belonging allow for children to feel safe, and even contribute to their enthusiasm regarding establishing social connections with children their age and with people around them. According to Kohut, just as our *awe* over our children contributes to their positive self-image and positive inner thoughts (▶ see Chapter 2), so does the experience of finding *similarities* between us and them contribute to their wanting to be a part of their social surroundings. Fascinatingly, it appears that it's actually through the experience of highlighting the similarities between us and each of our children, that our children will grow and develop their own individual selves.

How do we nurture similarities and "twinship"

To nurture your children's sense of "twinship," find—with each of your individual children—the similar aspects between the two of you ("*We both have the exact same smile*"); the things you both like to do, the things you like doing together (playing, swimming, hiking, listening to jazz, taking a walk in the park…). It doesn't have to be complicated—even watching reality TV or soccer games holds much significance. At the same time, and as your children grow older, find the character traits of yours that align and emphasize them. Even if your teenagers imply that *"the last thing they want is to have anything of theirs that is similar to you"*—don't believe them. Every child, deep down, wants to feel connected to their parents; to feel as if they belong.

By the way, I'd like to point out that the feelings of resemblance between children and their parents can be especially important and relevant when concerning children who are adopted, or children who were born through sperm or egg donations. In such cases, the similarities will mainly lie with finding shared hobbies, character traits, and common interests, rather than relying on physical attributes.

At this point, I'd like to emphasize two important reservations:

Firstly, when I refer to finding aspects of connection between us and our children, it does not mean that we should become their *friends*. There are enough people in the world lined up for that role, and they do not include us. Children will only gain from having parents who stay in roles of *parents*. The fact that you and your child both like cats, or rock music, or taking a long nap on weekends—doesn't mean that you instantly become each other's friends. While a friendly relationship is based on equality and mutuality, child-parent relationships are best to be based on authority, keeping a sense of *asymmetry* that naturally occurs between children and their parents.

Secondly, remember that the need for finding similarities does not contradict the fact that you are both different and unique individuals, nor does it contradict each of your children's wishes to develop their own sense of self. It's through this area of connection and belonging that their personal ambitions will grow, and their unique "true self" will thrive.

Father's son, mother's daughter

This may not sound "politically correct," but when regarding the issue of finding similarities between children and their parents, there is a special significance to the similarities between a child and a parent of the same gender—mother and daughter, father and son. Children very much need to feel close and alike to each of their parents; however, the closeness to the parent of the same gender—especially during their teenage years, though before so, as well—can hold a particular significance in forming their self-identity. Thus, assuming that you're raising your children as a couple—mother and father—you should pay particular mind—and time—to thinking about the relationship you build with your child who is the same gender as yours.

Remember that your children look up to you: they want to know that you love and appreciate them, and they also want to feel close and alike to the person you are. In other words: Dad, you've got a particular role when shaping your son's self-image; Mom, you've got a huge influence on your daughters' self-image. You should nurture these significant bonds: spend time with them just the two of you, find points of similarity and connection. And if you feel like something isn't right in your relationship, that something went wrong (maybe the relationship is too volatile, too sensitive, too rife with criticism) don't merely accept the situation as is. Do everything in your power to better this relationship; the responsibility of improving it lies on you, the parent.

And what if you're raising a child as a single-parent, or as a same-sex couple, and you don't have a parent "of the same gender" in your family (for example, a single mother raising a boy, or a gay couple raising a daughter)? You'll be happy to hear that research has found absolutely no evidence of this harming the personal self-identity or gender identity of children in such situations. Nevertheless, you can still contribute the sense of likeness to a same-gender parental figure, through strengthening the bonds between your son or daughter and close people around you: a loved uncle, a good friend, grandparents, etc. In many cases, bonds such as these occur naturally, if we don't interfere in their making.

When a child feels fundamentally different to his parents

The wonderful film *"Billy Eliot"* tells the story of an eleven-year-old boy whose mother died, and his father pushed him toward a boxing career. But, to the father's horror, Billy finds himself drawn to *ballet*. The film follows the complex, developing relationship between father and son, who are both so fundamentally different.

And it's true; at times it's not easy to find similarities between children and their parents. Sometimes, the child is born with very different traits to their parents—and that makes them go around feeling rather detached and foreign in their world (*"There's no one on earth who can understand me"*). Many adolescents who are attracted to their same sex—especially before coming out—report feelings of such foreignness and not belonging. A similar situation can occur, however, when an athlete father has a child who "doesn't like sports;" when a child has severe learning disabilities and the parents "don't know where it came from;" and in countless other situations, too (► see also the next chapter, regarding the gap between the "imagined child" and the "actual child," and in Chapter 28, regarding parenting children with special needs).

The feelings of likeness and "connection points" between children and their parents are so important, that we really can't give up on them. Moreover, it's our responsibility as parents to find the points of similarities between us and our children—to emphasize them, and "catalogue" them. So, if you feel as if one of your children is fundamentally different than you—make sure to find what you do have in common after all (*"We both like making faces in front of the mirror;" "We both like gadgets;" "We both fall asleep in a matter of seconds, no matter where we are"*). Stress these points of similarities, but still be sure not to try and change or nullify your child's individuality. Similarly to the process Billy Eliot's father goes through in the movie, such complex situations call for you to find your inner resources that will allow you to accept your child "just as they are." Children should not grow up feeling as if they are a constant source of disappointment and discontent to their parents; they shouldn't feel as if their parents are trying to change them or fit their personalities to their own needs. This ongoing experience can greatly harm the child's developing self, and the person they are growing into.

THE BOTTOM LINE

One of the ways children develop their individual identity is through emphasizing connection points and similarities between them and their parents. This experience stands as a basis for the development of the self; through this basis, they will continue to grow and find their own path, give hold to their preferences, and build their unique individuality.

There is special significance to the bond formed between father and son and mother and daughter. However, the establishment of similar hobbies, characters, and traits, between you and your children does not mean you have to become their *friends*. Not at all. Children need authoritative parents, parents who can be counted and leaned on. They do not need friend-parents.

In certain situations, children develop character traits and preferences that are far removed from those of their parents, thus making it particularly hard for parents to find the similarities between them and their children. In these situations, it's our responsibility as parents to find those attributes anyway—character similarities, hobbies, and shared interests. At the same time, it's important that we do everything possible to accept our children as they are, without trying to make them fit into our own individual needs and preferences. Read more about this in the next chapter.

CHAPTER 10

GOOD CHILDREN— "TOO GOOD" CHILDREN

The nature of "true self" and why our children shouldn't be "too good"

- *This boy has to be a footballer!*
- *My son won't dance!*
- *My daughter is going to be a math whiz!*

Who among us do not hold expectations—"what kind of children would we like to have?" Have you ever asked yourself how much your expectations contribute to your children or how much they can potentially harm them? Is there a price for parental expectations? We would all like for our children to "behave themselves," for them to "be *good* children," but can that "good" be "too good?"

False self: Mother only loves me when I'm happy

Donald W. Winnicott was the first to make the differentiation between the true self and the false or fake self. Winnicott's starting point is a repetitive theme in this book: a child's personality doesn't evolve in a "vacuum." It evolves through the interactions between them and the adults who surround them—most particularly, their parents.

The assumption is that each child holds an inner core with their own special and unique qualities: their talents, their heart's desires. However, the extent to which that inner core can develop, grow, and burst out, depends greatly upon the environment parents provide. Winnicott believed that parents who give their children adequate room to grow, a space where there is the option to play, experiment, create, and discover new things—these parents allow for their children to fully develop their **true self**. This includes a flexible, comprehensive experience of their true selves, including the feelings of vitality, creativity, calmness, and happiness. You can akin this to a small sprout that receives excellent environmental conditions: good soil, water, sunlight—all of which allow for it to grow from a small sprout into a beautiful little plant.

However, there are parents who, for whatever reason, need for their children to be exactly as they wish—their own child of their dreams. It happens, for instance, that parents can't stand certain qualities of one of their children; they go against their children's wishes, refusing to allow them space to experiment and fulfil their wishes (*"My son will not start dancing;" "My daughter won't be shy;" "This child has to be an athlete"*). Another kind of situation may present itself when the parents themselves are depressed and look to their child to be a source of joy, to pull them out of the complicated mental state they are in (*"These children are my whole life. If it wasn't for them, I wouldn't be able to get out of bed..."*).

In situations such as these, there is a true risk of the children developing a fake sense of self, or as Winnicott put it: a **false self**. It's important to remember that children at any and every age need their parents' love. When parents cannot accept a quality or aspect of their children, when they have a too rigid set of expectations, the children may end up suppressing their true wishes, hoping to adhere to their parents' wishes and expectations (*"Mom only loves me when I'm happy, so I'll never cry;" "My dad has to have a footballer for a child, so I'll go out on the field and pretend to enjoy playing, even though I really hate the game"*). The price is steep, but the children are willing to pay it—what wouldn't we do to gain parental love?

This situation is unwanted. It lays a huge burden on the child's shoulders, and can sabotage their ability to feel a wide range of emotions, and eventually become their "true selves." And what happens to our child's "true self" in such situations? Winnicott believes that the true self never fully goes away. It shrinks, gets pushed into a dark corner of our psyche, and waits for the opportunity to burst forth.

The drama of the gifted child

Many people have heard about "*The Drama of the Gifted Child.*" This book, written by the Swiss psychologist **Alice Miller**, created waves across the world; though not everyone is familiar with the particular drama, and who the gifted child actually is.

These gifted children of whom Miller writes, aren't gifted in the normal sense. They are not necessarily the smartest children in the class, and it's entirely probable that they aren't exceptional when it comes to mathematics. These children are *emotionally* gifted: clever, alert children, who have the ability to listen honestly and possess a particularly high emotional understanding; they manage to read adults' needs, get a sense of them, and follow them perfectly.

So, "perfect" for whom?—definitely not themselves.

These emotionally alert children can recognize the needs of their parents, and from a very young age, direct themselves accordingly. So instead of the *parents* being attuned to their child, allowing them a healthy sense of self as should happen, the *child* becomes attuned to the parents. Rather than the child acting per their heart's desire, they act in a way that would bring joy to their parents—all in a way of complying to their parents' needs. And so their true self is pushed away, and they develop a form of "false self." This is what creates children who are, in fact, *too good*.

So, how can we help our children develop their "true selves?"

Up until now, I've centralized the importance of parental love. Parental love is, indeed, an essential and fantastic resource. However, for your son or daughter to eventually grow into their true selves, you should acquire an additional quality. Alongside the love you give your children, you should also develop *curiosity* regarding who your child actually is: who are they? What do they enjoy? What are their unique attributes?

If you'd like, conduct a short exercise: take a pen and paper and write down, regarding each of your children separately, what are their special and unique qualities; what characteristics do they have that aren't directly "inherited" from either of you (*do they possess joie de vivre? Are they opinionated? Courageous? Extremely optimistic? Do they have a special sense of humor? A unique creative ability?*). Think about it: how wonderful it is to be able to see a child possess a quality that is wholly and entirely their own; a quality no one can truly tell where it came from. In the end, it's a kind of magic, watching children grow into who they truly are (▶ read additional aspects on this in the next chapter that deals with mentalization).

Stemming from that same curiosity, it's also important for us to be attentive to our children's true desires, for us not to confuse them with our own. If you'd dreamed your whole life about becoming a dancer, it is not your daughter's job to fulfil *your* dream. You can sign her up for dance class, but do so only if it's something *she* truly wants to do. Alternatively, if you were a successful basketball player, you son doesn't necessarily have to follow in your footsteps. Perhaps his dreams pull him in the direction of a certain musical instrument, instead—or maybe his interest is in a completely different sport?

Playing and creativity enhance the development of the children's true self.

When children are in a playful mindset, their "true self" shines through and has the opportunity to be fully expressed. It is specifically in those imaginary, make-believe realms that children can encounter meaningful, exciting "true self" experiences. And it's for this reason that we should encourage our children—no matter their age—to play as much as possible, without our interference (▶ see additional information on this in Chapter 5).

The imaginary child, the actual child, and everything in between

Sometimes, psychological terms get their time in the spotlight, and become known to the public at large. This happened with the professional terms "**imaginary child**" and the "**actual child**." The Israeli film director, **Avi Nesher**, combined these terms in his excellent movie "The Other Story" (▶ search for the trailer on YouTube), and through that brought the terms out of the psychology books and into the consciousness of hundreds of thousands.

"When a child is born," the protagonist's grandfather says, *"Two children are actually brought into the world: the child you imagined and the actual child; and at some stage, you must choose between the two..."*

Indeed, it seems that each of us holds in our heads a certain image of our perfect child. The image begins to take form well before we become actual parents, and this is the *"imagined child."* We dream about whether we'll have a boy or a girl, what characteristics and qualities they'll have: what they will look like, what they will be good at, and what we will enjoy doing together.

But the fact of the matter is that our *"actual child"* isn't born to fulfill our every dream. They are born to become themselves—their "true self"—with all the attributes that come with that: their own specific wishes, talents, dreams, and difficulties. And it's this gap between the imagined and actual child that we have to be aware of and check ourselves against. Which of our ambitions for them are legitimate to push for? Which are for their own benefit? In which areas and aspects do we fall short and wish for our child what we instead wished for ourselves?

It's important to say that the gaps between the imagined child and the actual one will always exist in some form or another. However, this gap widens when the child has special needs or certain disabilities that affect their daily lives (▶ see too Chapter 28). At times, this gap may appear when the child has different heart desires than what is "normally" accepted in society—such as when a boy or girl come out as members of the LGBTQ+ community, or those who choose to follow a lifestyle that sets them apart from their family. In the movie "*The Other Story*," the gap between the imagined and actual child presents itself in the protagonist, Anat's, choice to become religious—something that is far removed from her parents' lifestyle. Anat's parents try and do everything they can to "bring her back" to their familiar way of life, but at some point, they begin to wonder whether their actions are for their own benefit and happiness or for Anat's own welfare. These are, without question, complicated and sensitive parental dilemmas.

So, what should we do with our expectations?

What is, then, the lesson we can take from this chapter? Are we, as parents, not supposed to guide our children? Should we suppress all our expectations for them to grow into their own true selves?

Well, the answer to that is a very clear, no. As parents, we most certainly should be in a role that directs and sets boundaries. It is parental guidance that helps children adopt positive values that assist them in behaving in a way that fits within society. It is natural for us to praise our children when they act in a way we deem appropriate, and we definitely should scold them when they misbehave and break the rules.

Moreover, for our children to become their true selves, they need our parental presence. A stable, safe, flexible parental presence is what allows children to experiment and acquaint themselves with their special qualities and build their self-image. Additionally, as I mentioned in the previous chapter, children benefit greatly from finding similarities between themselves and their parents—as long as the similarities come about honestly and not forcibly.

To help our children formulate their true identities, the key point is to find the right balance: not too much and not too little. Parenting that lacks expectations is neglectful, while too many expectations can suppress the child's true self. To find the right balance, it's important for us to be aware of our children's actual needs—and our own needs, as well. If we believe the two contradict each other, we must check ourselves—what are our expectations? Why do we expect such things? Are there any additional options?

The well-known sculptor Michelangelo believed that within the marble, a sculpture was merely waiting to be uncovered. The sculptor's job, in this case, is to chisel away the superfluous material, and to uncover the art. This metaphor can fit well with the way we should view parenting. We don't *create* our children, nor do we sculpt them into our image or according to our wishes. Parenting, thus, should allow our children to burst free and be who they truly are.

The writer and poet, **Gibran Kahlil Gibran**, put it beautifully to words:

> *Your children are not your children.*
> *They are the sons and daughters of Life's longing for itself.*
> *They come through you but not from you,*
> *And though they are with you yet they belong not to you.*
>
> *You may give them your love but not your thoughts,*
> *For they have their own thoughts.*
> *You may house their bodies but not their souls,*
> *For their souls dwell in the house of tomorrow,*
> *Which you cannot visit, not even in your dreams.*
> *You may strive to be like them,*
> *But seek not to make them like you.*
> *For life goes not backward nor tarries with yesterday.*

THE BOTTOM LINE

Parenting is a complicated, complex matter, and holds within it the art of balance. On one side, we cannot raise children without certain expectations and guidance; on the other side, we must be careful not to overdo it, to not burden our children with our personal dreams for them and their developing personality. In many parenting situations, a gap is created between the "imagined child" and the "actual child"—and that is completely normal. However, children who grow up with too many expectations can develop a "false self;" can suppress their true heart's desires and direct themselves according to their parents' wishes—all to keep their parents' love and affection. For this to be avoided, it's important we build a healthy amount of curiosity regarding the question of who our children truly are; it's important we watch over with a sense of joy at the person growing forth from the child—with all their talents and wishes included. It's important to allow our children a space to experiment, play, imagine, and create. Through doing as such, we can greatly contribute to our children's developing true self, and there is no gift more meaningful.

CHAPTER 11

TO SEE THE OTHER FROM WITHIN, TO SEE MYSELF FROM THE OUTSIDE
The key factor of mentalization in parenting and child development

Love… confidence… a positive self-image… communication… empathy… mentalization…!

"M-e-n-t-a-l-i-z-a-t-i-o-n?!"

It is highly unusual for a new concept to move so quickly to the forefront of the professional lexicon, gaining an honorable position at the sides of known concepts like love, security, self-image, communication, and empathy. This is the precise thing that happened with *mentalization*. The British psychologist and researcher **Peter Fonagy** was the first to coin this concept at the close of the previous century. And here we are, a mere handful of years later, and the concept of "mentalization" has become one of the "hottest" terms in psychology of parenthood and in the realms of mental health in general. A long line of research proves this is a fundamental key to people's mental health, and something we cannot do without.

Even if you've never encountered this concept before, I fully believe that once reading this chapter, you will be convinced as to the importance of mentalization—with regards to child rearing and in general.

So, what is mentalization? Why is it so important? How can we develop it in our own children? We will soon find out.

Mentalization—a pleasure to meet you!

It's no easy feat to define mentalization. Officially, mentalization is defined as our ability to attribute meaning—in terms of emotions, intentions, and thoughts—to other people's showed behaviors, and to our own behaviors as well. Even if the official definition sounds complicated and complex, the examples for it are simple and easy to understand.

"My son is once again having a tantrum—perhaps he's hungry?"

"My daughter is incredibly nervous lately. It seems that having to say goodbye to her favorite teacher has had much impact on her."

"He's only twelve and already he's slamming doors—looks like he's heading into adolescence..."

As parents, we hope to understand what motivates our children, what is hidden in their inner world: their thoughts, feelings, what drives them and makes them behave as they do. Our basic understanding that everyone has their own unique inner world that includes a multitude of needs; the curiosity we hold regarding our child's inner world and our wish to understand it—*that* is mentalization.

At the same time, we consider our own motives:

"Why did I yell at her? I think I may have overdone it…. she wasn't at fault for my having such an awful day at work."

"I've been really preoccupied lately, and I've been taking it all out on the kids."
That, too, is mentalization.

In other words, mentalization refers to the understanding that every expressed behavior has a basis in inner motives—motives we're at times unaware of and do not necessarily fully "know." Additionally, it refers to our mere curiosity—toward other people's inner world or our own. In a picturesque way, we can treat mentalization as our ability to "see the other from within; to see ourselves from outside."

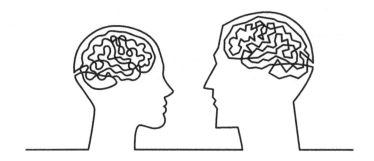

Our ability to understand misunderstandings

Imagine yourselves patiently sitting in a traffic jam, when suddenly someone overtakes you, cutting through the jam, taking up the space in front of you. Automatically, you will start feeling anger toward that extremely rude person. But what if you find out that, in the passenger seat, there is a pregnant woman about to give birth? Then you will surely move out the way and do all in your power to allow the driver to reach their destination (*"Good luck, and congratulations!"*)

Think how many fights and arguments could be solved if we were simply more aware of the misunderstandings that occur between us and the people who surround us—all of which simply happen due to not knowing the other person's motives.

Here is a routine example from the parenting world: assume your daughter invited a friend for a sleep over, but in the middle of the night, the girl suddenly burst into tears and asked to go back to her own home. Your daughter, in response, was highly insulted ("*She doesn't want to be with me... she doesn't enjoy my company... I'm not going to be her friend anymore!*"). Here, however, *you* must come in. You have to widen that set of possibilities, help your daughter imagine the guest's feelings, and explain to her that her friend most likely simply missed home, that she was still unused to sleeping away, and that shouldn't be a negative testament to their friendship.

This, too, is mentalization: the understanding that we cannot judge another person by merely what is outwardly presented to us, and that we may never be privy to the person's inner world. We can only *guess* the goings on and try and understand as best we can. And so, we must assume we do not know everything, that other people's behaviors—and our own—can stem from different inner motivations.

"Mom thinks of me—thus, I exist"

Nowadays, we know that developing mentalization in children is, foremost, a parental task. The mere fact that we treat our children as people with their own inner world, with thoughts, feelings, wishes, and hopes that are all their own; that we treat them as separate individuals "worth knowing," helps them eventually view themselves in the same way, and greatly contributes to their ability to treat others correspondingly. Sounds vague? Allow me to explain further.

The process begins with the child's first breath:

"*My beautiful baby, it's so wonderful seeing you happy!*"

"*Oh no... why are you crying, my love? Does your tummy hurt?*"

When a baby grows up with a parent who guides and treats them as an individual with their own specific needs and inner world, the baby indeed develops a concept of being as such. This process begins with us—with our simple recognition as parents that our babies are unique individuals, who hold personal needs, thoughts, and feelings; individuals who possess an inner world we're excited to get to know more about. Our *curiosity* regarding our children holds tremendous value for their development.

In other words, as parents, we try to "capture" in our own consciousness the inner world of our young children, and by so doing, we allow that world to exist. A baby whose parents are well tuned toward them will become a child capable of identifying the goings on in their own inner world: *"I'm tired... I'm hungry... I'm jealous... I'm annoyed now."* Even if, as parents, it's not always pleasant to know what exactly our children are feeling, it's best to remember that a child's ability to recognize their own inner feelings and thoughts, creates a mental basis that will serve them well throughout their whole lives. Such children will regulate their emotions in a better way, and will become adults who recognize thoughts and feelings—of themselves, of others, and one day, of their own children as well.

Here are a few basic principles that can assist you in promoting your children's mentalization abilities.

Help your children understand what they're feeling

Have you ever noticed what the first thing a young child does after they fall and hurt themselves? In most cases, they immediately look around and search for their parents' gaze, in order for them to work through and understand what happened. If the child sees their parent panicking (*"Help! Call an ambulance!"*), then the child will start crying hysterically—turning the uncomfortable hurt into a huge deal. However, if the parent expresses calmness to the child—*"You got hurt, I saw. Don't worry, let's go clean it up and it will feel better really soon"*—it's more likely that the child will manage to wipe away the tears, push through, and carry on playing. Well, we as parents are a vital source of information for our children—information regarding their own feelings and sensations.

The way we treat a child's hurt is only an example, of course. Our job as parents—helping our children recognize their emotions—is just as important to do when they are older. Let's assume that our child comes back from school extremely upset and declares: *"This was the worst day of my life!"* If we automatically react with extreme upset and worry—call the teacher, principal, anyone and everyone we possibly can—the child's tempest will only grow. Rather, it's better if we switch out that "exclamation mark" with a "question mark:" *"What happened? When? Let's figure out together what you felt when it happened? Maybe we can figure out a different way for you to react next time?"*

This isn't always easy. In many cases, our children are unaware of their exact feelings. As parents, we are in the position of helping them turn their general emotions (*"I feel good / bad"*) into more specific feelings. To do so, we must show an interest in listening to their experiences, help them translate their emotions into words, and pinpoint their sensations:

"I went out for recess and had no one to play with..."
Parents: *"That must have made you feel really uncomfortable. Did you feel alone? Were you sad? What happened then...?"*

"The teacher sent me to the secretary to get an eraser for the board, but I couldn't find my way back to class..."
Parents: *"Aww, what a horrible feeling! Were you embarrassed? Stressed? What did you do? What else could you have done?"*

"I can't take these exams anymore! It's too much stress!"

Parents: "*It really is a very stressful, busy time. You've got a lot on your plate, but I know you can handle it. The pressure will let up in a couple of weeks. If you manage your time better, it might help you feel less stressed out... let's think about this together—what can help?*"

Research has shown that children (and adults) who learn to correctly identify their emotions and specifically name each one, handle stressful and frustrating situations better, while regulating their unpleasant feelings. In many cases, there is a huge importance to the mere process of translating emotions into words; beyond that, when we say what we feel, it's easier for us to think what we should do next time when encountered with similar situations. Your parental presence allows your child to do all this. And so, this makes our most important parental role to simply "be there" for our children—to listen, take an interest, to help them recognize their emotions and regulate them, all without canceling out or denying the more unpleasant feelings. So, yes, this isn't always easy to do.

"~~Nothing~~ Something happened"—validate your children's feelings

Life is filled with frustrating situations. Let's assume, for example, that your son found out that his best friend canceled a playdate with him, only to ask someone else over—something that seriously hurt your son's feelings. An uncomfortable situation, no doubt. Or, another example could be: let's assume your daughter had been working toward a role in her youth group for a long time, only to eventually have her best friend get it instead. It's a huge disappointment (with a side order of jealousy, too).

So, our children come to us, upset, angry, hurt, disappointed, jealous, and so forth—and we, filled as we are with good intentions, desperately want to eliminate their bad experiences and make them happy: "*Nonsense—you'll have much more fun on your own,*" or: "*Who would even want that silly role? Now you have more time to focus on your studies.*" Well, no. That's a mistake. When we dismiss our children's difficult emotions, when we simply say, "*Nothing happened,*" we may fail in serving as a reliable source of "information" for their feelings ("*Mom, Dad, you just don't get what I'm going through!*"). Because to them—something did, indeed (!) happen.

Additionally, children who consistently have their feelings dismissed, may end up feeling confused and mistrustful regarding their abilities to recognize their feelings. In other words, for our children to successfully handle different life events and their rising emotions, they need an attentive adult in their corner to validate their feelings—not dismiss them. It's specifically our recognition of their difficult emotions, our allowing them room and support, that lets our children feel calmer about having them. By so doing, they eventually have room for other, nicer feelings.

It's at this point, however, that matters start to get a little more complicated. It's true, we should give room and validation to our children's feelings; however, if your emotional reaction is too strong, it can be problematic, too.

Avoid overreacting and overly identifying with your children

Let's return to the example of a friend canceling a playdate with your son, and choosing instead to meet up with a different friend. These social, uncomfortable situations may cause us to remember our own unfortunate childhood events, or otherwise simply "drive us mad" or "make us lose it." These reactions can cause us to respond in ways that are too explosive for the given situation: "*Poor thing! That is terrible! Stay away from him! You don't need to be his friend any-more—don't let him hurt you again.*" But, in actual fact, such a reaction is the last thing your son needs. When encountered with such a situation, rather than have your child recognize their own emotions and insult, rather than deal with it in a way that will calm them, they can feed off the negative stormy emotions you yourself exhibit. And so, instead of having the conversation be a source of calm and comfort, it is instead an additional element of pain, frustration, and trauma.

You can akin this to someone drowning in a stormy sea. Does that person need someone else to come and drown alongside them? Of course not. The drowning person needs someone else—someone to stand poised on the shore, who can recognize their plight, and who will hold out a hand to help them out of the waters (▶ see Chapter 7, regarding emotional regulation).

In other words, when our children encounter an emotional storm, they need us to remain poised and secure, not anxious and worried. They need our ability to notice and validate their distress; they need our empathy—but in moderation ("*I see, that really is insulting. But it's much more likely that your friend didn't want to hurt your feelings... I'm sure you can see him another day*"). Moreover, in most cases our children hardly need us to give them specific advice, or for us to tell them what to do. When our children are upset, first and foremost they need our *validation* of their emotions, and they should feel and understand that their stormy emotions are different than ours. This understanding will allow us to help them regulate their difficult emotions, without getting sucked into a storm of our own, or entering a state of over-identification.

The art of moderation—to watch our children from the right distance

Our need to keep a proper level of moderation continues. We all know that for us to better see our reflection in the mirror, we must stand at a proper distance—not too far, but not too close, either. If we're too far from the mirror—we see ourselves blurrily, but if we're too close—we'll end up not being able to see a thing.

The mirror metaphor is also relevant to our relationship with our children: for us to best see them, and for them to best see us (!)—we must find the optimal distance; not too far but not too close. Fascinatingly, parenting is, in many ways, a true meeting between two people—a parent and child. Two people with space between them: the space of interpersonal relations. The relationship we establish with our children is an excellent opportunity for them to learn about the give and take of interpersonal relationships, about the differences between people, of the other's humanity.

This learning cannot occur if we position ourselves "too close" to our children. And, indeed, there are parents who do everything they can in order to be attuned to their children at any and every given second, no matter their child's age (▶ see too Chapter 3, regarding helicopter parenting). Parents such as these sometime "press" pause on their own lives in order for them to "perfectly" answer their children's every need (or, more accurately, what they *believe* to be their children's needs). Those parents won't go out in the evenings so as not to leave their child under someone else's supervision; they won't move ahead in their job, nor will they develop their own hobbies—all so they don't hurt their children. In extreme cases, they may even choose not to expand their family.

However, children whose parents stand "too close" to them can feel as though the world in its entirety revolves around them. These children may find many life experiences hard to deal with; they may find difficulty in getting to know their own selves, may find trouble in getting to know other people and developing friendly relationships with those who surround them—all because they got used to having others *serve* their needs at all times. These children lack the opportunities to discover that others have their own inner worlds—worlds that are most often fascinating and worth knowing.

On the far other edge of the spectrum, are the children whose parents stand too far off—children whose parents hardly watch them: who don't interact with them or take an interest in their lives. These children, too, may develop problems with creating friendly interpersonal relationships.

As parents, it's best we position ourselves in the middle of the spectrum—between the two problematic extremes. It's best we look at our children from a proper, moderate distance, show them ample curiosity regarding their actual selves, and feel gladdened at the opportunity to get to know them—all and every characteristic included.

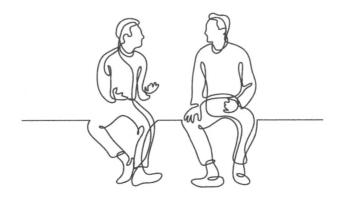

To allow our children to get to know us as human beings

When parents become overly attuned to their children, they can harm their children in yet another way. Not only will the child be incapable of "getting to know themselves" and look properly inwards, but they also miss out on getting to know their parents as human beings.

Children most certainly need adults guiding them and answering their needs to a certain degree (*"well enough"*). However, we now know that children also benefit from having their parents live their own lives, for them to be a part of additional things that are interesting and meaningful, and that have no direct correlation to their role as parents. Children benefit from their parents having meaningful and interesting jobs, hobbies, and healthy romantic relationships. They benefit from having parents who have their own social circles. When all these aspects occur, our children have the exciting, invaluable opportunity of getting to know us as human beings, apart from merely being their parents. Thus, in the same way we wish to get to know our children, we should offer them the wonderful possibility to get to know *us* as humans.

We can assist this special interpersonal relationship to develop by sharing different aspects of our own world with our children: tell them what happened at work, where you went out the other day, how you felt hurt when your friends went out without you—and how you forgave them when they apologized. At the same time, you can also share stories from your own childhood, when you were a child. Children are always happy to discover that their parents weren't *born* "adults" and "parental."

When we put effort into the interpersonal relationship we have with our children, we help them build up additional meaningful relationships with other children and adults, and greatly contribute to their ability to find worth and pleasure in them.

Practically—what can we do to promote our children's mentalization abilities?

- **Name emotions, feelings, and thoughts:** *"You're so excited!", "You seem disappointed.", "You're frustrated—and you have a good reason to be."*
- **Don't fall apart when encountered with your children's difficult, stormy emotions—but also don't dismiss them.** Treat them with the right amount of gravity: a moderate measure that includes a validation of their feelings; it's containment and regulation, which will finally bring them a relief from it.
- **Play with your children.** Playing—in all its forms—is an excellent way to promote mentalization skills.
- **Share experiences from your own world—both your inner world and outside one.** By doing so, you can help your children get to know you as individuals, and encourage their curiosity regarding meeting other people.
- **Be alert to misunderstandings. Apologize when needed.** Remember that children learn much by watching other people's behaviors. When we provide them with a personal example of people who look inwards and take

responsibility for their actions, they, too, learn to do the same.

- **Remember that your children are different than you (and different than the child you once were).** There is great value to recognizing the distinctions between us and our children, and to keep being curious regarding our children's unique inner world.
- When your child acts in a way that angers you—if they have a temper tantrum, if they lie, slam doors—pause for a moment and take a deep breath; don't react automatically. **Try and identify the meanings and thoughts behind such actions.** Try and look at it in a different way. In many cases, the mere pause and look inwards is enough to view the situation through a new angle—and hopefully provide the element to escape such unpleasantness.

THE BOTTOM LINE

Mentalization is one of the key foundations for a healthy mental state. It evolves from the relationship between parents and child, and there is much we can do to help this process occur. When we treat our child as a whole person from infancy, a person with their own special and unique inner world, we contribute to their ability to perceive themselves as such and, later on, view others in the same way. It's important to keep a curious mind regarding our children's inner world, and to accept the fact that we may never fully understand it.

When our children share their experiences with us, it's important that we are "there" for them—but this must be done in the right amount: not too much (over identifying with them), and not too little ("*Nothing happened*"). Additionally, it's important for us to get to know our children as human beings and allow them to get to know us. This process happens through conversation, mutual sharing of experiences, and playing together. The most important thing to remember is to enjoy the road together and appreciate the real relationship we create with our children.

CHAPTER 12

"YES—I CAN DO IT"
Helping our children believe in their ability to succeed

> *"Whether you think you can, or you think you can't—you're right."*
>
> **—Henry Ford**

Mom, Dad,

- *Show me how to do a handstand...*
- *Help me solve this math problem for my finals...*
- *For my next birthday, I want a fondant rainbow unicorn cake...*

When encountered with any one of these requests, it's highly likely that you'll tell your adorable children: *"Tell me, have you lost your* minds? *A fondant unicorn rainbow cake? Your* math *final?"* Or perhaps there's more of a chance you'd say: *"Of course, honey—though I'm not sure I'll manage, I can certainly try..."*

Your answers to these questions are all connected to the term "**self-efficacy**."

So, even if there's no chance you'd try and do a handstand, bake a unicorn cake, or solve a math final—knowing this term can be one of the most important gifts you can give your children, a gift that will last them throughout their entire life.

Self-efficacy—lovely to meet you!

Can you estimate what your children think regarding their capabilities: Does your son think of himself as a good friend? What does your daughter think about her musical talent? How do they appreciate their math abilities, or their sport skills?

The American psychologist **Albert Bandura** coined the term **self-efficacy** in relation to the extent to which we believe we can execute a certain task or role in our lives. The self-efficacy varies from one field to another—so that someone can hold high self-efficacy when it comes to athleticism (*"If I train hard, I'll be able to run as fast as I want"*), but a low self-efficacy when it comes to technical matters (*"I'm never going to manage to change a car's tire"*). We all have different levels of self-efficacy when it comes to parenting (*"The extent to which I believe I'm a good parent to my children"*), we have perceptions regarding our abilities at work, and through every other aspect in life. It's expected that our self-efficacy can evolve and change during different times as per the experiences and trials we go through.

And why is this important? It's important because the level of our self-efficacy regarding any given matter will determine our willingness to try and engage in any particular task; it will determine the level of effort we'll put into the task, and it will affect our eventual achievement levels. Thus, a magic circle is created. When we believe we can complete a certain task (let's say, a ten-mile run, baking a truly impressive cake, or learning to play the guitar), we give it a go. Our mere attempt ups the efforts we put in and raises our eventual chances of succeeding. Our eventual success further ups our self-efficacy regarding the task, something which can encourage us to try similar things in the future and succeed at them, too.

Is there a chance I can run ten miles?

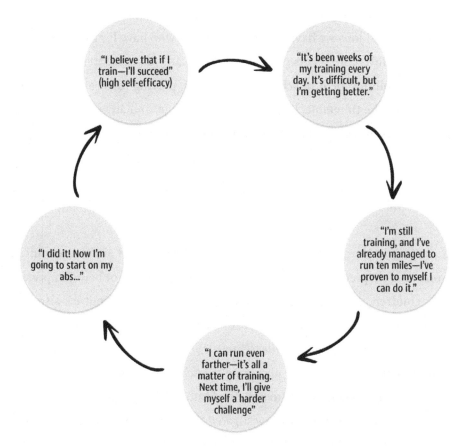

This cycle, however, can also work in the reverse. If we don't believe we can run those ten miles, or bake that special cake, or learn to play an instrument—we will pre-emptively avoid such tasks, not giving it a minimal effort ("low self-efficacy"). In this situation, we are expected to have less chances of success; we will receive the "confirmation" that we *cannot* run / play / bake… and will decide to avoid trying again in the future.

Here I would like to make an especially important point: the level of self-efficacy is not predestined. We can most assuredly improve and develop our own levels of self-efficacy—and our children's self-efficacy, too. And when regarding our children—the process is very much in our own hands. In other words: one of the vital parental jobs we have is to raise children who have high-efficacy abilities in many different aspects. We want to (and can) raise children who believe in their capabilities: be it in schooling, in sports, playing musical instruments, remembering the timetable, learning a new language, and any number of other things. How is this done? There are numerous guidelines that can assist us.

"You're so clever" or "Good effort?"

Who among us doesn't praise our children for being smart and successful? In the previous chapters I clearly emphasized the importance of being impressed by our children. And it's true—parental enthusiasm is vital, but it's also vital that we pay attention to what we choose to praise. Surprisingly, it appears that compliments such as *"You're so smart!"* and *"What a wonderful student you are!"* are not something our children need; rather, such compliments might even sabotage our children's willingness to put effort into reaching higher achievements.

The researcher **Carol Dweck** investigated this topic and arrived at some fascinating conclusions (▶ watch her TED talk on YouTube). In one of her studies, Dweck gave a group of ten-year-olds the task to complete a mid-level difficulty puzzle. Once the children finished, half of them received feedback along the lines of "Well done! You're so *smart*," while the others received: "Good job putting in so much *effort*!" The second stage of the research consisted of the children having to *choose* between an easy puzzle and a difficult one. Can you guess what happened? Take note of this: 70 percent of the children in the first group—the ones whose *intelligence* was complimented—preferred to take the *easy* puzzle. On the other hand, the second group of children—those who received positive feedback regarding their *effort* and *dedication*—70 percent of them requested the *difficult* puzzle (!)

Can you guess the reason as to why the children who were crowned as "intelligent" preferred to put in less effort?

Here's the explanation: when we compliment our children on their cleverness and achievements, we put them in the position of having to carry on proving their worth. These children will fear failure, for failing will mean losing the status of "clever" or "excellent." That's the reason the first group requested the easy puzzle—they didn't want to fail.

Think about it this way: if your daughter receives an A on her test and you tell her, "*Well done! You're so smart!*" what would she come to think about herself when she receives a C? Unfortunately, being "clever" goes hand-in-hand with being rather "foolish."

However, when we give children positive feedback regarding their efforts and dedication, we pass on the message that the difficulty itself is the challenge, and that putting forth effort always pays off. So, next time your daughter brings home a test with a good grade, it's best you tell her, "*Well done—you studied so well. You put in so much effort and dedication.*" Down the road, when she receives a C, maybe she will be able to tell herself: "*I guess that this time I didn't try hard enough. Next time I'll put in more effort and do better.*" Meaning, instead of complimenting your children on their cleverness and achievements, compliment their efforts. Compliments such as these are key aspects for your children's future progress, development, study habits, and willingness to handle new challenges.

But, is it only the words we use? Or is the process deeper? Dweck carried on studying the subject in order to better understand why some children shy away from challenges, while others view them as something they want to meet head-on. She discovered that, at the basis of it all, lie the parents' and their children's presuppositions regarding the nature of human abilities. Allow me to explain.

"I was born this way" or "The sky is the limit?"

Musical talent... language aptitude... special awareness... being mathematically inclined... emotionally intelligent... technologically inclined... a wonderful cook and baker...

Regarding each of these aspects, how deeply do you believe that our talents are predestined ("You either *have it* or you don't"), or do you believe that the differences and improvements you make rely on your will and motivation to practice and experiment—or in other words, believe that "the sky is the limit?"

Apparently, there are children and adults who believe that brains and talents are set characteristics that cannot be changed; meaning, they believe in a **fixed mindset**. These people tend to fear challenges, and in many cases, would choose to put in little-to-no effort. On the other end of the spectrum, are children and adults who believe that skills are something we can improve and develop— **growth mindset**. It's these people who put in huge efforts and push through difficulties and challenges, and they are also the people who eventually reach impressive and monumental achievements.

That said, today we know that in most aspects you need a mixture of both: a talent you were born with, combined with trials and learning. However, more and more evidence is building up proving that practice and effort have a greater impact on our achievements than our predetermined talents. Furthermore, it seems that there is a huge value to the mere *belief* children and parents have regarding the importance of practice and training. Children who believe that their abilities are inclined to improve if they work hard—are the children who put in the effort and reach higher achievements. As parents, we can influence our children's conceptions. We can teach them that our brain is a flexible organ that doesn't stop developing and improving. Each training session or new experience contributes to the making of new neural connections, so that the more we practice, the more and more we'll improve. There is no limit to our ability to learn—and that is a proven fact. Believing in that can pave the way to impressive, vast achievements. It's this concept through which we can positively influence our children's brains—and that is one of the most beautiful gifts we can bestow upon them.

Moreover, in the last few years, accumulated evidence showing that early intensive learning, and the continuation of learning new things throughout one's whole life, strengthens the brain, and may even prevent its lessening functionality as we grow older. These findings can be an excellent reason for *you*—the parents—to start learning Spanish, or how to play chess, to play the piano, or any number of unfulfilled dreams you may have.

It's hard—and unadvised—to be a perfectionist

We were once taught that during job interviews, if we were asked what were the qualities that might get in our way of doing the job, we should answer: "*I am a perfectionist*"—as though perfectionism is a positive attribute that merely disguised itself as a bad one. However, today we know that perfectionism is indeed a problematic and difficult quality, and one that causes people much suffering and redundant frustration.

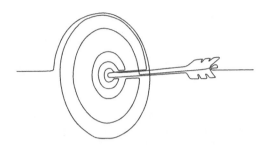

The root of *perfectionism* comes from the word perfect, of course, so at the basis of this quality is the underlying belief that things can actually be done "perfectly." Through that assumption, anything that is less than "perfect" can be perceived by the perfectionist as a failure. And indeed, perfectionist children are those who get disappointed when they get an A- on their test—they're also the ones who have a tantrum when their picture doesn't turn out just right, when their letters are a little wonky; or, when they're older and get a zit on their forehead… or, really, the long of the short of it is—most of the time.

In our society, which greatly emphasizes the connection between success and ambition to competitiveness (just look at all the reality TV programs: each has a winner, losers, and—most emphasized—those who are eliminated), it seems that perfectionism has become an actual pandemic. However, the price of perfectionism is heavy: more and more children, adolescents, and adults suffer from a continual lack of satisfaction and feelings of failure. That said, perfectionism isn't a life sentence, and we can help our children get rid of this problematic characteristic—or at least ease its influence.

Continuing the point made about fixed mindsets against growth mindsets, the source of perfectionism holds within it the assumption that there is a certain criterion for success, thus any who fall short of it, fails. However, it's entirely possible to doubt this assumption. Think, for instance, about the task: "Passing my French test" against "Learning to speak French." If the set task is succeeding in passing the test—then there is a clear criterion, and it's one that can be checked and measured. Alternatively, if the task is learning to speak the language—there's no limit to our ability of learning, improving, and pushing forward. In that case, there's no room for frustration when something doesn't go as planned, because that's simply an inseparable part of the learning process. This is also true with "coloring in the lines" instead of simply "drawing," or "playing this musical piece with no mistakes" instead of "learning to play the piano."

People who hold the belief that there is a certain criterion for success, are destined to experience much frustration throughout their lives. However, people who believe that the sky is the limit, will keep pushing forward, and view every failure as an important learning experience.

If your child has a tendency toward perfectionism—refuses to lose a game, gets frustrated and angry at every botched drawing, is disappointed about getting an A- on a test—explain to them the information written here. Explain the value of their mere experience and attempt, and that on the road to learning—there is no set criteria; that there are no limits to our ability to learn and grow. The things that may seem like failures are still important parts of the road and process.

INTERESTING TO NOTE

"Girls aren't good at math:" Preconceptions we have regarding our own selves, and the danger of comparing ourselves to others

In the last few years, some high schools around the world implemented a trial program for learning final-level mathematics. As a part of the program, girls studied independently from the boys. There was no religious basis to the separation. So, what, after all, was the logic behind such a decision? Apparently, many girls tend to drop high-level mathematics in high school, something attributed to their low self-esteem when comparing themselves to the boys in the class—who are considered, in general, more mathematically inclined. However, studies show that there is no inherited difference in mathematical abilities between boys and girls. It seems, instead, that the differences stem from prejudices and the girls' low self-esteem when compared to the boys. And indeed—schools that implemented the program saw a wide increase in the number of girls who successfully passed their finals—all because they were separated from the boys in their class. The girls' success rate was the same as the boys'. A large part of the explanation for this has to do with the girls' self-efficacy, which rose exponentially once they no longer felt as if they were being compared to the boys.

It's important to take note of this. In many situations we tend to form an opinion regarding our abilities to perform a certain task—all the while, comparing ourselves to others. Yet, such a comparison can do us harm, and affect our motivation and willingness to partake in the given activity. Think, for example, about a girl who desperately wants to sign up for gymnastics, but chooses not to—*"Because I'll never be as good as my older sister, who won second place at the school competition."* Isn't that a shame?

So, next time your child gives up on some activity, *"Because I'll never be as good at it as someone else"*—remember that the comparison is redundant, and only harms the child's accomplishments and ability to enjoy the activities. It's true that in a family or in our children's social circles, we cannot execute the same sort of artificial separation performed in the "girls only" math group; but our awareness of the issue of comparisons can free our children from unnecessary expectations and instead allow them to participate in whatever activity they choose—all without comparing themselves to others.

I gave it my all… and I failed—what does that say about me?

"I tried out for the student council and… I wasn't chosen;" "I sang in front of the whole school in the show… and I was off key;" "I asked a lovely girl out… but she said no."

So… what now?

When we think about children with high self-efficacy (meaning: children who believe in their ability to succeed), we tend to picture "successful children." However, it seems that what influences our capability levels more than anything else is actually measured through the way we handle failure. After all, our lives are riddled with trials and challenges, and we cannot always succeed. In situations when failure occurs, we all learn valuable lessons—centered, above all else, around the inner conversation we have within ourselves. In other words: it connects to the way we attribute the failure. And here, once again, you, the parents, have a key role in these situations: your attitudes toward your children's states of failure become, in time, your children's own inner voices.

Let's assume that our child received a grade of D on their science test, or perhaps tried out for the student council and wasn't chosen. They can attribute their failure to *outside* elements (*"The test was particularly hard;" "I'd left my notebook at school;" "There were a lot of candidates this year"*); or they can think of it as related to *inner* elements (*"I didn't study enough;" "I didn't put much effort in my election speech"*). They can attribute their failure to it being *permanent* (*"I just suck when it comes to science"*); or they can view it as *temporary* (*"I didn't sleep well the night before, so I couldn't concentrate"*).

Children who tend to take the failure unto themselves (internal attribution) and see it as permanent (*"I suck at science;" "I've got no chance of managing—ever;" "Children in class don't like me, so they won't choose me, anyway"*)—those are the children who will choose to avoid repeating such experiences, thus making their self-efficacy low. However, children who attribute their failures to external situations (*"The test was especially complicated;"* or *"There were many really good candidates"*), or to inner, but *fleeting* matters (*"I didn't put in enough effort—next time I'll try harder"*)—those are the children who are expected to try and try again, to put in additional efforts, and eventually reach impressive achievements.

At the same time, we should also ask ourselves how we and our children define failure. Let's assume that your son moved ahead in the sorting for a delegation from his youth group, but didn't pass the final stage. Is that a failure? And if your daughter played wonderfully in a school show but missed a few cords—is that considered a failure? In situations such as these, it's important that we remember the whole process—the efforts and pleasure it brought—and the many smaller successes that led up to the conclusion. You shouldn't allow one pointed non-success "paint" the whole picture in gloomy colors.

Practice leads to excellence—the 10,000-hour rule

If your daughter wishes to go to a ballet class, but you suppose she will not be particularly talented at it—will you allow her to go? And how would you react if your son wants to play an instrument, but you believe his musicality is lacking?

We were all raised on the myth of the "child prodigy," as though children were born being exceptional musicians, fantastic athletes, or "simply genius." However, it appears that "child prodigies" are a very rare phenomenon, so rare that it's doubtful it even exists. When regarding any aspect, the talent we're born with holds only a small component in the question of ultimate success. What matters worlds more than the given talent, is dedication, practice, and the belief in succeeding.

Malcolm Gladwell, in his book *"Outliers,"* pays particular attention to this issue. He referenced many research papers that followed the lives of people with extraordinary talents and accomplishments. And apparently, in every area of practice—musical instruments, sports, engineering, chess, and countless others—they needed a training regimen of 10,000 accumulated hours, usually spread out across a timeframe of approximately a decade, to finally reach an exceptional level of expertise. According to Gladwell, there is no such thing as a "child prodigy." There are children with talent, who are ambitious and possess a huge amount of will, who practiced and practiced and practiced, and only then became exceptional musician, wonderful chess players, brilliant developers, and so forth. "*Practice is not what you do when you are exceptional,*" Gladwell writes. "*It's what you do* to be *exceptional.*"

And so, can your son who doesn't possess rhythm, become a talented drummer, if only he practices? If he enjoys drumming and is willing to put in the effort—there's a good chance he will manage. And anyway, regardless, it's worth trying. Remember—the important part isn't the final destination (not that one truly exists), but the practice, the constant bettering of one's self, and above all, the pleasure in the process.

THE BOTTOM LINE

Children, by nature, are curious and look for challenges. They like to work hard and succeed. It's vital for them to feel as though they are, indeed, capable of it!

Self-efficacy is one of the biggest and most important gifts we can give our children. Children's and adolescents' beliefs regarding their ability to perform a task are directly correlated to their willingness to participate in different activities and to succeed in them.

To encourage the children to act, it's important to praise their dedication and efforts—not their cleverness. It's just as important to teach our children that their skills are not predetermined, but evolve due to their experiences and willingness to try, and the efforts they put in. Failure, ultimately, is an excellent chance to learn from our mistakes and continue trying at a further date.

Children and adolescents who believe that the brain is a flexible organ, and that efforts can improve their abilities—challenge themselves, try harder, put in the effort, and are, in the end, the people who reach impressive achievements.

CHAPTER 13

"I CAN AND I WANT TO"
Raising responsible, motivated, and aspirational children

> *"If you can dream it, you can do it."*
>
> —**Walt Disney**

Have you ever asked yourselves:

- *How is it that, while in daycare, they always pick up all their toys once they're finished playing with them, yet, at home, they* never *do?*
- *How is it possible that my child knows the names of every one of the NBA players and knows the rule book inside and out—yet they refuse to learn in the same way when it's for a history test?*
- *How can our adolescents put endless effort, 24/7, for the preparations for their youth group's summer camp? What motivates them to work so hard? (And, somehow, when it comes to issues of home and family, they don't put in half the amount of energy?)*

In the previous chapter, I put emphasis on the vital importance of our children's capabilities: their self-efficacy levels. However, beyond their own skills and abilities, their *will*, passion, enthusiasm, forward-pulling motivation, curiosity, and also their ability to *dream* and set up goals, are no less important. In this chapter, we will try and understand what are the triggers that cause motivation in children and adolescents, and what can—unintentionally—sabotage it.

Raising responsible children

As parents, we want our children to be responsible: for them to set the table; do their own homework and study for their tests; engage and play with their siblings; clear the dishwasher; take out the dog ("*You promised you'd be responsible for him!*"); practice playing their musical instrument; keep fit; etc. And of course we want such things—who doesn't want to raise children and teenagers who are responsible?

No matter their age, children can do certain tasks on their own: starting with picking up their fallen pacifier, getting their own cup of water, and culminating with cooking a meal for the whole family. You might be surprised to hear this, but children, by nature, *love* working hard and taking up responsibilities. However, at times, quite unintentionally, we sabotage their inherent capabilities—and especially their willingness—to do as such. Apparently, one of our biggest mistakes concerns the *incentives* we offer them in order to try and up their motivation.

The slippery slope of "if-then"

The researcher **Daniel Pink** wrote in his book "*Motivation*," important insights regarding strengthening our children's motivation. Most of us tend to think that if we wish to motivate someone to do something, we must give a reward for the wanted behavior—one that will act as positive reinforcement. Well, against our given logic, it's apparent that external rewards—given in the form of "if-then" ("*if you tidy up your room—then we'll go have pizza*")—harms our willingness to perform certain actions that would have otherwise been done well even without such rewards.

For example, let's assume you've reached the stage when you can ask your eldest child for help watching their younger siblings. You've used their help on and off for a few months already, and, so far, it's been going rather well. But, then you think about possibly paying your child a small amount of money for each "babysitting duty" ("*to keep up their motivation to help*"). Well—that's a mistake. From the moment children (or adults) get monetary rewards for their actions—or any other kind of external tangible rewards—the action they previously did "naturally" becomes a "chore." Even worse than that—an "unenjoyable chore."

Please note: if before, your child agreed to your request out of inner motivation, and especially out of the feeling of familial obligation, the external reward sabotages that inner motivation, turning it into an external one, instead. It's as if an inner voice whispers in your children's ear, subconsciously: *"I'm only doing this because I'm getting paid—I don't enjoy doing it, and I won't continue doing it unless I keep getting paid. If I get a better offer or something more important comes along—I'm out of here."* It's that thought process that you desperately want to avoid.

When we offer our children a dollar for every time they empty the dishwasher, or when we promise to buy them football cards, or "an expansion pack" for their favorite computer game if they do well on their upcoming test. External rewards in the form of "if-then" change the natural action, done out of commitment and inner motivation, into actions that are undesirable and forced upon us.

By the way, this may be one of the reasons your children despise tests—tests that culminate in a given grade. If we would offer them the opportunity to learn a subject of their choosing through the doing of an interesting, creative project, it's likely that they would enjoy the process and learn through curiosity, pleasure, and inner motivation. However, from the moment we set the goal of "succeeding on the test," the motivation for learning changes to one of an external source (getting a good test grade), and the process becomes subjugated as an unpleasant and uninteresting task—even if they did do well in the end.

Where have the positive reinforcements gone?

You must admit, the messages here are rather confusing. Does it mean that we were totally *wrong* in assuming that it's important to give children and adolescents positive reinforcements and praise? The answer here is, *of course not.* It's not a mistake, at all. Praise and positive reinforcements are a vital tool in the path of education—ones that are impossible to do without. Positive reinforcements help in passing on to our children our most important values; but it's imperative we give them correctly.

Firstly, as I wrote in the previous chapter, it's best to give children positive reinforcements for actions or efforts, and not for talents or smarts. Secondly, it's best to lessen the use of "if-then" that categorize different actions into unpleasant and unwanted tasks. Instead, you should give those positive reinforcements only *after* the task is done, and to be specific regarding the points of which we are impressed by. The American-Israeli psychologist and researcher **Dan Ariely** in his book "*Payoff—The Hidden Logic that Shapes our Motivations*" calls this: acknowledgment. "*Acknowledgment is a kind of human magic—a small human connection, a gift from one person to another that translates into a much larger, more meaningful outcome.*" Indeed, research has proven that our acknowledgment and recognition of someone else's efforts greatly contributes to upping that person's motivation. So, for example, when we ask our eldest child to watch their younger siblings, and they do so, we can say something along the lines of: "*Well done! It's a pleasure to see you watching your siblings—you play and engage them so wonderfully, and we're really appreciative of it.*" Such feedback can increase the possibility of being able to ask them to watch their siblings again in the future.

Additionally, it's important to give our children the feeling that their efforts are meaningful and not simply arbitrary ("*It helps us so much when you watch your siblings—it allows me to easily focus on other things*"). It's also important for the reinforcements to be genuine and not forced—children are very sensitive to any form of falseness or insincere or overdone compliments. So, let's not allow ourselves to be confused regarding this: children (and adolescents!) wish to gain our appreciation through our recognition and feelings of awe. Allow yourselves to give them away plentifully, though in an appropriate manner.

And when are reinforcements such as "if-then" acceptable?

You can use reinforcements such as "if-then" when regarding simple actions that are, by nature, regarded as not particularly pleasant, and ones that don't demand our child to have inner motivation. For instance, if your child is scared about getting an injection or vaccine, you can say that once it's done, you will take them out for ice-cream. Situations such as these are perfectly logical and acceptable instances to use "if-then" reinforcements. We would hardly expect an injection or vaccine to be a part of their inner motivation set. Similarly, when we try and eliminate one of our children's unwanted habits (such as children who continually creep into their parents' bed at night), you can give them positive reinforcements for managing to change their behavior (sleeping a full night in their own bed). It's important to make sure that the positive reinforcements given remain small and symbolic—a sticker, for example, rather than an expensive gift. You can also say that after your child accumulates five stickers, they will receive a surprise—a small one, again, nothing expensive. Why is it so important that the rewards are small and symbolic? It's important so that the message given to the child is that they are doing the behavioral change for themselves—and not for the gift. If you keep at this, it's likely that after a while, prizes and rewards will become redundant, but the wanted behavior will remain.

Raising curious children who love learning (and doing homework...)

And here is another issue where it seems that we fall through and act incorrectly.

If you give a child in daycare a workbook in math or language learning, it's likely that they will do it with pleasure and enthusiasm (they may even ask for you to give them more work to do). A mere matter of months later, while giving them the same workbook, but terming it "homework for first grade"—they will do everything they can so they do not have to do it, only to delay the inevitable chore. Well, what went wrong in the process? Where was our mistake?

The issue of homework has oftentimes drawn arguments among professional educators. Without going into the deeper aspects of the question of whether or not homework is necessary for the process of learning, there is still no doubt that it becomes—right from first grade—an unwanted and burdening chore. The fact that children hate doing their homework (and that *we* hate doing *their* homework…) should greatly concern us.

And what is our own part in this process?

We all carry memories of our time in the educational system. If we, as children, hated doing our homework—there's still no reason for us to pass on that hate to our children. Beyond that: when we sit and do their work with them, check over their work, correct it, erase things, or even do it for them—our children receive an undeniable feeling of stress, frustration, and judgment. Who would want to complete their homework in such an atmosphere?

Moreover, there are times during which our main communication with our children is based on the struggles around doing homework. Isn't that a shame? Rather than talking with our children about the good things that happened throughout their day, rather than hearing about funny or interesting things that went on at school—we are constantly busy with chasing after them to complete their work.

It's important to know that in many ways, *responsibility* cannot be present with two different people at the same time. As long as you are the ones who hold the responsibility of your child's homework, you cannot be surprised that they will struggle with taking over the responsibility themselves. And if we hope that one day our teenagers will take full responsibility for their finals or any other activity or task they wish to perform (which is definitely something we all hope for), then we must start the passing of responsibility at a young age—as soon as possible. In the lower grades of elementary school, it's all right to remind the children of having homework, to make sure they sit and do it, to be available for any questions they may have—but nothing beyond that. In the future, as the children grow, our level of involvement should considerably lessen.

Remember that it's your children's homework—not your own. It's also vital to remember that your children's homework shouldn't be "perfect"—mistakes are an inseparable part of any learning process. Additionally, no great calamity will occur if your child shows up at school without doing their homework once in a while—and also takes responsibility for that (*"I'm very sorry, we celebrated my sister's birthday yesterday, and I couldn't finish all the homework"*). Your child's ability to take responsibility for themselves, and the keeping of good relations between child and their parents—complex and deep relationships that aren't "colored" by arguments regarding homework—all these goals are more important than completing another page in a math book.

Remember that children, by nature, are curious and love learning. It's important to find ways to preserve their curiosity and not shut it down. Learning out of curiosity is active learning, in an atmosphere that includes the freedom of choice, and the feeling of infinite discoveries waiting at our fingertips. Such magic can't occur when surrounded by feelings of stress and compulsion, nor in an atmosphere filled with judgment and limitations.

Raising children who put effort into hobbies and extracurricular activities

Gymnastics, basketball, arts and crafts, young magicians, young scientists, dog training, young chefs, playing musical instruments, debate club, programming, and countless others—there's no limit to the myriad of extracurricular classes available today. There's no wonder, in that case, that our children find choosing so confusing—they try, change their minds and quit, try again, before quitting once more. It truly is very confusing. Research regarding decision-making shows that the more choices we're presented, the less satisfied we are with our final choice. This phenomenon is called the "*Paradox of Choice*" and it's explained by the fact that each of our choices emphasizes the *loss* of all the *unchosen* possibilities. In this aspect, perhaps it was easier in the past, when all the classes we had to choose from were ballet, painting, football, or judo.

Yet still, extracurricular activities and classes hold much value for our children's development. The different classes expose our children to different hobbies and interests, contribute to their overall creativity, allow them to develop talents—and by doing all that, contribute to our children's self-image. For all these wonderful things to actually come to pass, it's important for you to be involved with your child's ultimate choice of classes—but not in an overbearing way. Above all, you should define the "framework:" how many extracurricular classes can your child choose (don't overdo it—your child needs downtime, too) and which kinds of classes should they choose (musical, physical activity based, artistic, and so forth). Beyond that, try and give your children the freedom to choose on their own. Children who feel as though they have control over their ultimate choice, tend to take responsibility for their chosen class by putting in the dedication needed, and enjoying it to its full capacity. Remember, only a few children continue from their local judo class to the Olympics. Assuming your child is not among them, remind yourselves that the goals are, in fact, about the exposure to new interests, the special, social gathering the class provides, and, of course, the enjoyment of the activity your child decides on.

A burdening task, or enjoyable challenge— it's up to us!

It's impossible to write a chapter about motivation, and not mention "*Tom Sawyer*."

Tom Sawyer, the exceptional protagonist of **Mark Twain**'s book, received a job that was far from enjoyable—to paint the surrounding wooden fence of his Aunt Polly's yard. Forlorn over his given fate, Sawyer found himself an ingenious solution. He divided the fence into numerous parts, and after some hard negotiation, he "sold" the *right* to paint the fence to some of his neighborhood friends. The fence was soon painted with a lot of enthusiasm by Sawyer's friends—without Tom having to lift a finger. His actions exposed one of the wonders of human motivation: apparently, the same task can either be a burden, or an exciting, enjoyable challenge—it's all about the way it is presented. I'm sure you can think about similar, relevant examples from your own lives.

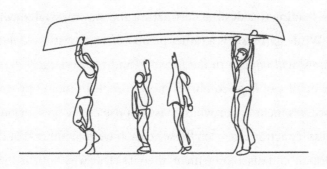

And indeed, the "Tom Sawyer Effect" can be successfully attributed in our parental daily lives. It's important for you to take this under consideration the next time you need your children's help—be it with building a cupboard from IKEA, cleaning up the paperwork on your desk, or making a salad for dinner. If we don't overuse this trick, there's a good chance we will rather than have to "force" our children to complete the given task—give them the "right" (!) to do it—just like Tom Sawyer.

Raising children who are ambitious and capable of dreaming

"What are your dreams?", "What are your aspirations?", "What do you want to be when you grow up?"—even if there's no real chance of your children giving any relevant answers to these questions (though, by the way, there's a very good chance of their future jobs not actually being invented yet), the mere raising of such questions holds an apparent great value. It is the field of *positive psychology* that brought with it the research of this special quality, called *hope*. The American psychologist **Rick Snyder** defines "hope" as the perceived ability to walk certain paths leading to a desired destination and stay motivated when walking these paths. While *optimism* is a rather passive characteristic—"*I tend to believe that good things will happen in the future*"—and is also largely determined by genetics, the quality of *hope* combines more complex thought processes. These thought processes include our willingness to pose challenges for ourselves and take the necessary actions to reach those goals. If we remember that the opposite of hope is despair and discouragement, then it's clear why hope is so vital. Much research has deemed that children with high levels of the hope quality manage to achieve higher goals—in all life's aspects—and to overcome many obstacles.

According to the theory of hope, a goal can be anything we wish to experience, create, do, or become (*"Being accepted to the Scout delegation," "Learn to play the clarinet," "Be a doctor," "Run a half-marathon," "To be more organized"*). Children and adults are differentiated through their levels of hopefulness. The more a person has high levels of hope, the more they will set themselves complex, long-term, and difficult goals. In order for us to actualize our self-set goals, people with high hopefulness will define themselves sub-category goals and will find alternative ways of action when they encounter obstacles. For this process to occur, we have to embrace a positive inner voice that will push us toward action (*"I can do this!" "I'm not going to give up on this," "Even if it's hard—I know it's possible"*). In this manner, we will be able to move toward our set goals, and eventually also make our dreams come true.

For example, this is what a teenage girl may tell herself:

"I want to be a youth group leader next year. In order to achieve this goal, I have to put a lot of effort in the upcoming course. At the same time, I should talk with the course leaders so they know it's what I want. There may be a lot of competition for the role, but I'm not going to give up on this. I want—and can do it. And if things don't go my way, if I don't get the role, I'll find something else—something even more meaningful, and I'll give it my best. If one of the youth leaders quits throughout the year, I'll try and take their place instead."

The combination of setting a larger goal, and translating it into smaller sub-sets, the positive inner dialogue, and the strategies for possible problems that may pop up down the road—that is what creates a high level of hopefulness.

And here is the most important message: hope is a way of thinking we can help develop within our children; we can teach children to dream big, to set goals for themselves and to reach them, too—step by step. We can teach children to overcome obstacles that appear along the way; and even provide them with that inner, positive voice that pushes them toward success and actualization.

Many professionals within the psychological and educational system believe that this is one of the most important missions of our everchanging lives: to teach children to dream, be ambitious, to hope, to set themselves goals, and eventually reach them.

THE BOTTOM LINE

Children and adolescents naturally wish to work hard and succeed. They want to contribute to their family and others. For this to happen, it's important not to give them external rewards along the lines of "if-then," for that lessens inner motivation rather than encourages it. However, praise and astoundment after the fact, the recognition of their efforts, and the importance of the task done—are all elements that increase children and adolescents' feelings of worth, and their ultimate willingness to behave and act as expected. Additionally, it's important for children to take responsibility for their homework and chosen extracurricular activities. If we involve ourselves overly much and put a lot of stress on our children, they will feel, right away, that the responsibility has shifted to be ours rather than theirs, and that is the exact opposite of our wishes.

Another thing we should remember is that the same activities can be viewed as either enjoyable and fun, or frustrating and stressful—it all depends on how we present it. This knowledge we can use to our advantage so that we encourage our children to perform out of a sense of happiness, enjoyment, and freedom of choice, and not out of necessity and force. Finally, beyond daily tasks, remember that you can and should develop within your child the ability to dream, hope, have ambitions, to set goals and eventually reach them, too. As parents we can develop within our children the faith in their own abilities, and their possibilities of actualizing their dreams.

CHAPTER 14

"MY MOM IS SUPERWOMAN"
Children idolizing their parents as a basis for acquiring positive values

> *"To the world you may be just one person, but to one person you may be the world."*
>
> **—Brandi Snyder**

Tony Soprano, the protagonist of the American television program "The Sopranos," is in a true bind. He acts as a family-man; a dedicated father to his two teenage children, but at the same time, "makes a living" through organized crime as the head of the American-Italian mob in New Jersey.

How are "both" possible to achieve? What values does the good, devoted father Tony wish to pass on to his children? And what should they write on the school questionnaires when asked about the parents' jobs? Such a conundrum!

Assuming your livelihood does not rest upon the high-crime syndicates, you most likely have good reason to wish for your children to look up to you with admiration, for them to hope to be like you. And why is this so important?

Various chapters in this book are centralized around the question of what makes children "human beings;" how our young children become fully functional, responsible, social, productive members of society; how they become people who hold good, honest values. One of the main answers to these questions has to do with the relations between us and our children, and the children's appreciation and admiration toward us.

This idea may seem a little far-fetched. Should our children truly admire us or idealize us? In our modern-contemporary world, such a perception is far from obvious. But parenting, by definition, isn't an equalized relationship: it's a relationship between an *adult*—big, strong, responsible, and knowledgeable, to a *child*—small, still learning, in need of support and protection. Allow me to explain.

My mom and dad can do anything!

Children—throughout most of their childhood—tend to believe that their parents are *omnipotent*: "*my father and mother can do e-v-e-r-y-t-h-i-n-g! There's nothing in the world they don't know, or cannot fix, or do for me.*" This feeling—though far from reality—allows a healthy illusion to take root in our children, and it's important to allow them to hold onto it. When we allow our children to admire us, to look up to us with shining eyes, our children aspire to be like us. It's through this process that they adopt positive, worthy values to themselves, and become the hoped-for "human beings."

With time, as our children grow older, they begin to gain slow exposure to the truth of their parents *not* being omnipotent, and that there are many things we don't know and cannot do. In a natural and hoped-for situation, this process occurs once the children are capable of "handling it," when their "self" is already quite developed. And so, as long as the process is done slowly and gradually, it doesn't harm the central goal: of helping our children gain positive values.

Listen to your own conscience (but before that—listen to mine...)

You may be reading this and saying to yourselves that you'd like for your children to choose their *own* way, which is not necessarily influenced by yours: for them to have their own political leanings, adopt their individual religious beliefs, decide whether or not to be vegan or carnivores, choose their ultimate jobs and interests. Of course, all these aspirations are important and correct, but they only become relevant once you've given your children your own basic, fundamental "basket of values." For example, you may want to pass on the importance of telling the truth, helping others, being a good friend, taking responsibilities upon themselves, avoiding violence, making moral judgments, and so forth.

In other words: we are our children's guides. There is no substitute for the parental modeling and guidance we provide our children with. Once we've set our children on the "right path," and have guided them toward the main values we wish for them to possess, we can allow them to find their own unique path.

It's also important to note: the process of value assimilation happens quite naturally, stemming from that appreciation and basic admiration children have toward their parents. For that reason, it's important we remain aware of it, that we pay close attention to our more "problematic" behaviors that sometimes happen in front of our children. When our children see us slip off course—driving too fast; yelling at each other; lying to our aunt who asked us over to dinner (*"What a shame, we're out of town on that date"*)—they pick all of that up, too. After all, there is no more powerful way of learning than through imitation. So, remember this next time you leave a mess in the park; cut the line in the restaurant; or answer the operator rudely when she annoyed you during your phone conversation. Remember, that as parents, we are on the job constantly—always and without a break under the observational gaze and learning eyes of our children.

Astoundment, similarities, and admiration: The three development avenues as coined by Heinz Kohut

The idea that children should look at their parents with astoundment and awe is taken by the wonderful *"Self Theory"* of the psychoanalyst **Heinz Kohut**. Kohut attributed three main avenues through which children become "human beings." They all connect with the special relationship that occurs between children and their parents:

- The first avenue is called **mirroring** and is attributed to our own astoundment of our children as a vital and central cause for the creation of their positive self-image and positive thoughts about themselves. I've expanded on this in Chapter 2.

- The second avenue is called **twinship**. It is attributed to the importance of finding similarities between us and our children. This is a basis for our children's feelings of connectedness and belonging, and it is important for the strengthening of their social skills. You've read about this avenue further in Chapter 9.

- The third avenue is called **idealization**, and it deals with the children's admiration toward their parents. It seems that the children's ability to look at their parents with astoundment and appreciation aids them in acquiring good and worthy values for themselves. This chapter concentrates on this issue.

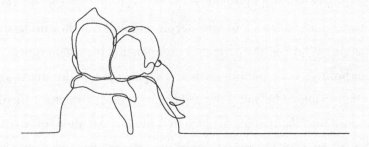

All of the aforementioned processes lean on the basic assumption that during the first years of childhood, our children's sense of "self" is still primal and not solidified. Thus, the children experience their parents as if they are a part of themselves—as though they are an extension of the child's sense of self (▶ see Chapter 2, page 35, regarding the term "**selfobject**"). These three processes of mirroring, twinship, and idealization help the children form their stable sense of self.

When parents go through rough life situations

We're not always easy to admire. Sometimes, parents get caught up in life situations when it's hard for them to remain subjects of admiration for their children. This can happen, for example, when one of the parents suffers a close loss, and experiences deep grief; or when one parent is sick for a long time, or hospitalized; it may also happen when the parents are getting divorced, or going through difficult financial troubles, and so forth. How do we handle such situations?

On the one hand, we may believe that there is value to our children seeing that we, too, are human. We have weaknesses and, at times, suffer rough patches and crises. On the other hand, our children require us to be "big and strong." Their existential security is undermined when one parent cannot function as a strong and stable figure in their lives. So, what do we do?

In such situations we should look at the big picture. Check with yourselves: what ages are your children, and how deeply and well can they understand the given situation? Which of the parents is experiencing the rough time—is it one of them, or both? Is the parent in crisis still capable of functioning as a parent? Is the parent capable of fulfilling the children's needs despite the difficult time? How well does the *other* parent manage to function? Are there other people in the family who can fulfil the parental roles until the rough patch passes—grandparents, other relatives, or close friends?

Based on your answers, decide how to conduct yourselves, and reconcile the complicated situation for your children. It's best not to hide what is going on from them, but still not share every single detail. In raising children, there is an important rule: always tell the truth, but not necessarily the whole truth. It's also important to try not to "fall apart" in their presence—at least not for long. Remember that our children have to be able to view us as strong, stable people, ones who can be leaned on and trusted.

Parents as a lighthouse rather than "on eye level"

Many people go into parenting with a set fantasy—being parents who inter-act with their children "on the same level"—meaning that they want to have a "friendly relationship" with them. However, as was written previously, your children do not need you as friends, and your relationship with them is not supposed to be "equal." They need you as adults who are stable and authoritative. Children need to look up to their parents, to appreciate them, and gain positive values from them; they need you as a *lighthouse* that will shine their way for-ward. Think for a moment about that "lighthouse:" high up above us, with strong lighting, can overcome and push through bad weather; it's always there, safe and stable, showing the way ahead for sailors. That's exactly how your children need you to be for them. They need that more than anything.

On the same subject, it's worth noticing people who grew up in difficult social circles; for example, those who were surrounded by crime and violence, but who still managed to pull themselves out of that darkness and give themselves a life full of value—supposedly against all odds. Such people often attribute that success to their parents, who guided them along and lit the way for them. Those people talk about their parents, and sometimes about additional figures such as teachers and educators, as those who fiercely passed on that "basket of positive values:" "You—don't you ever steal," "Don't ever lie!", "Work *hard, put in effort,*" "*You—you're going to be a good person.*" There's no doubt that parents have a huge amount of power to make a change and influence. Such processes are relevant, of course, also to those who grew up in more comfortable social situations.

THE BOTTOM LINE

Children become "human beings" mostly through their relationship with their parents. When our children watch us with eyes full of admiration, they assimilate good, worthy values through the model we give them. For this reason, it's important to allow our children to look up to us with admiration. As parents, we guide our children toward the values we find positive.

The children's feelings of admiration toward their parents is part of the process of cementing their own stable and healthy sense of self. Stemming from that, our children will continue to grow and find their own unique path; their own values they find important. It's impossible to give up this role. It arrives hand in hand with being a parent. Remember that our children watch us and learn from us. As parents, we're never off the job.

CHAPTER 15

GOOD CHILDREN—"BAD" CHILDREN
Every child wants to be "good," though sometimes it's hard

"...And how well did you behave today? Were you a good girl? Were you a good boy?"

From a very young age, children hear the expression, "be good." However, children and adolescents don't always manage to live up to their parents' expectations.

- *"Did you talk back to the teacher—again?"*
- *"You didn't study, and you got* another *bad grade...? (This laziness didn't come from me...)"*
- *"You fought with your friends again? You won't have any left with the way you're going."*
- *"You cut school again?"*

And the parents... the parents become exhausted, after being called to the day-care / elementary school / high school over and over—hearing how their child has been violent, rude, or how they cheated on their test. *"How many times have I told you, already."*

Every child misbehaves at some point or another. It's normal, natural, and, to a certain degree, even wanted (▶ see Chapter 10, with the matter of "too good" children). However, there are some children who consistently and specifically find it difficult to follow the expectations required of them: children whose parents, teachers, or the other adults around them, have to put a continual effort into dealing with them.

This chapter will deal with coping with children who struggle: children who are facing difficulties, and we who face difficulties with them.

Every child wants to be "good"

This is an important basic assumption to remember: children want to behave well. Every child, no matter their age, wants their parents to be pleased with them, and to be appreciated by the adults around them. You may be surprised to hear this, but even the "naughty" children want to behave well and be "good;" the "bad" students want to do well in school (yes, the teenagers, too). No child enjoys failing or being punished, getting a low test grade, or disappointing their parents. No child chooses to be the "bad child" or the "lazy" one.

Moreover, it's important to know that the child's or adolescent's success in their educational system acts as one of their main "life missions." In the same way every adult wishes to do well at their job, to be appreciated by the people around them who they hold at high regard, so do children wish to do well in school.

So, then, what might still sabotage their success with their main objective?

not necessarily

"It's emotionally based"

For us to be able to help our children effectively handle difficulties, we must first understand their origin. Children's struggles may stem from different sources: they may come from dealing with emotional or social issues (you should check from time to time what goes on in their smartphone…); sometimes the struggles have more to do with the child feeling a lack of their parents' involvement in their lives; in other cases, there is a physiological background to the struggles—learning disabilities, attention deficiencies, regulation difficulties, or other clearly medical centered conditions. This possibility requires additional expanding on.

In the past, children who behaved "badly" were fast labeled by their environment as "disturbed" or "problematic." Today, thanks to the growing awareness that children don't simply "behave that way," there's a tendency with adults—teachers, and parents alike—to attribute most of the children's problems as *emotionally* based: *"She's jealous," "He's competitive," "She doesn't have much motivation," "He's trying to get more attention,"* etc.. Sometimes, it is indeed the case, but certainly not always. In many situations, the behavioral problems of children, or their learning struggles, do not stem from an emotional or behavioral source, but from another: an organic-physical one. It's important to make a clear distinction between the situations, and not confuse them.

We should be well aware that an emotional *influence* is always present—it accompanies every human condition and behavior. However, for the rebellious, inattentive, or lazy behavior to be one that *stems* from an emotional *source*— there should be, at its foundation, recognizable emotional reasons. For example, if your family recently grew; if you moved house; if your son or daughter are socially excluded; if you're going through a rough divorce; if—God forbid— someone close to you passed away—these are all reasons for emotional distress, that can, most certainly, express itself through behavioral problems or learning issues. On the other hand, if you cannot find the central emotional reason for your child's learning or behavioral problems, and if all your efforts to set boundaries, to talk with them, to encourage them, fall through—then it's advised to start looking for the reasons for the problems elsewhere.

Troubles with learning, for example, mostly don't stem from the child's "laziness," or their reluctance to learn. They may be caused by different learning disabilities, organizational difficulties that accompany attention deficit disorders, and sometimes, even from pure medical problems regarding the child's senses: eyesight issues, focusing problems, hearing problems, and so forth. From the moment you recognize the problem, you can accurately and efficiently handle the issue. And what about behavioral problems? These, too, can stem from different physiological conditions that are far from being under the child's control.

Invisible disorders—nice to meet you!

One of the most common causes for children's behavioral problems is ADHD—Attention Deficit / Hyperactivity Disorder. Many tend to think that this is merely a "learning" issue, so, if the child does reasonably well in school, or—if they can sit concentrating for hours in front of the computer, then they probably don't suffer from it. In actual fact, that is far from the case. Firstly, "Attention Disorders" are a generalized, far-encompassing name for a wide range of disorders, ones which include different elements, among which are: impulsiveness, hyperactivity, and lack of attention—with different combinations and strengths regarding each. Secondly, it's important to know that in many cases the vast expression of the attention disorder is through behavioral issues—not through learning problems. Children with attention disorders often have trouble behaving in a way others expect of them. They know the rules, but have trouble following them. In such situations, a child may be continually rude to a teacher, hit someone who was mean to them despite knowing that it's not allowed, and even without meaning to actually do it. What seems from the outside as "behavioral problems," stems instead from a physiological difficulty, one that can be traced and treated.

The illusive nature of attention deficit disorders led to them being called "invisible disorders." Why invisible? Because from the outside, everything seems fine. The child is healthy and functioning. If the child was walking around with a bandaged arm, we wouldn't expect them to unload the dishwasher or play basketball. However, the attention disorders are "invisible." They're present in the child's life and affect their functioning, but we can't see them. This complicated situation brings about a foundation for arguments, anger, and misunderstandings.

Adjacent to the attention disorders, there are additional physiological reasons that can stand as the basis for problematic behavior in children and teenagers. Such difficulties include certain types of regulation problems: children who experience the world around them either too intensely or too dimly. Other problems can include "purely" medical conditions, that weren't diagnosed and thus untreated, like: asthma, allergies, celiac, diabetes, and many others. Such conditions can cause children to feel nervous, spacy, suffer a lack of energy, not manage to regulate their emotions, and so forth. And so, before casting a child's difficulties on an "emotional background," it's important to conduct a full *physical* assessment and to remember that many of the same troubles stem from physical problems rather than the initially thought emotional ones.

Excelling at being "the bad student" or the "bad child"

Whatever the cause may be for your child's difficulties, it's important to avoid attributing them a label: "*lazy*," "*wild*," "*a coward*," or, heaven forbid, "*a monster*." We won't manage to push forward from there. It's important to note: sometimes children lose their faith in their ability to "behave well," so much so that they try and "excel" at behaving badly or gaining the title of "the worst student in class." They then "modify" their problematic behavior, pushing it all the way to the "edge"—"*so that no one will be confused enough to up their expectations.*" A similar process can happen when a child doesn't do too well in school. A child who suffers from ongoing learning problems, at times prefers to simply stop trying—"*I'll be the student with the* lowest *grade in the class; at least* that *I know how to do really well.*"

To avoid these types of situations, it's important not to put your child or teen-ager into a column of them being "the problematic child" or "the bad student" (through their classmates' eyes, their teachers', your own eyes, and—worst of all—their own eyes, too). It's vital to allow your children to start afresh, to never stop believing in them, their abilities, and their willingness to do well (▶ see too Chapter 7, regarding the issue of emotional regulation, and the next chapter, which deals with setting boundaries).

Private lessons or football practice—what's better?

> *"We must enhance the light—not fight the darkness."*
>
> —A. D. Gordon

So far, I've related to the parental copings with different sorts of children's hardships. As parents, we have gotten used to thinking about how we can *treat* and *manage* our children's difficulties: remedial education, occupational therapy, psychotherapy, art therapy, riding therapy. Sometimes it seems as though everything around us has become "therapeutic." Well, treating our children's problems is indeed vital, and in many cases, definitely not something to give up on. However, parallel to dealing and treating a child's issues and problems, it's no less important—and perhaps even *more important*—to magnify the child's strengths, to give center stage to their talents and other wonderful qualities. Or, as **A. D. Gordon** put it, "We must enhance the light." And so, if your child has a learning disability, but also possess an incredible talent for football or music—though it's important for them to get the remedial education they need, it's still just as important to allow them to practice football or play music and develop their talents. When we turn that spotlight onto what exists and "works," rather than only what's missing or needs "correcting"—we help our children build up positive self-esteem.

In other words: your child's self-esteem, their own self-value, are just as important—and again, perhaps even more so—than treating specific, complicated difficulties they suffer from. At the end of the day, the child is the same child. When we show wonderment at their talents (that special sense of humor, their dancing talent, technological sense, creative thinking, impressive imagination, or any other wonderful quality), the value and mass of these positive aspects grows, as does the child's self-worth, while the difficulties, on the other hand, shrink (► see also Chapter 2, page 40, regarding game tokens).

So, practically what can do we do?

Be curious regarding your child's difficulties—try to understand their origins

If your child doesn't behave appropriately, or if they don't function as expected in school, it's worth putting effort into understanding the foundation of the problematic behavior. Try and ask yourselves: When did you first notice the issue? Has it been consistent? Do the difficulties appear in different situations, or are they attributed to a specific teacher in school? Or perhaps it's only at home, when your son "let's loose" and disregards the rules? Is your daughter under particular stress lately? Are one of their friends picking on them? What do their teachers say? What do they, themselves, say?

The answers to these questions will help you understand: Does the difficulty stem from an emotional plane? Perhaps it's more along the lines of a social problem? Has something in your parental availability changed? Are your boundaries not as clear as they should be? Or perhaps the difficulty comes from a completely different aspect? For instance, perhaps your child is suffering from an objectively physical problem that explains the behavior? If you can't find a clear reason for your child's behavior, you should widen your circle and get additional advice: talk to your pediatrician, the school counselor, a child psychologist, an occupational therapist, and if there's a suspicion for ADHD—a child neurologist or child psychiatrist.

Adapt your reaction to the source of the problem

If your child is suffering from an emotionally stemmed issue—talk with them, encourage them. Try and lessen their emotional distress. If your child's problems are socially related—talk with the teachers, the counselor of the school, the other children's parents. In no way or form should you accept a situation in which your child feels lonely or socially excluded. However, if the issue turns out to be *physiological* rather than emotional—there's no point in getting angry at your child for not studying properly or not managing to regulate their emotions adequately. Instead, it's important to treat the source of the problem (perhaps they need remedial teaching? Perhaps they need medication?).

The distinction between these situations is highly important, since if we rush to assume that the difficulties stem from a behavioral source or an emotional one, we also assume the child holds a level of control over their problematic behavior. Beyond that—we also believe that there's something *we* can do in order to pull our child from the clutches of their problems (set additional boundaries, get angry, punish, give them additional attention, or perhaps take that attention away). But, if we're mistaken, and the true source instead is, say, physiological rather than emotional—it would be akin to getting angry at someone for needing glasses for reading.

Make your child feel as though you stand with them rather than against them

Children who suffer from difficulties tend to feel as if no one understands them and that everyone is quite against them: against them and their low grades, against them and their fears, against them and their behavioral issues, their daydreaming, and so forth. It's a difficult place to move forward from. One of the most efficient ways to deal with such situations is to create "a shift in alliances" within the family circle. Meaning, rather than have your child feel as though you're working "against them" and against their manifested symptoms, allow your child to feel that you are actually working *together*, as a team, against the *symptoms*. *"You and I will win when faced with the violent reactions (or organizational difficulties, low grades, fears, etc.)."*

And what does this change actually mean? After all, on the surface of things, we hardly did anything at all—but in actual fact, the change is highly significant, and one which children sense and react to positively. When your child ceases being defensive and instead chooses to stand in a single front with you—all against the troubling symptom—it's easier to find effective ways to overcome it and be released of it, or at least have the symptom lessened significantly.

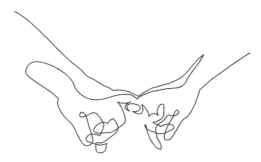

Remember, your child's self-esteem is more important than their math grade

When we deal with a child who faces difficulties, it's important we ask ourselves what are the most important things to us in relation to them. Is it worth—for a math grade—having our child think that they're lazy and stupid? Is it worth—for the sake of having a tidy room—that they believe themselves to be messy and unkempt? The answer is, pretty certainly—not. This doesn't mean we should accept the given, unwanted situation—the messy room or lack of studying—but it's still vital not to set conditions our children cannot meet and not to hurt them.

Remember—every child wants to do well. All children wish to have their parents be proud of them and for them to be happy with their behavior. The matter of maintaining their self-esteem is much more important than many other tasks or achievements.

Create awe-inspiring events for your child

Continuing the previous section, in order to nurture a positive self-image within our children, it's important to note their strengths and wonderful qualities and talents. We must nurture them, empower them, and give them center stage. Remember that the positive self-image and their positive self-worth are what give your child the emotional fuel they need in order to deal with given difficulties. Moreover, magnifying their talents and strengths is an easy, simple, and more enjoyable process than merely concentrating on the issues that need treatment. Doing so can have an important and impressive positive influence.

Check whether or not your expectations meet reality

To conclude, it's also important we check ourselves—for sometimes the problem has nothing to do with the children themselves, but with the high, overreaching expectations we hold of them. Many parents seem to believe that "other people's children" do everything "by the book:" they're all responsible, study without being pushed to do so, are polite, arrive places on time, and leave the bathroom tidy once they're done showering. Well, you shouldn't be so sure. So, before we lose our minds, before we get angry at the multitude of bad behaviors our children have—we should ask ourselves: do all children their age prepare their schoolwork alone? Do all children their age read books? Did we, ourselves, not "cut" school from time to time? So, perhaps our expectations were a little over the top. Perhaps, everything is just fine.

THE BOTTOM LINE

All children want to behave well; all children want to rise to their parents' expectations; they all wish to do well at home and in the educational system. If your child has difficulties in these areas, it's important to check the source of it. Children's difficulties can be explained through an emotional background, a behavioral one, a social one, or a physiological one. It's vital we differentiate between them so that we can give our children the care and treatment they need.

If our child deals with some kind of difficulty, it's important we not categorize them as "a problematic child," and it's vital that their educational system doesn't attribute them negative labels, either. On the contrary: it's important we "separate" our wonderful child and the difficulty they suffer from; it's important to help them handle their difficulty in an efficient manner, and by so doing, allow them to continue being "good"—as every child wishes to be. At the same time, when our child suffers from acute problems, one of our most important tasks is finding their *strengths* and magnifying them. This is just as important as treating the child's problems.

CHAPTER 16

ENOUGH IS ENOUGH!
The function of boundaries and parental authority in raising children

To punish or not? Is it ever allowed to give them a smack on their bottom? (No! never!) And what about when they really push the line—what then? How does all this connect to countries? And triangles?

Setting boundaries and the establishment of parental authority are questions and issues that are at the center of an active argument, posing dilemmas for both parents and therapy professionals. Some say that these issues are among the most important when regarding the question of parenting and child raising; however, other parents are prepared to swear that their children grow up and function perfectly well without them having to deal with the aspects of boundaries and the establishment of parental authority. Could such a situation truly exist? Is it possible to raise children without being constantly "on guard" and expending energy on setting boundaries?

To answer these questions, let's think, for a moment, about countries. A developing country, or a country that suffers from an existential risk, fights for its borders. Their main resources are bound for the establishment of the country's borders and their subsequent protection. In these situations, the matter of the country's borders is an important issue—one that's central to their survival. However, when the country is one that is well-established, with set, stable borders, the country can allow itself the possibility to redirect many of its resources to other things: questions of economy, education, culture, human resources, and more. Yet still, even a well-established country needs strong, stable borders.

So, what is the "border" situation in you little, private "country?" To what extent do you have to be "on guard" regarding the setting of boundaries, and how free are your children to handle other matters? In this chapter, I will concentrate on some of the important aspects of boundary keeping, which are relevant for every homestead—the ones where "border fighting" is a daily occurrence, and the ones where the "borders" are stable and well-established and are in the periphery of parenting.

Daddy! Our roles are reversed!

Have you ever encountered the phenomenon of parents calling their young child "daddio" or "baba?" Even if this is said in jest and affection, isn't it a little odd to call a little child—daddio? Could this expression be a clue for what is happening, or what may happen, to the relationships we have with our children?

You should know it wasn't always like this. Children's position in our society has changed dramatically in previous years. A mere century ago, children were regarded as small, under-developed beings, well on the bottom of the familial hierarchy, while in the last dozen-or-so years alone, that pyramid has become completely upturned, with children standing at the head of the social and familial ladder (▶ for additional information on this, view Chapter 31). However, it seems that at times the pendulum is pushed too far, too radically. This change in the children's position and the parental perceptions we hold, puts us at a potential risk for role-reversal. It happens when children become important—at times overly so—and take on the mantle of "customer" (yes, the one who is always right), while the parents are delegated as the "service providers." In these situations, parents can decide that *"if my child doesn't get the teacher we want—we can have them change schools."* There are also parents who choose to forsake their own careers and their personal self-developments, all for being able to "perfectly" answer all their children's needs—no matter their age.

Yet, we should be well weary of these processes. It's true, there's no doubt about the vital and crucial importance of the childhood years, but we still mustn't confuse our children for being "customers" we need to service. Above all else, we must understand that our children *do not need it,* and would, instead, lose out because of it. Children and adolescents need a strong and stable adult, one they can lean on and look up to. Children and adolescents also need boundaries—where they know what is allowed and what is against the rules; what is expected of them, and what is well beyond those lines. Only when we set those boundaries, can they conduct themselves freely, even go beyond the "borders," occasionally—being as it's an inseparable part of learning.

On parents and triangles

Assuming your child has two parents (be if you live together or apart), imagine a triangle. Your parental triangle should look like so (>image i) and not any other way:

i.

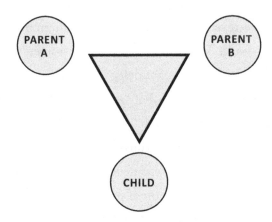

And translated: that would mean that children of all ages benefit from having two authoritative, responsible adults, who care for their education and well-being—together. Even if you're divorced, you have the joint parental responsibility to raise your children. It's true that a single parent can do an excellent job and raise happy and healthy children alone (▶ read more on this point in Chapter 29), but if you're *two* parents, you have to *both* stand at the head of the pyramid.

Any other positioning of the triangle—is problematic:

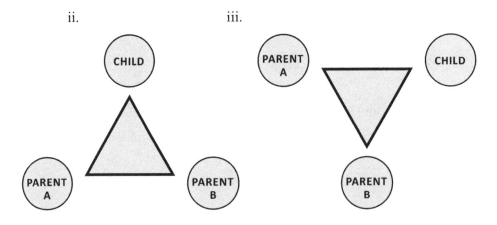

A child whose parents are *bound* to them (not to mention when they are *served* by them), is an unhappy child (image ii.). In this situation, the child receives too much power, something which will eventually cause them anxiety or create a narcissistic experience—as though they are the ones who dictate the world around them. This kind of starting point is not a positive one for your child to adequately handle future life challenges. A child who is in a "coalition" with one of the parents—against the other—also cannot benefit from it (image iii.). It so happens, that a child who sleeps in bed with their mother, pushing their father out to the living room couch; or a child who feels as though they can direct their father to their side "against" their mother (*"Mom, listen, Dad and I decided we will be getting a dog!"*)—are children who grow up confused about their roles. They receive excessive power, power they do not need, which can ultimately harm their development.

Foregoing the triangle will be just as problematic:

iv.

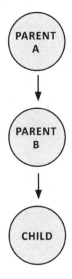

In households where the child knows that their father is "bound" to their mother's decisions, or the opposite (▸ image iv.), then a valuable parental resource is lost: the fact of the child having two responsible co-parents, who can confer with each other regarding key factors of their child's education. This doesn't mean that you, the parents, have to see eye to eye regarding *all* aspects of child raising. Such a goal isn't only unrealistic, but isn't wanted, either. However, the feeling that comes through co-parenting, the children's understanding that they have two parents who are stronger than they are, and who protect them together—that's the best starting point for parenting.

We shouldn't be confused by this: setting the triangle with the parents at the helm does not make your children less important. On the contrary: it allows them to grow and develop in a safe and stable environment. Similarly to a country with stable borders, children who have a homelife with set, clear boundaries, are available to deal with other matters: they're free to develop, learn, establish social connections, think creatively, and much more. For it is only children who live in a safe environment, one where the boundaries are clear and stable, who can allow themselves to play, dream, create, and experience true joy.

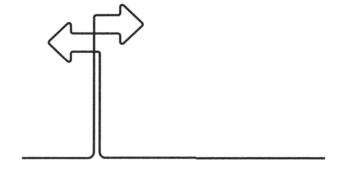

Out of four parenting styles—one is crowned victor!

Many parents ask themselves: "What kind of parents do we want to be? Easy going ones? Decisive ones? Perhaps ones who take things on at eye level?"

The American researcher **Diana Baumrind** created a distinction between four types of parenting styles, created from a combination of two dimensions. The first: the dimension of *emotional warmth*, which includes the levels of acceptance and support a parent shows their children; and the second: the *authoritative dimension*, including matters of order and boundaries. Note the chart:

- Parents who are highly characterized with elements of warmth, support, and acceptance, and simultaneously lay down clear boundaries and demands of orderliness—they are the parents who have the **Authoritative** Parenting style.

- Parents who express warmth and acceptance toward their children, but do not have high levels of authoritativeness; they do not insist on boundaries and proper behavior, and are characterized with a **Permissive** Parenting style.

- When the insistence on boundaries is high, but the warmth levels are low, an **Authoritarian** style of parenting develops (don't confuse this to the Authoritative style). Authoritarian parents are parents who put a massive weight on the issue of obeying their rules, all without paying much attention to the child's wishes, nor providing them with emotional warmth.

- And finally, parents whose boundary levels are low, and also don't show much warmth, are attributed to an **Uninvolved** or **Neglectful** parenting style.

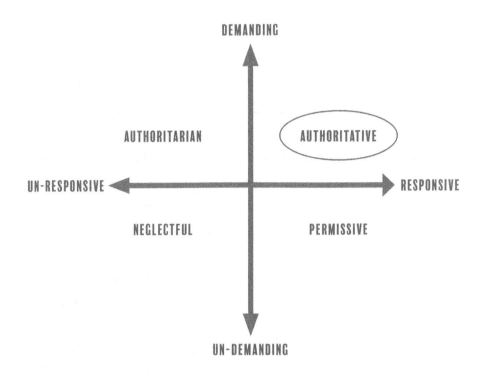

This distinction between the four parenting styles was corroborated by much research. Fascinatingly, the psychological research consistently and clearly exposes the benefits of the **Authoritative Parenting style** over all others. The many research papers and the extensive clinical experience gained, prove that parents who combine setting clear boundaries and demonstrating emotional warmth and a willingness to fulfil their children's needs, contribute to their children's overall emotional welfare. These children tend to be happier, hold a higher empathic ability, have better social interactions, and even do better in school when compared to children whose parents take a different approach to parenting. Thus, all the advantages remain embedded in one reigning parenting style: the Authoritative Parenting style.

In this context, it's also important to note that differently than what we often believe, setting boundaries and keeping order and discipline do not negate providing our children with warmth, love, and the fulfilment of their needs; the two matters remain on different planes from the other. And so, it's possible, and even advisable, to combine them: to set your child clear boundaries, but to still be warm and attuned to their needs; meaning, be Authoritative parents.

"Go to your room! No screen-time for a week!"—How to handle punishments?

We cannot mention boundaries without noting the times when our children "cross over the line." At times, they really can drive us up the walls. They do things they know they shouldn't; they lie; they give you backtalk; they make us lose our minds. We know we can't hit them (▸ see framed text). So, we pull out the only other weapon we believe we still possess—punishments. *"Go to your room!" "You're not allowed to go on play-dates this week!"* or: *"From today—you're not allowed to be on your phone or computer, or have any screen-time for a week!"*

Are we doing the right thing?

Differently to physical punishments—which is categorically forbidden—the matter of other punishments is more complex. Let's try and dive into the array of considerations we need to take into account.

Firstly, we must ask ourselves—are punishments effective educational tools? Does the act of giving the punishment assure that the child will "learn their lesson" and not repeat their unwanted behavior or actions? Surprisingly, in most of the cases, the answer is no. Apparently, children learn much faster through positive reinforcements; through praising them and giving them kind words—and less so through punishments. In order to properly grasp this, think about yourself in your workspace. Let's assume that your boss scolded you over every mistake you made. Let's further assume that your monthly salary was cut after each "screw up." Would these sanctions stop you from making additional mistakes? Probably not. In most cases, sanctions like this only create anxiety and a tense atmosphere; additionally, anxiety harms our learning abilities, and our capability to learn crucial lessons from our mistakes.

Secondly, we also have to ask ourselves, "*Who is this child*? Do they truly "need" to be punished?" It is my belief that there are children who can reach the "finishing line" of the age of maturity without having been punished even once. This can be aligned to road etiquette. Just as there are drivers who can go a lifetime without being pulled over by a police officer, and without being fined for driving well over the speed limit, so, too, can there be children who manage without punishments. These children usually grow up in homes where the limits and boundaries are clear—homes where the "young drivers" know perfectly well what the speed limit is, and where a "no entry" sign remains. Additionally, it's usually true that these children were also born with good regulation abilities: they can understand what's expected of them, and follow the rules set. This doesn't mean that these children *always* do as they are told. Yet still, with these children, it suffices to simply scold them when they cross the line, without needing to punish them at all. If we return to the road metaphor, they are like drivers to whom merely giving a warning is enough—with no need for fines or taking away their license.

But, not all children are like this. Sometimes, we're truly left with no choice. When a police officer catches a drunk driver going well over the speed limit, the driver must be "taken off the road." So, too, when a child knowingly does something that is very severe, after having received numerous warnings beforehand—there really is no choice but for us to react and punish them. However, at this stage, we must choose the punishment wisely.

Here are a few principles that can assist with this:

- It's important that the punishment be relevant and connected to the transgression. If your child violently snatched the remote from their younger sibling—it's reasonable to not allow them to watch television in the minutes after the fact. On the other hand, it would not make sense to ban them from going to a friend or their youth group the day after.

- Here I will raise another principle—it's important for the punishment to be given as closely as possible to the transgression, and more importantly—that the punishment be short. A child who feels as though their parents are angry with them over a long period of time, that their punishment is "never ending"—loses their motivation to improve their behavior and get back to the "straight and narrow." A child who suffers through a week-long punishment of "*no screen-time*" or "*We won't be celebrating your birthday this year*" can feel as though they have nothing to lose, since their parents are already angry and punishing them. This never-ending punishment, rather than eliminating the problematic behaviors, can actually worsen them.

- Treat your children's transgressions as an opportunity for you to pass on the messages you deem most important. Even if your children angered or disappointed you to a very high degree (let's assume they lied to you or took money from your purse without permission), alongside your decision to punish them, try and treat the problematic incident as an opportunity to educate your child and pass on essential values. For example, explain to your children the extreme importance of telling the truth and establishing trust. Treating it like this ups the chances of being able to take advantage of the difficult situation and turning it into a learning experience with lessons they can keep for the future.

- Additionally, when you punish your children (in the case when you decided punishments are unavoidable), it's important to give them the honest chance to apologize for their actions. It's also just as important for you to *forgive* them and allow them "to start afresh" (► see too Chapter 7, page 114). When we don't let go of our anger and "hold grudges," we don't allow our children to escape the negative cycle they become trapped in, preventing them from eventually returning to behaving well.

- Finally, it's important that the punishment you give doesn't hurt your children overly much. Remember, the goal isn't to "win against" or "defeat" your child—the goal is to educate and teach them. And so, if your daughter is an extremely social person—don't try and keep her from her important social connections, for they are an asset for her. If she lied or was rude, or did something else that had crossed a line—choose a punishment that will adequately clarify the mistake she made, but won't "break her spirit" and hurt her to the extreme.

Beating children for "educational" purposes? —what does the law say?

As I stated beforehand, the approach to parenting has changed greatly in the last dozens of years. An actual gap grew between the parenting styles prominent thirty years ago, and the concepts prevalent today. One of the most clear-cut examples for this has to do with how parents (and the law) attribute the question of hitting children for "educational" purposes and discipline.

The expression *"He that spareth his rod hateth his son"* is from the *"Book of Proverbs,"* and is attributed to King Solomon, the wisest of men. According to this saying—at least if taken literally—a parent who doesn't use their cane to educate their children—wouldn't be fulfilling their parental duties, and, by so doing, will end up harming their children. *Truly?*

Unfortunately, many of today's parents grew up in the light of this perception—the belief that sometimes you have to beat your children in order to properly educate them. This concept was also accepted in the more enlightened households. Luckily, things have changed. Today, there is an overwhelming agreement that hitting children, harming them physically in any way, is not allowed—not in the name of education, or any other reason. And so, the matter doesn't fall under parental (or professional) questioning—the law clearly states that harming a child in any physical manner is forbidden.

The following presents the clear-cut legal view on the matter of physical punishment of children in Israel:

"Corporal punishments of children, or the degrading of their dignity as an educational tool by their parents, is wrong in every way. It is a remnant of a long-rejected social-educational perception. The child is not the parents' property; they cannot be treated as a punching bag the parent can use to their will, not even when the parent wholly believes that through such actions, they were fulfilling their parental duties and rights regarding their child's education. The child is dependent on their parents, they need their parents' love, protection, and soft hand. The act of punishments that cause pain and humiliation contributes not at all to the child's personality and education, and furthermore, harms their human rights. It harms their body, feelings, dignity, and proper development. This distances us from the aspiration of reaching a society

that is free of violence. Thus, we should be aware of the fact that any physical punishment done by the parents, or punishments that degrade and humiliate the child in the name of education, are fully prohibited in our current-day society."

(An excerpt from an article written by the Israeli judge Haim Cohen, 2000)

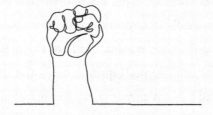

I will point out that this approach at times contradicts some cultural norms. But the bottom line remains—you are not allowed to hit your children, no matter your personal views.

THE BOTTOM LINE

The boundaries set by parents, and the question of parental authority, are a vital and integral part of a child's healthy psyche, and their ability to live a life full of creativity and joy. No matter the child's age, children need parents who are stronger than them, for them to be someone they can look up to. For this reason, we must be weary of "role reversals" between us and our children, and not allow our children to become "customers" whom we must serve.

Sometimes, when children cross a line, we are left without a choice but to punish them. This, however, must be done smartly, measuredly, and with respect—while still reminding ourselves of the ultimate goal of educating, teaching, and guiding our children, and never harming them. That said, any physical punishment method of children is prohibited entirely—by law, as well.

2
PART II
ENJOYING THE WAY
PLACING OURSELVES AT THE CENTER (TOO)

ENJOYING THE WAY
A PREFACE TO PART II

In the first part of this book, we got into the car and set out our destination: our parenting goals. We defined the aspects we'd like to nurture in our children: love, the feeling of safety in the world, a positive self-image, inner motivation, a stable sense of self, worthy values. Now it seems we are better equipped to achieve all that. But, hey, *we are here too*! And, really, what about us? Do we not deserve some introspection and to be able to place ourselves at the center?

The chapters in the second part of this book concern *us*, the parents. This time, *we* are in the center of the matters, and not the children. But—who exactly is there in the center...? Is it the *parent* part of us? Is it the *person*? Is it perhaps even the *child we used to be*? Is separating these identities even possible?

While flying on a plane, the safety precautions for passengers dictate that in order to best protect our children, we have to first adhere the oxygen mask to ourselves. Only when we are breathing easy can we be available to help our children. This situation is relevant to parenting, as well. In order for us to be good parents, it's important to also look at ourselves, to invest in ourselves so we can feel good, too.

Chapters 17-20 were inspired by the saying: *Good parents are parents who feel good about themselves*. First, we should try and understand why parenting is so challenging; further on, we will examine the wide array of connections between parenting and happiness (prepare yourselves for a complex and multidimensional answer here).

In Chapters 19 and 20, I will pose surprising answers to the question: "How can we be happier when concerning our parental lives, and happier in our lives in general?" In this matter, the answers are straightforward and accessible to everyone. They concern our ability to train ourselves to be fully present in the "here and now," and concern too for our more friendly approach to ourselves (Mindfulness and self-compassion, nice to meet you!).

In latter chapters, we will broaden our perspective, in the spirit of the saying: "it takes a village to raise a child." Chapter 21 concerns the matters of the fathers' involvement and cooperation in parenting; another chapter will be regarding the connections between our romantic relationship and our parenting (if you're divorced, read Chapter 27); furthermore, I will shine a light on the relationships we create with the people in charge of educating our children in daycares and schools.

In the final chapters of the Second Part, in Chapters 24 and 25, we will meet the child within us, and examine the parenting style we were raised with. We'll see how these processes affected the person we grew to be today, and later also shaped our own parenting style. Such a perspective may help us raise our own children and shape our parenting style as we would actually wish it to be.

And if some of these topics seem heavy and complicated, it's true, but let's remind ourselves that parenting is one of the most wondrous and meaningful roles we have in our lives, and we deserve to enjoy it.

Are you ready…? Let's carry on our way!

CHAPTER 17

WHY IS IT SO COMPLICATED?
The challenges of our generation's parenting

"Making the decision to have a child—it is momentous. It is to decide forever to have your heart go walking around outside your body."

—Elizabeth Stone

If you are honest with yourselves, how much does the issue of parenting concern you? How often do you think about it? Ponder it? Ask yourselves what kind of parent you are? What are the things you do well and what could be done differently? In what ways are you different from your own parents? How attuned are you to your children?

Apparently, if the answers to these questions were multiple choice ones, we'd all choose answers ranging between: "Yes, parenting concerns us quite often," to "It concerns us to a very high degree."

This situation is not one that can be taken for granted. Parents have always been around; there's nothing more natural than being parents. However, it seems as though during these last few years, more so than ever before, parenting has become a particularly challenging and demanding role, one that takes extreme amounts of energy from us. If you ask your parents, it's likely that you'd find that they hadn't been as preoccupied with their parenting as you are with yours, and it's more than likely that the term "parental guilt" wasn't part of their daily lexicon (there are many reasons for this change; you'll be able to read about them here in this chapter, and in Chapter 31).

In this chapter, we will try and understand why parenting is so all-consuming; do we take it too far? And—what can we do to lighten the load a little?

Irreversible role

Think about the different roles you fulfil in your lives: the relationship you have with your partner, the role you have in your workplace, the friendships you maintain. Well, differently to all other aspects in our lives, *parenting* is one of the only roles that is one-directional and irreversible. We can change our careers, break it off from our significant other, cut social relationships and renew them years later, but from the moment our firstborn comes into this world, nothing can change the fact that we are parents. We are parents to this little human—and to all others that follow—forevermore.

When this change first comes to pass, we find ourselves astounded by the wide range of responsibilities that become our reality overnight. Those nine months of pregnancy can't fully prepare young people to the coming shift. From being adults who are independent and almost worry-free (*"What did we even worry about before they were born?"*), we become responsible, around the clock, for a helpless, tiny baby. We have to feed, wash, put to sleep, diaper, and also play, educate, and set boundaries for them—countless new roles that are incredibly demanding and different from each other. And all of this—forever!

Parenting without a break and without an expiration date

And not only that it is an irreversible role—parenting, by definition, is conducted without a break. We can take a couple's vacation without the kids on the other side of the world, or immerse ourselves in a very important work meeting—but if we see the daycare or school's number flash on the screen of our phone, instantly our parental mode takes over (*"What happened? Is everything okay?"*) From the moment our first child is born, we become parents "nonstop."

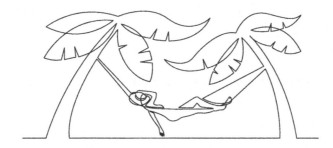

And what is the parental "finishing line," if you will? Is there even such a thing? There are some who try and hold onto that point of the children reaching the age of maturity, as though with their legal independence some massive change occurs, and our parenting role is concluded. Is that true, though? Try and tell that to the parents of the thirty-year-old student who hadn't yet found her professional path; or the parents of the divorcee who once again started searching for a relationship (or simply think of your own parents). Parenting is constantly at the forefront of our minds—even when our children are adults themselves. Additionally, parenting can oftentimes spontaneously reintroduce us with the child we once were, or expose us to behavioral patterns our own parents had when they were younger—something which may cause us to reevaluate our relationship with them. There are times when these "encounters" are wonderful and bring up nothing but positive emotions, but that is not always the case (▶ read more about this in Chapters 24 and 25).

"Say what you will—just don't tell me I'm a bad mother!"

If all of that isn't enough, parenting is also considered to be the most sensitive role a person can experience. We are prepared to take criticisms from friends, employers, customers, and partners—but the second our *parenting* comes into play, we instantly take offence. And why is that?

Throughout our lives, we build our self-esteem, layer after layer. The first "layer of self" deals with our *basic self-identity*, and it develops around the end of our adolescent years; that's usually the point when we become more settled on the issues of who we are, what our different qualities are, what are the things we're best at. Farther along the line, we develop our *professional-career-based self*, and also our *romantic-relationship-based self*. Layers upon layers that make us who we are. But, what about the *parental self*? This "layer of self" develops once we become parents, and it's considered the most sensitive part of a person's psyche. It's hard to say why exactly the issue of parenting is so sensitive; perhaps for the reason that we sometimes see our children as an extension of ourselves, or perhaps because we treat them as if they are our "business cards."

Whatever the reason, we feel the powerful need to be good parents (perfect, if possible), and when something in that process threatens to fall apart (when our children disappoint us, or when someone around us criticizes us or our children)—we may be particularly hurt by the outcome. Everything would be so much simpler if we merely reminded ourselves that our children are not, under any circumstances, our "calling cards." They're wonderful (though, at times, also annoying); they're ours (but first and foremost they belong to themselves); and above all, there's no aim for them, or for us, to be perfect. "Good-enough parents" is an excellent thing to be, especially being as there is no such thing as *perfect* parents (and, luckily, children don't need parents like that in the first place).

Parenting is not everything!

In addition, it's difficult to be parents since we tend to put such a massive weight on the importance of the role, as if we are to blame for every wrongdoing our children do. Imagine a child having a temper tantrum in the middle of a supermarket, or a young teenager shoplifting a pack of cigarettes from the corner store. When children and teenagers misbehave, we instantly turn accusing eyes to their parents ("Who raised them?", "Irresponsible parents!"). When it's our children who screw up, we tend to immediately blame ourselves. So, yes, it's true that parents have a vast amount of influence on their children (this is, after all, what this book is about), but yet, it's also important to remember that parenting isn't everything. Our children's behavior is affected by many different things: for example, their genetics (some are more prone to taking risks, others are more introverted), and the older the children get, the more they are exposed to outside stimuli and meaningful social interactions ("*All my mates are drinking already*"). Not everything stems directly from parenting. However, as parents, there's no escaping taking the responsibility and dealing with any difficult or complex issues our children may bring forth. We are, after all, their parents.

Children, are you happy?

Continuing the previous section, many parents feel as if they are also directly responsible for their children's happiness. We work "overtime" so that we can make sure our children do well in school, that they "live up to their potential," that they have friends, and, most importantly: for them to be happy. In the name of these goals, we often send them to many after-school classes, have them weighed down under different psychological theories, dietary plans, and—above all—those endless expectations of ours.

This problematic scenario is directly correlated to the times we live in. As I mentioned in the previous chapter, in the not-so-distant past, children weren't so vastly important. For many years, children were seen as a cheap workforce, and their main mission in life was for them to grow up and help the adults around them, whether in the field, in factories, or doing housework. Fortunately, this has drastically changed in the last few decades, with **Sigmund Freud's** revolutionary ideas being among the key reasons for the shift. Freud helped the world understand just how important those first formative childhood years are for our future development into adults. Thanks to his ideas and the accumulated research that began to grow at the time, the whole world realized that children are exceptionally important little people (▶ read more about this in Chapter 31).

These processes are important and have to be properly appreciated; we must also be thankful for them. How wonderful is it that we raise our children out of the understanding that they have to be nurtured and loved. Yet still, it seems we may have gone too far with the perception of the children's centrality. This means that there are many parents who raise their children while feeling anxiety and pressure, all out of the deep sense of commitment for the children's happiness.

This is unsustainable and could eventually harm both our children and our parenting experience. Have we not taken it too far? Can any person truly take responsibility for another's happiness?

Once, there was a village

To all this, we should add on the fact that in the western-modern society, we raise our children in relative seclusion, something which complicates and causes the parenting process to be more stressful. In the past, a baby was born, and all the women in the village—grandmothers, aunts, older sisters—would help raise them. The men, by the way, stayed out of the picture, because "someone had to be the breadwinner…" This situation changed exponentially in the last decades. In our current culture, children grow up in apartments or four-walled structures, with relatively small nuclear family units around them. The responsibility for their care falls fully on us, the parents, despite many of us having never taken care of a baby before having our firstborn (*"I wish they would have come with an instruction manual…"*). It's important to say that these changes also brought on significant, positive, and wanted processes (women who work and build careers, men who are involved in the childrearing), yet the relative loneliness we experience as parents challenges and threatens our happiness.

So, what do we do with all this complexity?

Let's start with taking a deep breath and treating ourselves kindly and compassionately. Everyone struggles, everyone finds it complicated; it wasn't invented by us. The children will grow, and it will become easier (hopefully). It's also very important to learn to accept help: it's easier to be good parents if we know how to be helped by others. On another note, it's also important we take care of ourselves and nurture the other identities we possess besides being parents (our relationship with our significant other, our professional lives, our friends, sports, music, hobbies; "*once upon a time we did, indeed, have a life*"). In conclusion, it's key to remember that though parenting is important—extremely important—it also isn't everything.

THE BOTTOM LINE

"Irreversible," "nonstop," "no expiration date," also a most sensitive role, with countless responsibilities, and—a role that tends to bring on feelings of guilt and self-blame… no wonder parenting is considered more complex than anything else. It's important to be aware of this. However, there are steps we can take to lighten the load—even the simple awareness of this complicated situation can help, even if only a little.

CHAPTER 18

CHILDREN ARE A JOY
On the complicated relationship between parenting and happiness

Children are a joy—it seems as though that is an indisputable fact.

With such a firm statement, the psychological research findings are quite shocking and surprising. A long line of studies shows the following:

- People feel a *diminished sense of happiness* once they become parents.
- Couples without children report *a higher rate of enjoying life* when compared to couples with children.
- Parenting is associated with *rising tensions between partners* and a less satisfactory couple life.

So… what is going on here? Were we incorrect with assuming "children are a joy?"

Well, luckily, after many years of accumulated research that show a *reverse* connection between parenting and happiness, the general approach today lies with checking what the actual factures which *mediate* between parenting and happiness.

Meaning, under which conditions are we expected to feel happy, and what may disrupt our feelings of satisfaction and well-being. Let's find out together.

To what extent do we enjoy taking care of our children

In 2004, **Daniel Kahneman**, an Israeli-American psychologist and Nobel prize laureate for economics, published a key paper in the reputable journal "*Science*." Kahneman developed a research method that was ingenious in its simplicity: he gave a "beeper" of sorts to the women participating in the study, requesting they kept it with them at all times. Whenever the beeper went off, the woman was asked to document what she was doing at the time and the feelings she was experiencing at that given moment.

The participants in the study were 909 employed women from Texas, U.S.

A number of days after the beginning of the trial, a list of 19 actions began accumulating regarding the things the women did throughout the day: shopping, calling their friends, talking to their superiors at work, interacting with clients, intercourse, cooking, and more. Among the list, of course, childcare was also included. Can you guess how high up in the list the women rated their pleasure from taking care of their children?

Hard as it is to believe, the research showed taking care of children was rated sixteenth on the list regarding the women's enjoyment. Sixteenth—out of nineteen actions! Napping, cleaning the house, shopping, and many other things—yet still, almost all other actions were rated higher than child rearing. How could this be possible?

These findings caused an uproar among professionals, and to this day it is still quoted often in the attempt to fully understand it. In this chapter, I'll use these findings as a gateway for understanding the interconnectedness between parenting and happiness.

Women's pleasure scale regarding their different activities throughout their day:

1. Intercourse
2. Rest
3. Social interactions
4. Physical activities
5. Watching television
6. Prayer / meditation
7. Spending time with friends
8. Alone time
9. Making food
10. Shopping
11. Housework
12. Screen time (internet and emails)
13. Spending time with their partner
14. Spending time with family
15. Travelling for work
16. **Taking care of their children**
17. Interaction with clients
18. Interaction with colleagues
19. Interacting with their boss

From: Kahneman, D., Kreuger, A. B., & Schkade, D. A. (2004). A survey method for characterizing daily life experience: The day reconstruction method. Science, 306

The importance of proper sleep times

Kahneman's research reflected what every overtired parent well knows—sleep is a critical component when regarding parental happiness. As simple as it is, so is its importance. The pleasure felt from parenting was significantly higher with the women who had more than seven undisturbed hours of sleep a night than with those who slept six hours or less. Kahneman pointed out that the differences were more significant than the variations seen between women who held an income of 30 thousand dollars a year, to those who made 90 thousand dollars a year (so, annually, that extra hour of sleep can hold the value of 60 thousand dollars…).

There is no doubt that tiredness causes burnout and greatly affects our personal happiness—so, too, regarding our parenting skills. In other words, to be good parents, to be able to give more of ourselves to our children, our most basic needs have to be met. It's hard to be a happy, fulfilled mother, when you're exhausted or terribly hungry.

"Where did the time go?" : Flow and Parenting

If we asked you during which moments in life you feel a great amount of happiness, what would your answer be?

An American psychologist named **Mihaly Csikszentmihalyi** devoted his life to answering this question. He conducted numerous interviews with a range of people from different cultures, ethnicities, and ages, all in the pursuit of discovering what gives people great pleasure. There was one concept that repeated itself throughout the interviews: people described themselves as happy during the moments in which they were so immersed in an activity, that everything else faded away. Csikszentmihalyi called this *flow*. Flow is described as a situation in which there is so much enjoyment in the experience itself, that we forget ourselves, act through incredible inner motivation, become one with the activity, and don't notice the time flowing away from us. Interestingly, flow is achieved oftentimes while there is a good balance between the perceived *challenge* of the task at hand, and our perceived *skills* regarding our inner ability to complete it. Think about it: *easy* tasks tend to bore us, while *too difficult* tasks make us feel anxious. However, when we have a challenging, complicated task to complete, and a true ability to see it done, that is when it is most likely for us to feel a sense of flow (▶ note graph). The feeling of flow may arise when we're busy with artwork, playing music, building something, immersed in work we enjoy, and many other things.

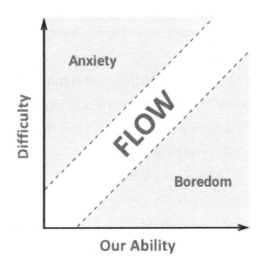

And how does this connect to parenting?

Well, Csikszentmihalyi claims that raising children seldomly brings on feelings of flow. Children, more often than not, cause us to be confrontational. *She wants her chocolate n-o-w, before dinner; he wants to go to his friends but they're all busy; they're glued to their respective screens; he lost the extremely expensive basketball shoes we bought only last month ("You have no value for money!")*. Each of these scenarios, and in countless others, flow is unachievable; thus, in most cases, flow and parenting cannot coexist. And why is this fact so important for us to understand?

First, for us to be more forgiving to ourselves. In this day and age, with social media so prevalent, it seems as though others are always happy: everyone is out enjoying themselves, everyone is smiling, and the family photos of others are all picture-perfect. Real life, however, is far from being so. We argue, we worry, we get angry and bothered—we ask them to clean their room a thousand times, to study for their tests, for them to be available when they're out late at night. All this and so much more is exceptionally hard and exhausting. There can be no flow.

Secondly, it's important to know this because at times such magic truly does occur. We have a deep, meaningful conversation with her; we build a Lego space-ship with him, acting like children ourselves; we take a run by the ocean; we take a family trip and, for a special moment, everyone is happy and content. These magical moments are worth noting, are well-worth feeling thankful for, and, if possible, should be tried to be duplicated.

Let's define happiness

It's impossible to relate to parenting and happiness without first asking—what is happiness? The positive psychology—a fascinating developing branch in these last years—gives an interesting answer to this question. Many of us associate happiness with fun and pleasure. However, today, though we know that pleasure is a *component* in the feeling of happiness, we also know it is merely a small aspect. It seems that happiness mostly stems from a *feeling of purpose*, and not from pure unadulterated pleasure. When we feel as if we're doing something meaningful and worthwhile, we have greater chances of being happy.

As we all know, raising children—especially during their younger years—can damage our daily pleasurable experiences. Child rearing often includes feelings such as worry, tiredness, overtasking, fighting (with your partner, the children, the in-laws), and feeling an increase of financial burden. Having children harms our ability to be spontaneous and forces us to change up our priorities almost completely. Yet still, it is no doubt that having a child is one of the most meaningful things a person can go through in their lifetime—perhaps even the *most* meaningful of them all. Fundamentally, there is also an evolutionary necessity we feel to "continue our legacy." And beyond that, the experience of creating a new life, raising them, taking responsibility for their upbringing and education, the values they eventually will hold… watching the wonderful person they grow into—what could possibly compare?

"No Regrets"

So, what happens in actual fact? There are many parents who dare not admit they are struggling; that sometimes they are simply fed up and wish for their freedom—the way they had it before their children were born. Such feelings oftentimes cause a build-up of shame and guilt. On the other hand, there are parents who never stop complaining, saying how difficult everything is for them, how exhausting being the caretaker is. Though, both sets of parents, and all others in between, would most likely never give up the experience of being a parent—not for any price in the world. People may regret not having become parents, or maybe not having *another* child. It's very rare to find parents who regret ever having children at all. So, where are you in this complex parental experience?

It's important to remember that all parents struggle, but beyond their hardships, their experience is deep and meaningful—and that greatly contributes to our sense of happiness. It is still essential to find ways to make our daily lives as parents easier. Allow me to address a few principles that may assist with it:

Allow yourselves a moment to relax

Take the occasional vacation—without the kids; have the babysitter come over and go out for the night while they're asleep; find time for that afternoon coffee while everyone else is busy; have your family help watch them in your stead.

Don't neglect yourselves and the things you enjoyed before becoming parents

Parenting can easily become so all-consuming that we forget that we have interests and hobbies that are unrelated to the children. We become people who only do the things that are "necessary." Such a tendency pushes us to exhaustion and harms our overall happiness. To overcome it, find the time for physical activities, for meeting up with friends, going to classes and workshops, to read, to listen to good music, to play music—or any other thing that makes you happy. Any other thing that makes you *you*.

Note the times when everything works, and try to recreate it

It's that small change that can sometimes create a monumental difference. When you ask your children to set the table—have on a song that they especially like in the background and watch as the atmosphere in the house changes in a matter of moments. When your children stop fighting for a moment and start playing together or being kind to each other—express your happiness at it ("*It's so wonderful to see you playing together!*"). By pointing it out, you'll encourage them to recreate those magical moments.

Nurture your relationship with your partner

Your relationship with your partner can easily be one of the central areas that suffer after having children—especially during the time when they're young. In other words, "you're not alone"— problems between partners are an issue shared by many families. It's important to be aware of such troubles and to find ways to overcome them: talk to each other, understand the source of the disagreements, be more forgiving, learn to work together as *partners* rather than people who work against each other. At the same time, it's important to keep your romantic relationship alive beyond merely being parents. Remember that your connection was there first—before you were parents. Your relationship is the base for your built family, nurturing it is important (▶ see Chapter 22).

Share your problems with others, don't keep it all bottled up

The 909 women from Texas revealed that we weren't the only ones who found parenting hard. Parenting holds within it countless small, daily tasks, some which are not always enjoyable. It's important to know that the hardship is temporary, and moreover, that the experience changes vastly as the children grow older. If you still find your burdens too heavy—don't stay alone with your thoughts. Share them with the people closest to you—your partner, a close friend, your relatives, and if necessary, don't hesitate to get professional help. Beyond all the hardships and daily bothersome tasks, you can't give up the right to love and enjoy parenting.

When parents feel difficult feelings toward their children

It's difficult to raise children. Children can awake within their parents—besides the feelings of love—many other emotions, too: sadness, anger and frustration. This is natural and normal, and it's important to be able to talk about it.

The psychanalyst **D. W. Winnicott** bravely regarded this issue in one of his classic articles—*"Hate in the Counter Transference"*—mentioning the vast range of emotions mothers can feel toward their babies. He wrote that apart from the incredible, wondrous feelings mothers feel, there are also moments when they feel hate toward their demanding, needy baby, the one who took their breasts and their freedom. Yes, even these feelings are allowed to be felt.

And what do we do with it? The answer is—it depends. It depends on how often the feelings arise; it depends on the other emotions you feel. If the difficult feelings toward your children are a momentary, fleeting matter, something that is well balanced with love and pleasure and countless other warm emotions—there's nothing more natural than this. You can calm down. However, if either you or your partner feel as though the rate of negative feelings keeps growing, that your children are taking too large a physical and emotional toll, that you simply can't see the sun rays beyond the gray clouds, or if you, God forbid, have thoughts of possibly harming your children—do not hesitate and immediately seek help. Share your stormy feelings and experiences with the people around you, ask them to help you find the assistance you need. Just like dark clouds in the sky, difficult feelings do not last forever. They too can pass, but in complicated situations, we may also need help to eliminate them so we can change our mood, so we can wake to a brighter day. This help can come from family members, friends, and professionals. You owe it to your-selves—and to your children, too.

THE BOTTOM LINE

Parenting is a complicated life mission, hiding within it countless tasks—both small and large. It's no wonder it causes burnout and oftentimes affects parents' mental welfare and happiness. However, on the deepest levels, parenting creates a sense of purpose and meaning, and that is a central key for feeling happy. As parents, we have to manage to find the balance between the difficulties and complex problems, and of the happiness and purposefulness we gain through our children. To succeed, it's important to be aware of the issue, and it's also important to take care of ourselves: to keep reasonable sleeping hours, regular meals, and to create time for our own hobbies and interests. In the hardest most stifling moments, it's essential to see the bigger picture of our parenting and the relationship we have with our children. All this and more can help us enjoy parenting and overcome the hardships it brings along.

CHAPTER 19

BEING PARENTS IN THE "HERE AND NOW"
What is Mindfulness and how it connects itself to parenting

> *"You are wherever your thoughts are; make sure your thoughts are where you want to be."*
>
> **—Rabbi Nachman of Breslow**

Have you ever had your son come up to you, wanting to share something important, and while he was talking, you suddenly realized you hadn't actually been paying attention? Has it ever happened that while playing with your daughter, you noticed that though you were outwardly present, playing with her, your thoughts had, in fact, wandered elsewhere—perhaps to the text message you'd just received?

Just like our life, parenting also continues without pause. Our children constantly demand our attention, the same way work, house chores, relationships, me-time, and various other tasks do. It's always been that way, but in the last few years it's worsened, with screen time sucking our attention, as well. It seems, at times, that we can barely be anywhere while also being fully *present*. Our attention never rests, jumping from one thing to another, and that's exhausting—a recipe for burnout and affecting our overall contentment.

In the previous chapters I've addressed the issues of parenting complexities and the consequential possible harm it can do to our personal happiness. Surprisingly, one of the ways to lessen the emotional burden of our content-filled lives comes from the Buddhist regions of the Far East.

In other words, allow me to introduce you to *Mindfulness*.

In this chapter, we will take a short trip into the fascinating world of Mindfulness, familiarizing ourselves with some of the deep insights it holds. Such ideas can positively affect your personal happiness levels, your daily functioning, and your overall joy as parents. If you're wondering *"How can this have anything at all to do with me?"* It's important for me to state that this chapter is meant for everyone; those of you who already practice Mindfulness, those who are, perhaps, curious about it and wish to try, and to those who've never heard of Mindfulness and don't have any intention to start practicing it.

What is Mindfulness?

The Mindfulness approach means turning our attention to what's happening in the present—in the "here and now" of our lives; all in a way that is open, friendly, and lacks judgment. Mindfulness directs us to notice the things that are going on at this exact moment: our thoughts, feelings, and physical body. And why is that important?

It's important merely because routinely we're not doing it; we have our coffee and our thoughts scatter in endless directions; we drive the car, and our mind wanders every which way. In fact, research shows that approximately half the time we aren't present in the things we do, and that our wandering thoughts negatively impact our well-being.

The reason for the endless wandering of our thoughts connects directly to the characteristics of our brains. The human brain is expert at processing information. Our brain holds the ability to evaluate and deduce the future; it allows us to plan, to worry, to imagine possible scenarios—both those that may happen and those that will never come to pass. At the same time, it also allows us to remember the past, to think on events, analyze them, regret them, perhaps miss them, too. This functional ability has many advantages: it is the reason we can make plans, handle ourselves in different and changing environments, imagine, be creative, and invent new things. However, this also comes with a price. As I stated above, research conclusively shows that wandering thoughts and the lack of presence in the moment cause us to be less happy.

Mindfulness resolves this situation:
- Mindfulness trains us to notice the occurrences in our bodies.
- It allows us to pay attention to our current thoughts.
- Mindfulness assists us in creating a "gap" between stimuli and responses, and that same "gap" allows us the freedom to choose the way we respond to different life events, while not reacting automatically.

This is the point to emphasize that hundreds of published scientific research comes out yearly, stating that practicing Mindfulness can positively affect brain function. Additionally, research also proves that practicing Mindfulness assists in our ability to recover from various medical issues, promotes mental welfare, assists in cases of depression and anxiety, and contributes to regulating emotions, empathy, and compassion (▶ see next chapter, too). Moreover, lately there have been scientific studies that showed Mindfulness to be a contributing factor in *parental* life; in improving the relationship with our children, and even assisting in our children's development process.

How Mindfulness connects to parenting

Mindfulness training teaches us to pay attention to our bodies and experiences, moment after moment, in the here and now. However, even without constant practice, the principles and insights of Mindfulness can integrate themselves into our parental lives, and vastly improve them.

Being fully present while interacting with our children (even for short spans)

Our children desperately need our attention, and that's not something which is always easy. In our day-to-day lives, we find ourselves mostly busy, overworked, worried, and our attention shifts from one thing to the other. It's for that reason specifically that we have to attempt at being fully present with our children, even if only for short spans—simply listening to them, being with them. When the children come back from daycare or school, give them those few precious minutes—listen to what happened to them that day. And then, wait for the next opportunity to be with them fully. This can happen throughout the day while playing together, or at night when you read them a bedtime story. It can also happen while driving around with your teenage daughter, who suddenly puts her headphones down and says, "*Mom, listen, I wanted to tell you…*" These moments are priceless, and what truly makes them so, is being completely present. By the way, your being present can happen while folding the laundry, walking the dog, or completing any other daily task (► see also Chapter 4).

Research shows that our ability to be present with our children greatly contributes to their emotional regulation (and ours, too), and so helps build their empathy, the awareness of their own feelings and the feelings of others.

Being fully present doesn't ensure "fun"

People who practice Mindfulness report a greater sense of calm and satisfaction regarding their own lives. However, let's not get this confused; moments of listening and being fully present in our children's lives doesn't ensure only fun and pleasure.

Parenting often puts us in situations filled with "unpleasant feelings"—both our children's and our own: anger, short tempers, disagreements, temper tantrums, frustrations, insults, stress, strife, and disappointment. What do we do with this slew of difficult emotions? If we try with all our might to fight them and dismiss them in order "to create a peaceful atmosphere in our house, just like (we assume) the neighbor has"—we're bound to become endlessly frustrated and unhappy. And so, if your son returned home angry from school; if your daughter failed an important test and she's sad and disappointed; if your children are fighting again and everyone is stressed, rather than try and *fight* such difficult feelings, it's better to take a deep breath and find the ways you can communicate and function alongside them. Our ability to accept that anger, that disappointment, that sadness, our ability to make space for them rather than fight them, will eventually vastly improve our mood, thus making the unpleasant feelings go away.

You can compare this to surfing waves. At times, the ocean is calm, but sometimes it is rough and stormy. If we fight the waves (meaning, if we struggle with each uncomfortable or unpleasant feeling we or others experience), we will be in danger of drowning. However, if we learn to surf the high waves, to accept the storm as it is, without trying to change or dismiss it—after a while, it will pass.

Please note that this statement isn't meant to have us *ignore* those stormy feelings or confrontations. It instead directs us to look at them, to find the ways to function alongside them without getting over-involved ("*Why are they doing this to me?*") and without "losing it" and noting our own emotional storm (▶ see Chapter 7, regarding regulation of emotions). After the storm passes, we can properly examine the events in a more calm and measured manner, and think: "*what happened? Why did it happen? Perhaps the storm could have been prevented? Was there a better way to react?*"

Thoughts floating away on a breeze

Emotional distress happens, most often, due to our tendency to get "stuck" on different thoughts and troubles, thinking about them over and over. Psychologically this is called "rumination," which means pointless processing of already-processed information. This tendency drags us down rather than help us forge ahead.

It's when we practice directing our attention to the present that we may notice that our thoughts are "merely" thoughts—they come and go, as fleeting at times as clouds in the sky. If I am worried about one of my children (*"He hardly sees his friends anymore…"*), I notice that I'm experiencing feelings of concern. The worries don't define me (*"Overbearing-worrywart of a mother"*); nor do they define my child (*"Unsocial"*). The thoughts are simply that, arisen in that moment. If I can pay attention to this—out of sheer curiosity and without judgment—a short time later the worries can pass, freeing up space for additional, different feelings and thoughts.

Expanding your attention toward the things that work, and being grateful

Hardships and problems are an inseparable part of life. Rather than being "stuck" on thinking about what doesn't work, it's better to expand our attention to additional aspects of our life (▶ see Chapter 8). This idea is especially relevant to our lives as parents. Things can, and do, go badly at times, and we constantly have something to worry about. However, if we can let go of our negative thoughts regarding everything that *doesn't* work, if we can expand our point of view and focus on the good—our overall experience is expected to change and be more pleasant and easy-going.

Allowing "contradicting" and different feelings to coexist

Practicing Mindfulness allows us to expand our emotional plane, and to eventually assist in figuring out that those "difficult" feelings can coexist beside the good and pleasant ones. Different sorts of feelings don't cancel each other out—there's room for them all. So, for example, you can be *brought to tears with sheer joy* due to a touching interaction between you and your son; you can be *sad and upset* over something that has happened to your daughter, and simultaneously feel *worried* about something concerning work. The ability to differentiate between different feelings, to make space for each, greatly contributes to our emotional welfare, even if the feelings themselves, in part, aren't "good" ones.

To better understand this point, you should take a few minutes to watch a fantastic, animated video "The Unwelcome Party Guest" on YouTube. This video is about a young man who decides to have a party at his house. He's very excited about it. Unfortunately, when his friends arrive to the party, he discovers that his neighbor, whom he is not fond of, came too, despite not having been invited. The young man goes above and beyond to try and get rid of the neighbor, though, in actual fact, the more he fought, the more he himself suffered, making him incapable of enjoying his own party. At some point, he decides to simply give in and allow his rude neighbor to stay at the party. His decision causes his whole experience to change, and he finally starts enjoying himself even though not everything is perfect or going exactly as he planned.

If we return to the point at hand, it seems that our ability to "host" unwanted feelings together with "positive" feelings and experiences, creates a balance, and furthers our overall satisfaction.

A puddle or a lake: our ability to stay stable when things go wrong

When we allow ourselves to feel a wider range of emotions, we reach a better capability of emotional regulation; difficult life events and "negative" feelings are less of a threat to our peace of mind. To fully understand this, imagine a stone landing inside a puddle of water. The stone greatly affects the puddle—"destabilizes" it—making water splash every which way. If we throw that same stone, just as hard, in the middle of a lake, the impact the stone has over the lake is negligent—practically non-existent. Similarly, when we allow ourselves to feel a wider range of emotions, we become more peaceful, measured; we no longer feel destabilized over everything that goes wrong.

Creating a "gap" between what is going on and our reaction

Parenting, as stated, often includes confrontations with our children. This happens, among other reasons, because we're simply different people; people with different needs, wants, and priorities (you want them to get in the shower already, while they are interested in anything but). Such matters can cause us to react—quite automatically—in contradicting and disproportional ways. (*"I lost it... I y-e-l-l-e-d at him to get in the shower already!"*)

Mindfulness helps us decrease the amount of automatic, uncontrollable reactions and, in their stead, react to confrontational situations with our children in a more proportionate way. If you're angry, and you *realize* you're angry—note the thoughts and feelings it brings;—your ability to choose the way you'll respond will improve. Paying attention allows you not to "lose it" and so, your reaction will also be more measured and thought out.

It's true that we're all human and that we all lose control at times, however, there is importance to how often it happens, the degree to which it happens, and our ability to correct any mistakes or apologize when needed (► see Chapter 7). Research indisputably shows that Mindfulness contributes to parents being more attentive and more controlled. Consequently, it assists in lessening the tension between us and our children, and helps create a more peaceful, familial atmosphere.

Where did Mindfulness originate from, and how did it seep so deeply into the Western culture

In the year 1979, a young doctor and scientist, a Jewish American by the name of **John Kabat-Zinn,** turned to his superiors at the public hospital where he worked, with a rather odd request. He asked for them to allow him the opportunity to have eight weekly meetings with a group of chronically ill patients who were admitted to the hospital. They were patients who suffered from pains and constant and prolonged mental strife, with the medical world having given up on helping them further. Kaban-Zinn's unconventional request raised many doubts, but was ultimately accepted. He received a large room in the hospital, and during approximately two months, worked with the patients on different meditational techniques. In a surprising and amazing development, the patients' suffering eased, their mental welfare greatly improved—all because of the meetings.

And how did this happen, exactly?

Numerous years pervious, while he was still a student, Kabat-Zinn was introduced, quite by chance, to a lecture regarding Zen-Buddhism. He started to practice the Buddhist meditation himself. He noted that the raw ideas of Buddhism had much to contribute to the Western world of knowledge, specifically regarding dealing with suffering and physical and mental problems. Until that time, there was a clear divide between the medical world and exact sciences, to the more spiritual realms of meditation and Buddhism. Kabat-Zinn wished to break that boundary. He chose to blur the aspects of Buddhist spirituality from the meditation techniques and began inserting exercises taken from the Buddhist world and transferring them to the realm of medical, conservative and orderly treatments.

It was thus that one of the most interesting and most popular treatment methods was born. It is also one of the most research-based practices in the Western world: the method of MBSR—Mindfulness-Based Stress Reduction. As stated, Mindfulness in its Western version does not necessarily include spiritual elements, but instead is mainly based on the act of training the brain to be fully present in the "here and now," all through turning one's attention to thoughts, feelings and physical sensations. This practice allows people to stop their automatic reactions, to reach a better inner stability, to grow their freedom of choice and the levels of their emotional regulation abilities.

The Mindfulness techniques are interwoven in many psychological therapies and conventional medical practices and, as mentioned, it holds a vast and unprecedented evidence-based affirmation regarding its effectiveness.

"Sixty seconds" on practicing Mindfulness

It would be thoroughly presumptuous to cover all of the vast Mindfulness principles in one chapter. There are whole books that deal with the subject, and they, too, find it difficult to cover everything. So, if the subject appeals to you, find the best ways for *you* to learn more about it (courses, guidebooks, apps, and so on), and begin practicing it. Even ten minutes a day of practicing can bring about a positive change.

Until you manage to do it consistently, you should know that one of the ways to increase awareness of our own body, awareness of the "here and now" of our lives, is to develop breathing awareness. Breathing is with us constantly, like a thread stretched out from the day we were born to the day we die—air goes in and air goes out. When our awareness is scattered, when we're bothered or worried, or notice how we're incapable of being fully "there," it is worth paying attention to our breathing. Breaths happen moment by moment; it's part of our present, and it's always there. Turn your focus inwards toward your breathing—see whether it's deep or shallow, comfortable or not. There's nothing you should change, simply be attentive as to how it is. Your ability to read your own body, even in unpleasant situations, without pushing to change it, trains and betters your ability to be in the present—holding everything it entails. By the way, children find such exercises a lot easier than adults do. They naturally live their lives in the moment. There's much to learn from them. Pause a moment and check your breathing: the air coming in, the air flowing out. Practice such awareness and, if you'd like, at times you can also do so with your children.

THE BOTTOM LINE

Mindfulness means creating the ability to pay attention to our present lives in a friendly, curious, gentle, non-judgmental way. In a world so full of stimuli like ours, where there is a constant battle for our attention, such a point is of vital importance. As parents, practicing Mindfulness lets us be present with our children, both in our daily lives and when things go wrong. These abilities allow for emotional regulation and happiness—ours and our children's. If these ideas seem too complicated or far from your reality, you should know that these skills are, in actual fact, simple and easy to apply; listen to your children with your full attention; expand your ability to contain different and sometimes conflicting feelings at once; learn how to "surf the waves" during difficult confrontations; feel gratitude for the positive things in your life.

In dealing with Mindfulness, there is a subtle and beautiful link between Eastern spirituality practices and Western science and research. Both worlds reach a singular, similar conclusion: practicing Mindfulness and implementing its principles can assist us and our children in being more emotionally regulated, calmer, and happier. There is no doubt we want to be a part of all this goodness—for ourselves and for our children.

CHAPTER 20

LOOKING AT OURSELVES WITH KIND EYES
The special role of self-compassion in parenting

> *"If you have no compassion for yourself, then you are not able of developing compassion for others."*
>
> **—The Dalai Lama**

"I hate myself for not spending more time with my children"
"Sometimes I stall at work, all so I don't have to come back to the mess going on back at home. I'm so disappointed in myself"
"They're stuck in front of the screen for hours on end—I'm such a terrible mother"
"The eating habits in our house are atrocious—it's a parenting failure of ours"

Do any of these descriptions sound familiar to you?

We tend to say that parental guilt is born together with the baby, so much so, that there isn't a parent, nor is there parenting, without guilt. Many parents walk around with a criticizing, judging, harsh eye following them around. That eye belongs to none other than us—we are the ones who judge ourselves, criticize ourselves, are exceptionally hard on ourselves. Think about it: sometimes we talk to ourselves in a way we would never allow anyone else to talk to us; in a way we would never dream of talking to anyone else. However, it seems that this negative way we treat ourselves does nothing to help us and may even harm us and our children.

We all want to be good parents—very good parents—but life is complicated. We have to juggle a huge number of tasks, and things often don't go as they should or as planned. It's at that point the self-criticism rears its head and starts judging us so harshly. And we listen to it—avidly! We do it because we think it's a way for us to get better and be better parents, only it's more than likely that we're wrong. In this chapter, we will see why this harsh self-criticism does not help us, and what could pose a healthy alternative for it.

Being our own best friend

Close your eyes for a moment and imagine a friend or a brother or sister—someone you love very much. Imagine that same person telling you that they are going through a particularly trying time: "*I don't have any patience for my kids, the house is constantly a mess, and the children are acting out. They're pushing boundaries, their screen time is over the top, having too many sweets, even their schooling is suffering... a rough, bad time.*" How would you react to that close friend? Would you tell them it's all their fault? That they're clearly a lousy, irresponsible, neglectful, harmful parent?—probably not. Then, what *would* you say?

Now imagine *yourselves* in place of that important person—"*Yes, it's me who's going through a tough, busy time; I'm not as available to be with the kids as I'd like; don't really give things my all... it's that kind of time.*" Well, that same warm understanding you'd give your close friend or sibling should be directed at *you*. Look at yourselves kindly, give yourselves an imaginary hug. Talk to yourselves without malice, be friendly—just as you would with your other loved ones.

If this idea sounds strange and foreign to you, it's only because we're not accustomed to thinking this way. Let's try and become more familiar with this way of thinking, and in other words: allow me to introduce you to **self-compassion**.

Self-compassion—the most important term you still don't know

Similarly to Mindfulness, so does the term compassion (for both us and others) come to us from the realms of Buddhism. Like with Mindfulness, the term compassion also receives a wide research-based affirmation regarding its importance and value for our mental well-being. However, differing from Mindfulness, which was accepted into our midst with open arms and spread out like wildfire though books, applications, courses, and many other mediums, the term compassion doesn't seem to assimilate as easily to our culture. Perhaps it's because we tend to confuse it with pity, or perhaps because it directs us into a completely different way of thinking from the familiar way that stems from the Western culture. But compassion is not pity, and if you read this chapter closely, you'll probably find how earnestly you want to adopt the approach and integrate it into your daily lives.

Compassion is defined as a warm, empathic feeling that arises within us when we encounter suffering or distress—our own or others'—and the accompanied will to ease the suffering or distress presented. Acceptance and compassion toward our own selves and toward others are, in fact, the opposite process of guilt and judgment: self-criticism and criticism toward others. And why is compassion so important? Different research has proven that self-compassion helps build of our own sense of wellness, it helps us adjust to changing circumstances, promotes our ability and willingness to take responsibility for own lives, and for us to feel optimistic and act to fulfill our goals and dreams. Before we dive into the elements of compassion, let's focus in on a few matters.

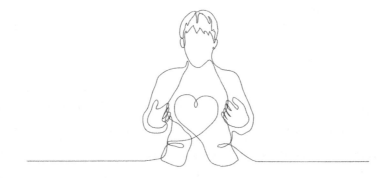

Compassion—toward ourselves or toward others?

When we were kids, we used to say, *"I'm rubber, you're glue."* Compassion works along that principle, only through its positive aspect: when we focus it on ourselves—when we're friendly and nice to ourselves—we also manage to pass that along to others. Moreover: our ability to be kind to ourselves, to treat ourselves with compassion, is a precondition for our ability to project warmth and kindness toward others. And here the magic happens: parents who manage to treat themselves and their life experiences with compassion and with kind introspection, are also more likely to show compassion toward their own children; and children whose parents show them compassion, tend to show more compassion toward themselves and others. Thus, a true model of a win-win situation is established: everyone benefits. So, if you had a bad day at work, take it with forgiveness and humor, find the chance to share your experience with your children. These qualities are expected to help children deal similarly with their own unpleasant experiences, for example, a test they failed, a fight they had with their friends, or any other frustrating situation. But does compassion lead us to mediocracy and a lack in ambition? Let us examine it more closely.

Say goodbye to harsh self-criticism

Western civilization tends to connect between mistakes and the acts of punishment and self-criticism. When we make a mistake, we get angry and criticize ourselves (*"I forgot to turn off the oven and the cake burned—I'm so stupid"*). When we make mistakes with parenting (*"I left work too late and then was late to pick up the kids"*), we tend to be especially angry with ourselves. In Chapter 2, I spoke about how the way we think about our children ultimately affects the way they think of themselves and their developing self-image. Children who receive an excess of criticism from their parents may develop an overly rigid sense of self-criticism, one which could end up harming their own sense of self-worth and their general happiness. Now the picture includes us, too: parents who are excessively critical toward themselves, end up hurting themselves, and if *we* get hurt—our children get hurt, too. Everyone gets hurt.

It seems as though the reason we get so angry with ourselves in the first place is because we wish to do better. Below that heavy load of self-criticism hides the hidden assumption that that is the only way for us to fix our mistakes. However, research consistently shows that parental guilt and self-criticism do not contribute in any positive manner, nor do they help us move forward in a better way. All they do is frustrate and weaken us, make us feel depression, desperation, and anxiety. Anger that's directed inwards and harsh self-criticisms activate physical systems that are correlated to survival and stress mechanisms. These systems harm our decision-making process and sabotage our ability to learn; they negatively impact our happiness levels, and over time, may even hurt our physical health. However, when we truly understand that erring is human—that everyone makes mistakes, and mistakes are simply a part of life; when we manage to treat ourselves more kindly and with humor—it is *then* that our overall mental wellness and our ability to learn from mistakes and function at a higher degree is expected to improve.

We all need a little mercy

The American researcher **Kristin Neff** dealt much on the issue of compassion (▶ you should definitely watch her excellent TED talks online). Neff identified through her research three components that, when combined, create compassion and self-compassion: a. friendliness and generosity (both toward us and others); b. the recognition of the joint aspect of humanity; c. Mindfulness. I'll elaborate on each of these aspects.

A. Friendliness and generosity toward ourselves

"It's true, I'm far from perfect, but that's what I've got to work with— and I'm a great mom."

When we look at ourselves with kind, friendly eyes, we relax and become happier. Just as being with a loved one releases the love hormone, oxytocin, into our system, so too happens when we are friendly toward ourselves. Love hormones contribute to our overall happiness and mental and physical health. It's also important to treat our mistakes with forgiveness and humor: *"Yes, it is I, the father who rarely manages to bring his children to school on time... ever;"* *"And I'm a mother who has no idea how to make meatballs..."* We can look at ourselves from an outside point of view and say to ourselves: *"I'd like to be a better cook,"* or: *"I'd like to be able to be more organized,"* but it's still best to do without adding in extreme judgmentalism, anger, or grudging feelings—*"Speak kindly to yourselves, please. Be gentle."*

B. Recognizing our joint humanity

"Everything is natural and human. We all experience joy, sorrow, positive, and negative experiences, sometimes even experiences that are too difficult to endure. That, after all, is life."

When we go through a difficult time, we may think that none other than ourselves could ever fully comprehend our awful feelings—*"Why the hell is this happening to me?"* In these situations, it's important to remember that we're not alone. At some point, everyone goes through a similar variety of human experiences. When you feel overloaded and frustrated—torn between work and wanting to be home with the children—the simple acknowledgment that many other people feel the same can contribute to our self-compassion and forgiving our own faults. So, too, when you lose control and yell at your children, all without meaning to. Please note, this doesn't mean that we should simply neglect these situations, such as the lack of balance between work and family, or our losing the fight against our anger. It very well might be that you have been working too many hours; you also may have been functioning with a "short fuse," and there is no reason for your children to be harmed by that. However, the assumption is that positive changes in our lives will stem from that friendly and forgiving place, and not from harsh self-criticism. Remember that we didn't "invent" the hardships we suffer. Self-compassion research proves that indeed "a sorrow shared is a sorrow halved."

C. Mindfulness

"I am really pissed off now;" "The noise in the house makes me lose my cool."

The third component of compassion is Mindfulness, which was expanded on in the previous chapter. This is the skill of paying a non-judgmental focus to the things we experience in the present, from everything we go through, moment to moment. Our ability to pay attention to our thoughts and feelings in the "here and now," to look at them with curiosity; without getting caught up in the endless thoughts of the past and future—this is one of the components of self-compassion.

Self-compassion is the right touch

For many years we were taught that it's vital to nurture our children's *self-esteem*. However, note that the term self-esteem, by nature, holds the comparison and competitiveness to others. For a person to hold a high self-esteem, they must think of themselves as "above average." Yet, how is it possible for us *all* to be above average—in sports, studies, professionally? Mathematically, it's simply impossible. Moreover, for someone to think of themselves as "above average," they have to lower the value they hold of others. That, in itself, is a recipe for an unhealthy competitiveness, perfectionism, and even aggression.

On the other hand, self-compassion is the right thing to choose for ourselves—it's directed inwards, all without harming other people. It promotes our happiness without lessening anyone else's. It isn't limited, isn't comparative, and gives us nothing but benefits. Letting compassion into our lives allows for us and our children to be better regulated, more empathic, and hold more positive and fulfilling interpersonal connections with the people around us. All these are priceless attributes, and they are not difficult to achieve.

THE BOTTOM LINE

Parental guilt and harsh self-criticisms do not elevate us, and, in fact, can harm our happiness levels. In their stead, it's best to adopt the aspect of self-compassion—to view ourselves with kind and friendly eyes, the same way we naturally do with our loved ones. Self-compassion includes being generous to ourselves, being tolerant toward our flaws, recognizing everyone has difficulties and stressors, and being able to turn our attention to our experiences in the "here and now." It encourages us to be warm and kind when encountered with our own and others' distress. Contrary to what we believe, self-compassion does not point us in the direction of mediocrity; quite the opposite: it allows us to develop a healthy sense of ambition, promotes our ability of regulating our emotions, and elevates ours and our children's overall mental and physical health: all wonderful qualities we wouldn't want to give up on.

CHAPTER 21

HELPFUL, INVOLVED, OR A FULL PARTNER?
Being a fully dedicated father

"Mothers, you have to bathe your child... lay them down to bed... feed them..."
"Dear mothers, you are hereby invited to a parent-teacher conference..."

It's hard to imagine it, but mere decades ago, parenting books were addressed and targeted only at mothers; fathers were not allowed into a birthing room, and parent-teacher conferences had an overwhelming female majority. Parenting was, quite frankly, only a mother's duty—a role in which fathers were barely involved.

Fortunately, this matter has drastically changed in the last few years. How much so? Well, that depends on who you ask. In many ways, we may only see the triumphs of this in several years, perhaps when parenting books don't have to include a separate chapter regarding fathers. Then, a father's involvement would be so easily taken for granted as fact, that writing about it specifically would be completely redundant.

And what about what goes on in *your* house? Are the parental roles evenly shared? How do you divide these roles? Who does what? Are you happy with the role division, or is it a cause for constant fights and disagreements? And also—which one of you is reading this chapter now? The mother or the father? It's an interesting thing to note…

Before we dive right in, allow me to point out that this chapter mainly deals with the active involvement of fathers in households where both the mother and father live together. That said, many of the principles that will come up here are relevant both to families where the parents are divorced, and, with certain shifts in perspective, households of same-sex parents, being as they, too, have a parenting role division between *two* parents (▸ if you are divorced or same-sex parents, you can read more on these subjects in Chapter 27 and Chapter 29).

A fully involved father—why is it so important?

In the past, the role division between men and women was exceptionally clear: the father worked outside of the house, providing for the family, while the mother stayed home and cooked, cleaned, did the laundry, and took care of the children. It followed the same lines as you would find in nature: the female takes care of the cubs, and the male goes out to hunt for food. Luckily, this reality has vastly changed since women were integrated into the workforce, approximately circa the mid-twentieth century. And just how women refuse to give up on their right to work, to build a career and accomplish themselves, the men, too, refuse to give up on their right to be fully involved in raising their children. And that is a good thing, because when a father is fully involved, *everyone* benefits.

Let's start with the children themselves: children highly benefit from having a father who is fully involved in their lives. Research has shown that children whose fathers are more involved in their lives tend to be happier, calmer, more emotionally regulated, have higher self-confidence levels, reach better academic accomplishments, and even have a higher IQ score; all those in comparison to their counterparts whose fathers remain less involved in their lives. Additionally, these children also tend to be less violent, handle competitive situations better, be more aware of their feelings, and even have better romantic relationships when they are older. How can we possibly give up on all these attributes?

Moreover, you'll probably not be surprised to hear that fathers who are fully involved in raising their children have wives who are more satisfied in their relationships. The mothers also report better functioning within their parental role—making the children benefit twice over. And what about the fathers…? You may say to yourself something along the lines of: *When I was a child, my father had only one main role, and that was to provide for the family—and now I'm meant to do both: be the provider and the nurturing father. I work a full-time job. I haven't got even a moment to myself.* Well, despite the stress and multiple roles, we clearly find that fathers also benefit from being involved in raising their children. Research shows that fathers who co-parent, live a more balanced life; they broaden their emotional capabilities; they feel less stress in their work life (which you may find surprising, but the fact is research-based); they experience a deeper, more meaningful sense of purpose, and above all: they report higher levels of satisfaction in their lives.

It seems, then, that paternal involvement in children's lives holds nothing but benefits to the entire family. The notion of a win-win situation was mentioned here before and will be mentioned again. My belief is that this principle is relevant to most all interpersonal relationships. The opposite of the win-win situation is, of course, the lose-lose one: the situation when everyone loses. So, if you can choose between a situation where everyone wins or between the other where everyone loses… how can you ever choose differently? In other words, how can a father ever choose not to be fully involved?

A fully involved and participating father—how is it actually done?

Despite the many advantages in having an involved father, this situation doesn't always happen, nor does it always happen sufficiently. Let's try and get to the bottom as to the reason for it; why paternal involvement can, at times, be a tricky concept. The awareness of these problems may help to eventually overcome the possible obstacles along the way, and help you not give up on the right and privilege of raising your children together in honest partnership.

A role without a model

Our parenting is highly based on the parenting models we ourselves experienced in our childhood. The way our parents treated and raised us affects—sometimes subconsciously—the parents we ultimately become. However, being as how in the past most fathers weren't involved in raising their children—fathers today, who do try and be fully involved in their children's lives, oftentimes find themselves lacking a role model. In other words, you want to be a father who bathes, feeds, plays, discusses your children and your own days, comforts, hugs and calms when needed… but you're lacking a model to help you do it. At times, fathers may feel as though being a fully involved parent makes them "less manly"—by doing things such as cook dinners, put their children to bed, or talk to their children about feelings. Fortunately, this situation is changing for the better year by year. Paternal involvement is growing constantly and is slowly becoming a given and a natural part of parenting. Already many fathers refuse to give up on the privilege of being fully involved in raising their children. And if you have indeed broken that glass barrier and are fully involved in raising your child, you can feel honestly encouraged at the fact that your children—when they grow up and become parents themselves—will have a true role model to base their behavior on.

There are many ways to be a "good father"

Differently to the maternal role which is quite clearly defined in our society (and highly demanding, besides), when it comes to the question of paternal roles, there seem to be many ways to be a "good father." A "good father" can be someone who takes their children to the park and teaches them how to ride a bike; a "good father" can be someone who comes back from work and reads their children a bedtime story; a "good father" can be someone who spends time with their children in the afternoons while the mother is at work.

There are many definitions and possibilities for "how to be a good father," and many families feel frustrated over the issue, especially being as it's an opening for arguments between parents. Despite a growing paternal involvement, many mothers still feel as though they are the ones who carry most of the weight of parenting; the ultimate *responsibility* is theirs. They are the ones to coordinate play dates, they are the ones who remind their children about tests and home-work, and they are the ones in constant communication with teachers and the school in general. This situation happens, at times, even in families where the father is with the children more hours than the mother, who works during the day. Many mothers feel as though the responsibilities are still theirs to bear, while the fathers merely "help out" or remain "involved."

If one of these descriptions sounds familiar to you, and if you feel uncomfortable with the role distribution between you and your partner, speak things through; try and make decisions regarding the changes you should make—ones that will fit in your family unit. However, before doing so, you should be aware of the "50-50 trap," and the trap of "exactly the same:" both are described below. Try not to fall into them.

The 50-50 trap

The many years of being educated in the benefits of democracy have cemented within us the concept that "co-responsibility" means "equalness," or, as the children might put it, "50-50." However, in many of life's situations (you can think about the biblical story of the judgment of King Solomon), a "split-through-the-middle" equalness does not necessarily present the most desired solution. As parents, you are expected to highly benefit from holding a joint responsibility regarding parenting. Still, this does not mean it has to be done through a 50-50 mentality. Parents who understand that co-responsibility does not necessarily mean half-and-half, are expected to save themselves a large number of fights, disagreements, and incessant dissatisfaction. After all, we have to admit that splitting something truly down the middle, is hardly possible in real life.

The "daddy is just like mommy" trap

In addition to the 50-50 trap, it's also important to understand that you shouldn't behave in "exactly the same way." You're two different people, and your children can most definitely benefit from each of you being involved in their lives in different ways: in the ways that fit you best. So, there's nothing wrong with Daddy being the one the children jump and horse around with, while Mom is the one the children go to for those heart-to-heart conversations when their social issues at school don't go the way they wish. It's also perfectly acceptable for Mom to be the one to help with math, while Dad plays football with them, or cooks with them—and countless other combinations that fit in your lifestyles and preferences. Research shows that these different interactions with each parent stimulate different parts of the children's brain, thus contributing greatly to their development.

Daddy wants to be involved—but Mom won't allow it

Let's admit it: sometimes a father can have trouble being a part of the parenting process because the mother prevents him from participating. And in some families (not *ours*, of course*)*, mothers encourage fathers to take part and do *everything* with their children—with the stipulation of the father doing everything in the exact same way as they do it (something we already know is impossible; we read about it in the previous section).

It seems, then, that this is another trap we have to avoid. I've written in earlier chapters about the "triangle" that represents the healthy, stable relationship between parents and their children: a situation in which the child has two authoritative parents who are responsible for their well-being—the two parents together and each separately. This is different from the situation in which one parent is subjected to the other's decisions. And so, the next time, before we go to Pilates and leave our significant other with a detailed "instruction manual" about how *exactly* they should put the children to bed, we should remind ourselves that our children benefit greatly from having a parent who treats them differently than the other, reacts to them differently, and puts them to bed in a slightly different way, too.

The importance of raising children while being on "the same page"

I've given heaps of praise regarding the natural differences between parents, and that is well deserved, but it also shouldn't be translated into allowing you to contradict each other or dismiss the other's decisions (*"Mom won't let us have candy, let's go ask Dad—he'll definitely let us"*). Children may benefit from the individual styles each parent has, but they need their parents to be "on the same page." It's recommended to aspire to a single set of values, that the rules of the house remain stable and consistent, and that you both stand behind those rules, and respect and hold up the other's decisions.

In praise of the triangle: the love of a mother and the love of a father as per Erich Fromm

The psychoanalyst and philosopher **Erich Fromm**, in his book "*The Art of Loving*," shines a light on the possible differences that can occur between the love of a mother and a love of a father. He perceives a mother's love as an unconditional love, a love that occurs by the child simply *being*. However, a father's love does have stipulations—the child has to meet certain achievements and adhere to a specific set of expectations in order to be rewarded with it.

Although this division into categories sounds artificial and old-fashioned (and, indeed, the work was published in 1956), it seems that there is a certain value to the simple distinction between two sets of "love." Children benefit from the combination of that unconditional, ever-present "maternal love," and the "paternal love" that is based on expectations, demands, and set of values. *We love you—for simply being you, for merely existing, and also because you behave as you should, you work hard, try your best, and do good things.* And so, even if we disagree with Fromm regarding the maternal and paternal set roles, it's important to note that there is still value to the different relationships we build with our children; to the combination of unconditional love, and a love that guides them on the right path of self-fulfillment, and accomplishments.

THE BOTTOM LINE

When fathers are fully involved and a consistent part of parenting their children, everyone wins: the children, the mothers, and the fathers. Sometimes, it's far from simple—we do not have a clear model of how to go about it, and each parent's expectations are different. The role division between you both can cause fights and arguments, but despite it all, it's worth it and vital to put the effort in. It's also important to remember that Dad shouldn't function in the same way as Mom does. There is much worth in the variety and difference in styles both parents possess. And the most important thing is to not give up on sharing responsibility for parenting your child.

CHAPTER 22

MAKING SPACE FOR ROMANCE (IT WAS THERE FIRST)
On the connections between being a couple and being parents

*"**Daddy**, sign Jonathan's permission slip for the school trip..."*

*"**Mom**, help Noa with her Geography homework..."*

How did we get to this point, you may ask. How is it that from being a couple—a loving, cool, close couple—we started calling each other "mom" or "dad?" How have we become people whose conversations, 90 percent of the time, are about children? Be it to coordinate play dates or who will drive whom, the kids' after school classes, their homework, even the food in their lunchboxes...

We promised ourselves—thousands of times over—that we'd never end up like this, that our romantic life will remain a priority. The children would come next, as wonderful as they are...

"Mom" and "Dad," is it possible that like most other couples, you, too, dropped the ball on this one?

Parenting, in most families, is a couple's job. The romance, in most cases, came before parenting, and was the basis from which parenting stemmed. But, parenting is such an all-consuming job, so demanding and exhausting, that in many incidences, it blurs the couple-life, overtakes it, and threatens to harm it. And if any of this is familiar to you, don't worry, it's only because you are truly not alone in this.

Let's not get confused by this—children are the most wondrous outcome a couple can hope for; new people were created out of the combination of the two of you—is there anything more exciting and beautiful than that? Despite so, research that checked happiness levels discovered that parenting tends to harm the overall happiness levels regarding a couple's life (▶ see too Chapter 18). And yet, you still have all the reasons on earth to hope and aspire that your couple life will be different. I'm sure you'll also be happy to hear that it is, indeed, possible to achieve, especially since it's largely in your hands.

This chapter is addressed to couples who are raising their children together, heterosexual or same-sex couples alike. (If you're divorced, you're welcome to read Chapter 27, and if you're single parents, read more about that in Chapter 29.)

Strong couple life makes for a win-win situation

In the previous chapter, I wrote about the attributes of a win-win situation: everyone wins (or everyone loses). There's no better example of this model than a couple's life. When one of you shows warmth and good-will to the other, your counterpart feels good and is expected to put the effort into being positive and warm back. In this way, the magic occurs: you both feel good, and that is expressed down to the children, too. However, the opposite of the win-win situation, the model where everyone loses, makes for a negative cycle that only grows and feeds itself: you're unkind, they're unkind back, and you both remain unkind to each other. It would hardly be logical to choose the option where everyone loses over the possibility of everyone benefitting. It's so important to put in that effort and choose the first option.

To clarify this idea, you can imagine a couple playing Frisbee. In Frisbee, both players have a similar goal: to keep the disc in the air for as long as possible. The players need to have good communication between them, and also must be constantly well coordinated. Differently from tennis, for example, where each of the players tries to *beat* the other, and one player's victory means the other's defeat, with couples your goal is *mutual*. There are no winners or losers. It so happens that either everyone wins, or everyone loses. This is true for the relationships between children and parents, as well.

The mathematics of a happy couple's life

"A religious Jew, an American, a psychologist, and mathematician"—it almost sounds like the beginning of a joke, only these descriptors are attributed to one man: the Jewish-American psychologist **John Gottman**, who, rather unconventionally, was a mathematician before becoming a psychologist. This fact helps explain Gottman's choice of attributing mathematical-quantitative principles to purely psychological matters.

Gottman stepped outside of the important and accepted presumption that a monogamous, romantic, sexual, prolonged relationship was, in fact, the most wondrous gift life could provide us with. His classic research dealt with the attempt to identify the causes that could sabotage healthy, happy relationships, and ultimately lead to divorce. In a series of brilliant studies, through watching the couple's communication, Gottman managed to predict, in an astoundingly accurate way, those couples who live their lives in a way that may elevate the chances of divorce or allow them to stay together (▶ see framed text). Only, fortunately, Gottman didn't stop there. As a psychotherapist, (who worked closely—however not—with his *wife* Julie who's, too, a psychologist), he attempted to translate his findings into simple actionable principles, designed to help couples live a more fulfilling couple life, and to ultimately prevent divorce.

For example, Gottman found that 69 percent of the things couples fight about are regarding "unsolvable" situations. These matters regard questions of set personality traits and the fundamental beliefs each of the partners hold. In light of this fact, he clarified that the goal for couples isn't to *prevent* fights, not even to *settle* them, but to first and foremost learn how to *reconcile* and move forward from each argument. Additionally, Gottman found that it matters less the *amount* the couples fought, and instead what truly makes a difference is the *proportions* between the couple's struggles and their good moments and positive gestures. Based on his research, he recommended a ratio of 5 to 1 at the minimum, meaning: five positive gestures at the very least, to every moment of tension or argumentativeness.

And if you thought psychology didn't include any recipes, Gottman, the mathematician-psychologist, thought differently. He created a "recipe" of sorts, consisting of six weekly hours—detailing them down to the minute—to ultimately help couples keep their strong relationship alive (▶ see framed text on page 314). And even if you don't follow the recipe down to the letter (you'd need a rather obsessive mindset to do so), the principles that appear in it can help you direct your functioning in your daily lives together, and ultimately contribute to your and your partner's welfare.

"Are you still married?"—Gottman's classic research

All couples fight from time to time. In that case, what characterizes the couples who will stay together for years to come, over those who will decide to separate?

As a talented researcher, Gottman understood that in order to answer this question, he had to survey couples while they were married, *before* the time when things started falling apart. In the context of one of his research studies, he summoned married couples to the "love lab" he created. The couples were asked to argue with each other for fifteen minutes over some random subject. During the argument, each of the partners' blood pressure was measured, and their facial expressions were caught on camera. Approximately three thousand couples participated in the study.

In another study, Gottman observed married couples who had agreed to move into a videoed house for a few days. The couples were requested to live their lives as they normally would, while the cameras constantly recorded the goings on between them (this was many years before commercial television started the "*Big Brother*" style shows).

In both studies, Gottman and his research assistances kept following up with the couples (the research participants) once a year. In the follow-up conversations, the couples were asked one main question: "Are you still married?" Gottman's goal was to find the connections between the interaction patterns couples had as they interacted in front of the cameras, to the ultimate chance that same couple would carry on with their married lives, or choose to divorce.

And indeed, Gottman found that the way the couples spoke to each other, even their tone of voice and facial expressions, could predict highly accurately—91 percent, to be exact—if the given couple will continue to live together, or choose to separate. Specifically, he found the serious damage that lay in four behavioral patterns:

- **Criticism within the relationship**: especially when the criticism was directed toward one of the partner's personalities, rather than their behavior.
- **Defensiveness of one of the partners** (*"Why do I deserve this? I did nothing"*).
- **Scorn, contempt, and resentment** while fighting.
- **Stonewalling**: closing up, aggressive silences, and a pulling away (this tends to be a male tendency, more so than women's).

> It's important to be aware of these points. It seems that the way couples treat each other—while fighting or during their normal day-to-day lives—the words we choose, the silences when we're angry, our tone of voice and facial expressions—all these have a huge impact on the relationship, both currently and in the future.

A good stable relationship: a gift for life

It seems that there is a consensus regarding the fact that a stable, good couple's relationship has benefits in every possible circle: for yourselves as adults, for your parenting, and for your children. Let's elaborate.

A good relationship is the basis of it all

One of the most complex challenges when it comes to romance and parenting, regards the need to maintain the relationship—to protect it and fill it with substance—independently from the given parental tasks. If you put effort into it and act accordingly (and have a little luck), then your relationship will last and flourish, even after the children move away and leave the nest (surprisingly, this happens much faster than you may believe). In order to preserve and nurture your relationship, it's important you set out boundaries and create time for yourselves—time that's apart from your parenting duties. Go out in the evenings just the two of you; go out with friends; set time aside each evening after the children go to bed or are in their rooms and not a part of your conversations; go out on a couple's vacation every once in a while. You'll all benefit from it—and not only the both of you, your children, too (see latter part of this chapter).

Your relationship creates a meaningful space for you to reach decisions regarding your children

Let's once again reiterate that parenting is a highly complex life mission. It combines countless minor details you have to manage, and numerous complex decisions you must make regarding your children. One of the wondrous benefits of a couple-based parenting unit, is that the two of you desperately want what's best for your children (by the way, this is relevant to those who are divorced, too). How marvelous for you that you can *share* the many parental tasks, that you can confer with each other, and focus together on those very important little people of yours.

A good relationship creates an important balancing system: to be there for the other and to regulate them

Who among us doesn't have weaknesses? Who among us doesn't have those moments when we simply break down? These weaknesses can be dependent on the time of day ("*My patience as their mother simply runs out after 21:00, come take over for me—now!*"); they can be subject dependent ("*I don't care if it'll bring on the apocalypse, I'm not taking them to the dentist!*"); and sometimes they can be attributed to a specifically bad time one of you is going through (*"These last few months I've been so occupied with taking care of my own parents. I know I've been more impatient and short"*). As a team—as parents—you can both be supported and support the other, take over for each other, balance each other out, or, in other words: *"How lucky you are that you're not going through this parenting thing on your own."*

A good relationship helps the children know their place

When you take care of your relationship and nurture it—give time to yourselves without the presence of your children, go out without them, have "grown up" conversations—you send your children the important message that they are not the center of the world; that you have interests of your own, conversation matters the children do not need to be a part of; or in simpler terms: "you have a life." Sometimes, children insist on not letting go: they want to know what you're talking about, they want to be involved, and they always have something of their own to add. Don't give up on your right to some privacy. Interestingly, and not necessarily intuitively, children need this experience—the understanding that they are not the center of the universe. The awareness of the fact that you and your partner are bigger and stronger than they are, that they are merely a *part* of your world (significant and central as it may be, but still, only a *part* of it), and do not take up every bit of it—gives them a sense of security and calmness. And in the same context—*let's talk in Spanish for a moment*—please refrain from changing languages and talking "over your children's heads." It's offensive, insulting, and disrespectful. Instead, simply give yourself the chance and space to talk privately about the issues that concern you, when the children aren't around.

A good relationship creates a stable network for your children

As I mentioned in other contexts, children benefit greatly from growing up in a household with two parents. Your child's ability to lean on each of you, to trust you both, greatly contributes to their sense of security in the world. Additionally, you should remember that your children also benefit from your being different people—from having parents with different characteristics, personalities, preferences, thinking patterns, occupations, and hobbies. In addition, your children also benefit from doing different activities with each one of you: going out for treks with one of you, playing an instrument with the other, watching a reality show with Dad, and skating with Mom, and much more.

Problematic relationships may end up harming your child

So far, I've focused on the many attributes of having a positive, good relationship. At the same time, it's important to note that studies have shown that a problematic, stress-filled relationship negatively affects the children. This situation is called the *spill-over effect*. Ongoing tensions and conflicts between parents tend to spill-over from the couple's relationship to the relationship between parents and their children. Such situations tend to make the overall atmosphere in the house dark and complicated, and impair the child's well-being.

Your good relationship is an important model for your children to learn from

Most of the parents aspire for their children to grow up and eventually build their own families: a home and family that is based on a good relationship—a relationship based on love, interpersonal communication, intimacy, and, perhaps above all else, a mutual commitment. When you conduct a relationship such as that yourselves, you are greatly contributing to the model your children receive, and heighten the chances of them indeed basing their family on a similar model. Allow me to reiterate that a good relationship does not necessarily mean you always see eye to eye regarding every subject. You are still different people, and it's only natural that each of you brings to the family dynamic something different—a different style, and even some differing values. As was written previously, it's still vital for you not to have clashing sets of values between you both, and that you don't cancel each other out in front of your children. However, differences of opinions and arguments are expected to happen—happen naturally, in fact—and it's even a positive thing that they do. It's important to remember that children are highly affected by the model of behavior they see at home; your behavior shapes and affects your children's perceptions regarding interpersonal relationships, and most importantly, a romantic relationship.

Six weekly hours to keep your relationship healthy—Gottman's "recipe"

- **Saying goodbye in the morning:** in the morning, before you part, tell each other your plans for the day (2 minutes * 5 times a week = 10 weekly minutes).
- **Meeting in the evening:** at the end of the day, talk quietly with each other for 20 minutes, with no television or background noise to distract you (20 minutes * 5 days a week = 100 weekly minutes).
- **Expressions of appreciation and affection:** a daily, honest expression of affection and appreciation (5 minutes * 7 days a week = 35 weekly minutes).
- **Physical gestures:** expressing affection through physical kisses, hugs, caresses, every day (5 minutes * 7 days a week = 35 weekly minutes).
- **An intimate weekly date:** a time you spend together just the two of you, for two hours (two weekly hours).
- **Conversational updates:** each week, you set aside an hour to talk about your relationship—you start with expressing your appreciation for the other person, and go on to discuss any difficulties you had that particular week and try and work through them (one weekly hour),

Overall: six weekly hours.

Gottman's studies and the practical meanings derived from them, are elaborated on in his excellent book: "*The Seven Principles for Making Marriage Work.*"

THE BOTTOM LINE

Parenting in most families is a couple's job, only in some cases, parenting can overshadow your relationship and take it over completely. Do not let this happen—take care of your relationship—it has a right of its own to exist. There are many ways to keep your relationship alive and to nurture it; a good stable relationship is based on trust, intimacy, and mutual commitment, and it's one of the most important gifts life has to give an adult.

Beyond the great value of the relationship on its own, there are also additional benefits to a parents' relationship. It allows for your children to feel a sense of security, both because there are two people for them to lean on when needed, and because of the inherent differences between you both. Additionally, by seeing that you have a life, that they are not the center of the world, you give your children some much needed life insight. A good relationship allows you the possibility and space to make important decisions regarding your children, it creates a set of balances between you both, and contributes to your emotional regulation. Finally, children who live in a household that presents a healthy couple's way of living, are expected to be positively influenced by it in their adult lives. All the benefits in one place.

CHAPTER 23

THEY'RE NOT AGAINST US—THEY'RE ON OUR SIDE!
Regarding the relationship between parents and the children's education systems

Close your eyes for a moment and think back to your memories of school, back when you were students. What memories are most prominent? What do you remember from daycare? Or elementary school? What was the name of your first grade teacher? Who are the people you remember fondly, and who would you rather forget?

Each year, when I do this exercise with my students who are studying for an MA in psychology, I find myself astounded at just how much we remember. We all walk around with clear, detailed memories of the educational system we were once a part of: memories of certain things we were told—or things that were not said in the end; experiences—some wonderful and positive, others painful and frustrating, and at times even traumatizing.

While so heavily equipped with this emotional baggage, we send our children out every day either to school or daycare. Some do so with a smile and a sense of calm, but others do it with a heavy heart and worry, and at times even ragefully.

Only, our feelings are not transparent—our children notice them. Even if we don't say a word, the feelings seep into our children's consciousness and affect them, so it's vital for us to be aware of them. And when you think about it truly—the challenge is indeed large and complicated. Our children spend many hours a day in the educational system, sometimes even more waking hours than they do at home. There is no doubt that the systems have a huge influence on their education, but yet, we still don't have a way to choose who will end up being the children's daycare teacher or schoolteachers. We can't decide what the content of their lessons will be, either. Furthermore, much of the children's way of perceiving themselves is cemented during the time spent in the educational system: *how I get along with other children, how social I am, what kind of student I am, how talented I am.* Research has shown that regarding these concepts, the school systems may end up having an even greater impact on our children than we, the parents, do (!). For these processes to work in our children's benefit, it's important we remain aware of the kind of relationship we build with the daycare or schoolteacher, and other people in charge of our child's education in these varied systems. Before I offer the principles and actions I believe can help with this, let's first look at the bigger question regarding the challenges of education in the 21st century.

"The terror of parent-teacher day," or: what is the true role of the teacher

One of the more vivid memories all former students have is about a biyearly occurrence: that parent-teacher conference. The teacher, parents, student, and grade sheets are all present—even a small plate with pretzels is added to the table. Most of all though, is the tension in the air: *What will the teacher say? What will the parents say? How will they react? And what will the final outcome be?* Everything is perceived as incredibly dramatic and dooming. This kind of atmosphere has to change. The stressfulness and pressure shows a pure lack of understanding in the ultimate role schools and teachers have. If we look at the big picture, the educational system nowadays handles large and fundamental issues regarding its ultimate goals. Everyone understands that "the transfer of *information* from teacher to student" is no longer the be all and end all; that knowledge, after all, is but a quick internet search away. What then *is* so vital and fundamental?

Now, the growing perception in the world is that the educational systems are, first and foremost, meant to *promote the positive mental welfare of its students*— both the personal and social. That is the overreaching goal (▶ for more on this, see framed text below).

And, indeed, the OECD adopted this overreaching goal, making it one of the most central future educational ambitions. The significance of this is that educational systems will aim to develop in their students qualities such as: inner motivation, flexible and critical thinking, creativity, emotional regulation, leadership, the ability to create meaningful interpersonal relationships, to give back to others, to take initiative, possess self-awareness, to be capable of expressing oneself, and more.

And if you ask how promoting this essential overreaching goal is possible, we now know that its eventual success is largely due to the interpersonal connections forged between students and teachers. Just as you, the parents, act as significant role models for your children, so can their teachers become major influences for them—people who will ultimately positively affect your children and allow them the possibility to express all their wonderful qualities and talents. For this to be feasible, the teachers themselves have to aspire to make it possible, and at the same time, we, the parents, have to *allow* them to step into that position.

So, yes, it's true that teachers will never hold the same influence and importance as parents do, but they are still more than welcome to join in the challenge education presents, and to contribute through their professional and personal attributes to our children's overall benefit. Even if we continue to view knowledge, academic achievements, grades, and learning skills as vital, it's still no less important for our children to be aware that their teacher appreciates them for who they are, that their uniqueness is taken note of, and that the teachers believe in them. When all this comes to pass, parent-teacher conferences will no longer be so dramatic and threatening.

Educational goals in the 21st century and the way to achieve them

What are the true goals the educational systems hold nowadays, and what will be their goals for the future? These questions have been occupying many professionals throughout the world these past years. The researcher and historian **Yuval Noah Harari**, in his book *"21 Lessons for the 21st Century,"* states that the last thing a teacher needs to do is teach their pupils more information. They already have far too much of it. Instead, people need the ability to make sense of information, to tell the difference between what is important and what is unimportant, and above all to combine many bits of information into a broad picture of the world. He suggests the schoolteachers switch to teaching through the basis of "the four Cs:" critical thinking, communication, collaboration, and creativity. Noah Harari states that the most important of all skills is the ability to deal with change, to learn new things, and to preserve your mental balance in unfamiliar situations.

As previously stated, the OECD and many additional countries have adopted such goals. But what happens in actuality?

Many teachers and education-workers claim that they fully identify with these important goals, but, in their day-to-day working environment, find them hard to achieve. The reason for this lies in the fact that their ultimate success is measured through the students' all encompassing, grade-based success. And truly, this makes for a complicated situation. As of today, the educational system at its core holds conflicting missions and values. Yet still, among the many didactic tasks schooling presents, it's important to remember that promoting the emotional and social welfare of the students is no less—or perhaps even *more*—important than acquiring knowledge and grades above a certain threshold.

Healthy communication between us and our children's educational system—how is it done?

You may be reading these lines while telling yourselves that the bottom line is that your children go to a "regular" school every morning, with teachers who are overworked and worn out. How can all these ideas be in any way relevant for us and our children? Well, if you feel that way, you should truly attempt to shift your perspective and adopt a more sympathizing view when it comes to your children's educational system. I will concentrate here on some key principles and actions that can assist you with this.

Combine forces with the system—don't fight it

"They're not against us, they're on our side!"—is the most important message of this chapter. Unfortunately, many parents go into attack mode the second they have to communicate with their children's educational system. Full of good intentions and a will to protect our children, we put on our fighting gear and charge off to war: furious, accusatory, disappointed, sometimes even threatening. When that happens, the "system" fights back—something that affirms our need to fight it in the first place. Only, there is no bigger mistake you can make with this. Contrary to what we may believe, there are no conflict of interests between us and the educational system; there are no conflict of interests between us and the teachers, the school counselors, or the principal. All everyone wants is what's best for the child—our children. If we can see the truth of that, if we can join forces rather than fight—there's no doubt our children will benefit greatly from it.

At school your child is not the "center of the universe"—and that's fine!

Sometimes, parents feel the need to fight against the system, believing themselves to be the only ones who see their child at the center of the matter, being as the teacher has to divide their attention between so many children at once. Yet, it's important to understand that though at school your child is indeed one of many, their teacher still wants what's best for them. Moreover, the fact that at home your child feels like the center of everything, and at school they become a part of a wide group of similarly aged children, makes for a valuable developmental milestone, allowing for the children to find their place in a team or group and function properly in society.

Share important information about your children with their educational system

As we said previously, our children spend many of their waking hours at school or daycare every day. So, in order for this situation to be beneficial for them, it's important to put your trust in the educational system and to allow your children to pick up on that trust, too. It's also important to share with the system any substantial changes or issues your child may have. For example, if your child is going through a rough time—no matter the reason (*"Our beloved dog passed away"*)—it's vital for their teacher to be aware of it, so that they can be more attuned and sensitive to the child's needs; or, if you noticed that your daughter needs to doodle in order to pay attention, let the team know and ask them to cooperate with allowing her do as needed (you'll be surprised how much the systems today are open and attuned to such matters).

Take the messages you receive from school seriously

If your child's school shares information with you regarding your children (*"He seems inattentive lately," "She was really rude to the caretaker this morning"*), don't take it lightly. Don't disregard the reports you receive from the school. So, if your son's teacher lets you know that whenever there are uncomfortable situations, he leaves the class in a temper—take the account seriously and try and help moderate and regulate your child's reactions; don't cynically reply something along the lines of: *"Sure, if he found class a little more interesting, maybe he wouldn't feel the need to leave."*

It's important to remember that having an open line of communication and trust between the household and the educational system is vital and necessary for our children. Also, if you feel as if the school was wrong in their approach, or in the way they treated your child—something that can most certainly happen at times—talk about it with the relevant sources, enlighten them, and listen calmly to the messages coming from their side, as well. It very well may be that in the end you and the educational team will still disagree on certain matters; it's not always possible to reach a complete consensus on absolutely everything. But still, communicating properly, letting there be a respectful atmosphere between you all, and, above all, not causing a *split* between you and the school is essential. Your children should not receive the message from you that they're going to a "problematic" place every day, to fight "enemies."

When the child moves between systems—pass on important information

If your child is just starting preschool or transferring from elementary school to high school, and you have information that the educational system may find relevant—don't keep it from them. For example, if your daughter suffers from ADHD or learning disabilities, or if your son suffered through some social issues in the previous year, share the information with the educational team in the new school and enlist them to help. Don't let them find everything out on their own, and don't put them to the test ("*Let's see if they notice...*"). Remember—the educational systems are on our side and aren't working against us.

It's true that many parents in such situations wish for their children to have a "fresh start" and hope to avoid having them stuck with negative labels that could potentially harm them farther down the line. However, in most cases, *sharing* the information will help your children, while *hiding it* will do the opposite and hurt them. The sharing of the information will help the new system put your child in the class that is the best fit for them, with the most appropriate teacher for their difficulties, or the right friends, and may even allow your children to receive the professional help they may need to get them ahead. And that is the exact outcome you hope for.

Note the fine difference between meddling and being involved

If you ask educators what the most complex part of their job is, it's likely that they will all say—unanimously—"the parents." And honestly, it's understandable. The way parents have begun treating the educational systems in the last few years has grown to be increasingly demanding and difficult. The social network groups allow parents to complain publicly—no matter if the issue is minor or major; the teachers being available by phone or e-mail gives us "permission" to call on them whenever we choose. In many ways, it seems as though we have lost the minimum of respect we should give to professionals who work hard and hold a huge amount of responsibility when it comes to our children's education.

Let's not be confused, however—my belief is that there is a huge importance to parents' involvement in the children's educational system. We have much to *contribute* to the system, and we can only better do so if we know how to properly cooperate with the parties responsible for our children's education. However, we mustn't allow our involvement to become meddling. We cannot interfere in ways that can undermine the teachers, make them loosen their grip, or make them wish for a different job… so, even if you do have some criticisms, if you have something to say—find the right way to do it: humbly, quietly, respectfully, and in a way that promotes listening and communicating properly. They're not against us—they're on our side, remember?

THE BOTTOM LINE

From a very young age, children enter the educational system and spend many hours of their lives in them. The educational system play a key role in shaping your children's image, affect their sense of self, their social interactions, and the adults they'll soon grow into. For this challenge to succeed, it's important to remember and believe that the educational system wants what's best for our children, and that there is no conflict of interest between us and them. Keeping an open, positive, and respectful line of communication between the system and your household; being constructively involved without letting the involvement turn into meddling; giving our children's teachers the chance and opportunity to be meaningful role models for them— will all help promote our children's overall emotional welfare. You're not alone in this—daycare centers and schools are fully cooperative in helping educate your children, and they do it together with you.

CHAPTER 24

"I SOUND JUST LIKE MY MOTHER…"
Intergenerational transmissions and how it affects our parenting

"Man is but the imprint of his native landscape."

—**Shaul Tchernichovsky**

Who among us is unfamiliar with this feeling? We promised ourselves we'd be different kinds of parents—that we wouldn't get angry when our children play rough and enjoy themselves, that we wouldn't look at them with a disappointed expression when they get a low grade on one of their tests, that we wouldn't suffer from anxiety every time they leave the house… that we'd be cooler parents, easier to get along with, more empathic… but more than whom? Well, more than our parents, of course.

And for some reason, it doesn't always work out as we wish. Often we find ourselves recreating the same parental patterns our own parents raised us with. You can hear your mother's voice come from your throat; you feel as if you respond in the same way your father did.

This fascinating phenomenon—our tendency to recreate the parental patterns on which we were raised—received the name **intergenerational transmissions**, and it connects, among other things, to the fact that we were all once children ourselves. We all experienced certain parental patterns, and these patterns affect us deeply—sometimes in ways we are not necessarily aware of.

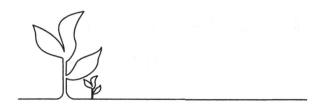

On the spectrum between wonderful childhood experiences, and traumatic ones

You may possibly be asking yourselves, "What connection do I have with this subject?" Well, it seems that on a certain level, intergenerational transmissions occur all the time, in all families. What changes, however, is the *content* of the transmissions: beginning with positive, bettering experiences, all the way through to difficult events, and even traumatic ones. So, if your childhood experiences were mostly pleasant and happy—you and your children have truly benefitted. But what about the parents who went through a less-than-ideal childhood? Parents whose own parents used to hit them whenever they behaved out of line? Parents whose own parents "disappeared" whenever one of the children annoyed them? Parents whose own parents were too busy with the everyday matters, and were not concerned about what was actually going on with their children…?

In this chapter, we will try and understand what stands at the basis for the intergenerational transmissions: in good and positive situations, in difficult and traumatic ones, and in the wide range between them. And since this subject may be extremely emotionally loaded and sensitive to touch upon, I will start by saying that even if the intergenerational transmissions are impossible to ignore, we still have much we can do to *deal* with them and let go of the past problematic patterns. Awareness regarding the unwelcome patterns we grew up with can help us overcome them. Read about it both in this chapter and the next.

Ghosts in the nursery

The psychological understanding regarding intergenerational trans-missions stemmed from the groundbreaking essay published in 1975 by the psychoanalyst and social worker **Selma Fraiberg** and her colleagues. In that essay, carrying the chilling title of "*Ghosts in the Nursery*," are depicted two extreme cases of very young mothers, who were raising their children under the terrible conditions of complete lack of emotional connectivity and apathy toward them. The babies' physical needs were met, but they received no parental love and no intimate connections. The children's development, in turn, took a sharp and disturbing downward spiral.

The emotional therapy for these mothers happened in their homes, under the umbrella of social services. Throughout the therapy, it was found that the young women themselves grew up in homes with ter-rible emotional circumstances. The young mothers had experienced a long series of neglect, parental abuse, and severe childhood trauma in their formative years—experiences they'd supposedly forgotten about. When the mothers started recalling the difficult occurrences and sharing their problematic life story with their therapists, they slowly found the ability of being able to hear their babies cry, to calm them, and answer to their needs. They began to function as mothers, and the babies reacted to the change in a positive and surprisingly fast manner. In an almost miraculous way, the more the mother recalled and shared the traumatic aspects from her childhood, the more attentive she became to her child, and the baby's development was set back to its correct course.

This paper has been quoted countless times since its publication, and has become a key factor in understanding the way to treat parents who'd been through traumatic events in their childhood years. If you are interested in reading the original paper—look it up on Google.

Intergenerational transmissions: how does it actually happen?

For dozens of years, researchers and therapists have been hoping to find the reason why we recreate with our own children the same patterns we grew up with. Nowadays, there is a quite good reasoning as to how and why it happens. Let us first look at the positive and functional aspects of this fascinating process.

Our second childhood—an easy accessway to the child inside us

> *"And through your eyes, my girl,*
> *I will discover the whole world anew,*
> *And through your hands, I'll learn*
> *To touch the waves of the ocean blue."*
>
> —**Ehud Manor** (translated by Elli Sacks)

In the wonderful Israeli song *"My Second Childhood,"* the poet, **Ehud Manor**, describes the true excitement of parents, who experience once again, through their young children, a variety of states and emotions: the first time they touch the sea waves, their true joy over hugs, the way they look at the world with fresh eyes. And indeed, our children create an "easy accessway" of sorts to the children we once were, the children hidden deep inside our adult selves. Parenting takes us back to our childhood and the ways our own parents treated and took care of us.

In many ways, this is the secret magic of parenting: we become parents overly much due to the positive parenting we ourselves received in our childhood. Our parents are the ones who plant the seeds of our future abilities to become good parents down the line. By the way, this characteristic is not unique for humans. In Chapter 30, I mention a study in which female rats, who'd been separated from their mothers not long after they were born, and did not receive maternal care, found it exceedingly difficult to become mothers themselves, and did not know how to treat their offspring. It seems that our parents, and parents of other mammals in nature, set up a kind of *model* that allows for us to one day become good parents to our own children.

Parenting as a "training board" in relationships

Many ask what the true purpose of parenting is: does it center around education? Setting boundaries? Determining key values? Well, our parental jobs include all of these aspects, of course, but it seems that above all else, parenting creates a form of invaluable experimentation for the relationships we build with others. When parents are attentive, when they listen to their children and are attuned to their needs, they ultimately equip their children with a set of optimistic glasses, ones that positively affect the relationships they have with other people (friends, daycare, or schoolteachers, and so forth). These children are expected to be able to enjoy and feel protected in their social relationships; their positive outlook will, most often, become a self-fulfilling prophecy (► see too Chapter 3). The same basic feeling of safety the parents give their children will continue to serve them when they themselves become parents—and there is a higher possibility of them passing the same along to their younger children, and so forth. This, then, is one of the key explanations for intergenerational transference: we recreate with our own children the same relationship patterns we ourselves grew up with.

The ability to be with our children and understand them "from within"

Other parental qualities that stand at the basis for the intergenerational transference (and have been mentioned throughout the book) are the parent's ability to be with their child, and the level of parental mentalization—meaning the way the parent manages to treat their child as a separate person with their own inner world, and helps the child perceive themselves as such in turn (► see more in Chapters 3 and 11).

Imagine a situation in which your daughter comes home upset—two of her good friends met up without her. In another scenario, your son missed a basketball shot, and his friends blamed him over the whole team losing. Would your children share their emotional turmoil with you? And if they did—what kind of reaction would they receive from you? Would it be criticism? (*"If you'd have only trained harder—you'd have made the shot!"*). Would it be an attempt at ignoring the difficult experience? (*"Nonsense, nothing happened. You have a thousand other friends"*). Or would it be actual, true listening, empathy and sympathy? (*"Being in that situation must feel horrible, I can only imagine what it feels like to be in your position"*). Parents who can *be with* their children, even through difficult, stormy situations, who can imagine the inner experiences the child goes through and contain it all without dismissing it and ignoring it, contribute greatly to the child's overall ability to regulate their emotions.

Research has proven that these parental qualities tend to be "passed on"—"inherited" from generation to generation, and by so doing, largely explain the existence of intergenerational transmissions. In other words: when we manage "to be there" for our children—physically and emotionally—we contribute to the development of their emotional capabilities. These emotional capabilities are what will one day allow our children to "be there" for their own children.

"It's all done out of good intentions"—being aware of intergenerational transmissions

Parenting is a complex life mission, and our parents—even if they did their very best—were not immune from making mistakes. When we become parents, many of us arrive along with plenty of *positive* past experiences, ones we wish to recreate with our own children (*"My father always gave me the feeling that I'm worth more than anything else on earth—I want to give my children the same exact feeling"*). However, with those positive past experiences we also sometimes have behavioral patterns, attitudes, and events we are adamant about *not* passing along to the next generation. It doesn't always work out. These patterns may include:

- **Over-emphasizing of certain qualities we don't perceive as vital** (*"With beauty like yours, you'll be able to get anything you want out of life"*).
- **Diminution of other qualities** (*"Music is such a waste of time. Learning math is much more important"*).
- **Being overly critical and having too high expectations** (*"You better not come back with a grade lower than…"*).
- **Impatience and parental apathy,** or perhaps **over-protectiveness and over-involvement** (*"I refuse for you to go out on school trips—not unless I come with you…"*).
- **Emphasizing things we don't truly find important** (*"You have to finish all the food from your plate!"*).
- **A lack of attention to the things that matter** (*"My own parents never asked me how I felt…"*)

And there are countless other characteristics of our parents that were, most likely, simply done out of "good intentions."

When we discover that we recreate with our children some unwanted experiences from our own childhood (being furious at them and losing control, being overly critical, ignoring them when they annoy us, being short with them, and more), we tend to be angry and disappointed with ourselves. However, it's important to know that the mere identification of these problematic patterns presents the first key to stop recreating them.

As stated beforehand, no one is immune from making mistakes. Our own children, no doubt, will one day criticize *our* parental behaviors, too. Yet still, if you recognize a problematic pattern that you "inherited" from your own parents—don't accept it as a simple fact of fate. Define the pattern for yourselves (or quality or characteristic), understand the place it came from, and make the decision: to change it, not recreate them. The choice is yours, and it's most certainly possible.

How is it that parents who experienced a difficult childhood could recreate the same patterns with their own children?

One of the more extreme situations of intergenerational transmissions is attributed to the transferring of evilness and abuse. We would expect children who'd suffered through abuse and neglect to do everything in their power *not* to recreate the same circumstances for the generation to come, but—there are families where this still occurs. It begs the question as to how it is possible that children who were hit by their parents, or who suffered through neglect, could become parents who harm their own children.

One of the main explanations for this phenomenon (that does not always come to pass) is connected to the mechanism of **identifying with the aggressor**, which was described by the psychoanalyst **Sándor Ferenczi**. To better understand the meaning of this mechanism, we have to remember that children get emotionally attached even to harmful, neglectful parents. The evolutionary need to be emotionally attached to our caretakers makes it so children love their parents, even when the parents are adverse or abusive. Here the drama occurs. The child loves their parent; they need them in order to grow and develop. However, when the beloved parent hurts the child—humiliates them, hits them—then the child has two choices: the first—to acknowledge the intolerable existence of the trauma, and understand that their mother or father does horrendous things to them. This possibility holds within it a very steep price, because it means that they lose the trusting, loving relationship with their parent—something the child still can't do without. The second choice lies with the child creating a kind of "split" within their psych: they *disconnect* from the traumatic experience and from the intolerable emotional pain that comes with it, deny the existence of the trauma, and by so doing, allow themselves to keep the aggressor parent as still-lovable and emotionally dependable. This is the mechanism of identifying with the aggressor. The young child preserves the aggressive parent as someone who is beneficiary for their well-being, at the price of recognizing the authenticity of their inner experience.

This mechanism explains how it's possible for this child—who'd been a victim of hurt, neglect, or abuse—to find themselves one day down the road harming their own child.

And why is this so important to know about and understand? First and foremost, understanding this mechanism is a first and essential step in trying to overcome it; in stopping the problematic intergenerational transference. Secondly, if you witness a situation when a parent hurts their child (whether you're the other parent, the teacher, neighbor, or any other adult)—do everything in your power to stop it. We know that the mere existence of one adult who is aware of the harming of the child and works to stop it—can help the child in the present and avoid the severe harm of emotional trauma.

Our parents are always to blame(?)—actually... not!

On the surface, we can claim that the theory of intergenerational transmissions does as what we seem to think all psychologists do—blame the parents. Everything is their fault. However, when we look deeper into the theory, we see a completely different situation. Even if we take the hardest and most complicated of cases of intergenerational transference—ones that concern parents harming their children—then we see that the theory encourages, above all, the *understanding* of the parent, and the understanding of the "place" they were acting from. All without being judgmental.

So, according to the theory, the same parents who harmed their children (the children who later grew into adults and became parents themselves), these parents—now grandparents—were most likely exposed themselves to problematic parental patterns. In other words, rather than blaming the parents, it's best to widen our perspective, to look at the parents with empathy and compassion, and to try and understand where they themselves came from, and the reasons as to why they behaved as they did. As I've stated before, recognizing the intergenerational transferences remains the first and most important part of the process of being free of them.

THE BOTTOM LINE

The parenting characteristics we lived through in our past become, at times, the attributes we ourselves have. This process is called intergenerational transmissions. You can hear your mother's judgmental voice coming from your throat—something that makes you feel bad after the fact; or you react with rage toward your children when they're playing a little too loudly—raising the "ghost" from your past that "makes" you react that way.

The intergenerational transmissions include both the positive parental patterns we experienced, and the more complex and troublesome ones. They connect, among other things, to the way our parents were attuned to us when we were children, how well they saw our inner world, and the amount to which they were present in our lives—both physically and emotionally.

Parents often find themselves recreating unwanted parental patterns from their past, and in many cases feel serious guilt and grief over it. Fortunately, psychology doesn't stop at simply recognizing the problematic mechanisms—it wishes to dig deeper into the understanding of how to let go of unwanted intergenerational transferences, and to avoid recreating them. Apparently, there are effective ways to do so. The next chapter is centered around that issue.

CHAPTER 25

TELLING OURSELVES OUR OWN LIFE STORY
Releasing our past unwanted demons

> *"Those who do not remember the past are condemned to repeat it."*
>
> —**George Santayana**

In the previous chapter, I explained the process in which parents feel as though they recreate with their children—sometimes unwillingly—behavioral patterns, situations, and experiences they experienced themselves in their own childhood.

If you grew up in a household with a positive atmosphere and experienced a childhood that was mostly positive and bettering, then you are likely less worried about this situation. But what happens to the parents whose childhood experiences included difficult ordeals? What happens to the parents whose own parents treated them in an overtly critical way, with indifference, or perhaps even harmfully and traumatically? How can we avoid passing on to our children the unwanted parts of the parenting methods we ourselves experienced as children?

Well, I promised an answer to this massive question, and here it is in a sentence: It culminates in our ability to look at our past openly, and to tell ourselves our life story in a cohesive, logical manner. In professional terms, this is called, "creating a coherent life story." Sounds vague? Read this chapter and you will see why it's so important, and how we can do it.

Telling ourselves our life story—why is it so important?

Parents' tendency to recreate with their own children unwanted patterns from their past is a powerful inclination that is not easy to be free from. However, there are still parents who manage to do so: parents who grew up in unideal circumstances, but managed to shape themselves into good, devoted parents to their children—sometimes, against all odds.

Many researchers and therapists have wished to find out *how* this happens: What allows these parents to *not* recreate the problematic patterns of their past? Apparently, the key lies with the parent's ability to tell themselves their life story in a coherent way. Research has shown that parents who can tell themselves their childhood story in a way that is cohesive and holds inner logic (what led to what), can "let go" of their past demons, and thus, are not doomed to recreate the problematic behaviors and patterns they experienced as children. This is in vast comparison to the parents who went through traumatic or difficult childhoods, but cannot "look back" at them, remember them, and give them order and sense; they cannot figure out what exactly happened, and why the events happened as they did.

At this point, it's important to clarify that a complete, coherent life story is not an *imaginary* tale a person chooses to adopt for themselves. It is, instead, a *true* life story, one that does not disregard the facts—even when they are difficult to process. Yet, it still holds the understanding of the connection between the facts. It's a story that usually holds a measure of compassion toward one's parents, and the deep understanding of the "places" the parents acted from. This is in direct contradiction to a situation in which the person holds a choppy life story, that is full of contradictions, makes no sense as to how the things came to pass; a story with traumatic elements without having processed the trauma.

But we can't change the past

"My father beat me every time I got a low grade on a test."
"My mother would just leave when she got angry with me. I never knew when she'd come back."

If you experienced difficult childhood experiences, you may be asking yourself how it could possibly help to recall them—the past, after all, can't be changed, and the memories can make us feel depressed and despondent. Well, you may be right. You don't always need to recall the traumas from the distant past.

Sometimes, it's best to forget them (>see framed text). But, if you feel as though your past baggage negatively affects your parenting—the most effective way to be free of it is to *recall* those past occurrences, to understand what happened, and to incorporate the difficult event in your life story. And this is the main message I would like to impart on this issue: while the past events cannot be changed, recalling them openly allows for us to create a fresh understanding regarding these occurrences. This process enables us to then incorporate these past events into the insights we hold regarding our lives, and by so doing, mitigate the negative and harmful influence they hold on our present.

So, for example, a man who used to get beaten up by his father could recall the difficult events, ponder them, and with time reach insights such as:

My father wasn't a bad man. I think he believed, deep down, that that was the way you should educate children. It took me years to realize that my father, who'd lost his father at the tender age of five, had no positive paternal role model who he could talk to, play with, and simply "be" with. Now, when I think about him, I believe he did his best, and it's impossible to have expected more from him. All things considered, we did have many good and happy moments together, and when I truly needed him—he did everything in his power to help me.

When we think back to our childhood events in order to understand them and incorporate them in our life story, we can "put them aside" and forbid them from infiltrating our present and sabotaging our parenting. In other words, although the past experiences themselves are difficult, and—without a doubt—put us at a disadvantage in our parental lives— they do not "doom" us or set our fate and future. If we can shape the story so it would make sense, so that we can ultimately understand our past and the place from where our parents acted—the difficult events from our childhood will stop infiltrating our present and "activating" us in negative ways. Instead, we can put these events aside and become the good parents we wish to be.

Our ability to understand our parents "from within"

In the previous chapters, we were introduced to the concept of mentalization, and the central role it plays in parenting. Mentalization, among other things, is attributed to our ability to understand the people around us and see them "from within." In the context of parenting, it usually regards our curiosity toward our children, and our attempt to understand them: what and how they feel.

When it regards the life story a person builds, mentalization acts in a different way. In these contexts, we refer to our ability, as parents, to look at our own *parents* "from within:" to think about our parents from an open and nonjudgmental perspective; to understand them rather than blame them or get angry with them; to be curious about them; to realize that our parents are humans, too, and they, too, acted out of their life circumstances. I mentioned this in the previous chapter, too: in most cases, blaming your parents is pointless. It will not help us move forward. Rather than blame our parents, it's better that we view them with compassion, understanding, and acceptance. It's this kind of perspective that will allow us to let go of our anger and not recreate the unwanted parental patterns.

Difficult and traumatic past experiences—to repress or remember?

As we know, trauma experienced in our childhood oftentimes is suppressed or the memories become subconscious. Nowadays, professionals tend to agree that repression on its own isn't necessarily a negative outcome, as long as it's done wholly and completely. Meaning, if a person completely repressed difficult parts of their childhood, and they live a full life without their traumas affecting them, then there is no need to bring up those difficult memories. However, in many cases with supposedly repressed childhood trauma, the events continue to influence our behavior in ways we can't explain. We then find ourselves reacting to our children with rage, indifference, contempt, or emotional outbursts we cannot understand. In these situations, it seems as though there is no escape from bringing up the past events, trying to understand them in different ways, and checking the ways they affect our present behavior, and the actions we can take to mitigate their harmful influence.

At this point, it's important to note that these ideas aren't "crack psychology"—they are all research-based and lean on some fascinating findings from the area of neuroscience. The American psychiatrist, **Daniel Siegel**, deals much with these issues. In Chapter 7, I mentioned the distinction he makes between the "**high road**" brain activity, and the "**low road**" one. Siegel found in his studies that rage and dysregulated reactions that we do not fully understand—usually are derived from the "low road" brain activity. They tend to be connected, in many cases, to childhood trauma that hasn't been properly and adequately processed. However, one of our parental goals is to function as much as possible through the "high road" brain activity, and not through the "low road." Researchers and therapists believe that recalling our past experiences and building them into a cohesive, coherent, logical "story," while combing the understanding of how the events affect our everyday lives—is the ultimate and central way to avoid problematic parental responses. That will lead to acting most of the time through the "high road."

How do we create a cohesive, coherent life story?

And now for the million-dollar question: How is it done? How do we create a life story that can let us be free of the difficult or traumatic childhood events, and allow us to avoid recreating the mistakes with our own children? Well, it's a complex process, but it's possible. Here are a few principles that may assist you with it. Please note that the different principles move from your past (as a child) to your present (as a parent).

Pay attention to the failing points of your parenting

The process begins with your day-to-day lives with your children, when you notice a behavior of yours you are displeased with: a tendency to anger quickly, cutting off contact with them when they make you angry, over protectiveness, or perhaps even the urge to hit them when they make you mad. When you recognize patterns such as these—stop and take a breath. Tell yourselves *"It's happening again,"* and check within yourselves—why is it happening? What reason, in your past, could have led you to behave in such an unwanted way?

Create "space" between the times of anger and the ultimate eruption

Difficult childhood experiences make us, in many instances, "lose it" and react toward our children in mismeasured and dysregulated manners. This situation is unhealthy, and we have to do everything in our power to overcome it. For us to succeed, we have to learn how to create a "space" between the anger or rage we feel (inside), and the (outward) eruption at the children. Our ability to stop for a moment before the explosion, to take a deep breath and pay attention to the things that happen in our bodies at the times of anger—all this can help us delay and alleviate the unwanted reactions (▶ see framed text in this chapter, page 348, and Chapter 19, regarding Mindfulness). When we manage to stop the dysregulated reaction, when we understand that it comes from our own issues, and that our children have little to do with it, we promote our ability to react from a place that is more measured and calm.

Find ways to recollect the difficult past facts in a supportive, containing atmosphere

Our failing points as parents make us recall unpleasant events from our pasts. This process can be painful and difficult. For us to manage, it's important to allow the recollection of the painful facts happen in a place that is both open and accepting: an atmosphere that can allow us to think them over and combine them into our life story. There are people who can do this on their own; there are people who'd prefer to use the support of a close friend or their partner. But if you are carrying around "heavy loads" from your past, you may choose instead to go through the process in therapy with a professional by your side.

Recall the positive experiences and the good people from your childhood

In the previous chapter, I mentioned the "ghosts in the nursery"—the difficult past events that "overtake" our parental lives and cause us to recreate them with our own children. Now, we know that it's not only traumas that get passed on from generation to generation, but also the positive experiences. And here the important influence of positively impactful people from our past comes into play: the "angels in the nursery"—the people who loved us and looked at us with awe. So, if you did suffer through negative childhood events, it's important to put the effort into remembering the good parts of your childhood, too: the pleasant and emotional times with your parents, or the people who believed in you and were kind in turn (your beloved elementary school teacher, the leader in your youth group, your wonderful grandmother who accepted you exactly as you are, or your high school principal who was tough, but made you feel worthy). The process of recalling the positive people who'd influenced you in your childhood, and the good, happy moments from then, too, help build the coherent, whole story of our lives, and allow us to let go of those unwanted past-driven patterns.

Remember that *your* parents are not the parent *you are* today

Despite our vast efforts—it's not easy. In many cases we still catch ourselves recreating the unwanted patterns of our childhood: treating our children with aggression or indifference, being overly critical or contemptuous—"*We've promised ourselves so many times not to do it again!*"

In these moments it's important to remember that though we may "stumble"—you're still not a carbon-copy of your parents. You're a part of a different generation, acting from a different place, and the mere fact that you're *aware* of the mistakes you make—that's a vital step in correcting and freeing yourself from many of the problematic behaviors and ultimately fixing them ("*I yelled at the kids again for no reason, just because they were playing around, making a mess, and being loud. It's probably a demon from my past that won't let me accept noise in the house; my mother was just like that, too. I have to let it go and start enjoying the simple fact that my children are having fun*").

Don't overdo "digging into" your past, and remember that no one is perfect

Continuing the previous section—it's also important that we don't overdo with our looking inwards. Self-awareness is important, but over-self-awareness and the over-handling of our parenting skills can actually do more harm than good. So, if you think you may be exaggerating the "looking inward" stage, it might be best to simply let it go, put the doubts, guilt, and self-criticism aside, and be calmer and more easy-going parents.

And finally, you should remember and remind yourselves of it over and over that no one is perfect. Fortunately, our children only benefit from having actual *real* parents (who aren't perfect), and who love them as much as they do, but who also make mistakes (yell sometimes, lose control, criticize, act overprotectively, or pull away when they are angry). So, if you made a mistake, if some demon from your past pushed you to do something you didn't mean—put the demon back into the bottle, apologize to your children when you need to, forgive yourselves, and move on. Self-compassion—remember?

THE BOTTOM LINE

You may have read through this chapter and hardly understood what it was all about. There are parents to whom these subjects are irrelevant, and if you're one of them—wonderful. You lucked out.

However, if your read this through and felt as though the words were directed straight at you, read it through again, and remember the main message from it: though you lived through difficult childhood events, and that they ultimately gave you a disadvantage at parenting, we also know that they do not "doom" our parenting in the present or the future. Their influence can be mitigated through remembering them and creating a complete life story that is logical, coherent, accepting, and full of compassion. The more logic you include into your life story, the freer you will be to put it aside and not recreate it. This is both important for your well-being, and for that of your children.

3

PART III
MANY DIFFERENT WAYS
PARENTING DURING LIFE'S
SPECIAL CIRCUMSTANCES

MANY DIFFERENT WAYS
A PREFACE TO PART III

In the first part of this book we defined our parenting goals and set out on our journey; in the second part we put our parenting in the center, and reminded ourselves to enjoy the way; and here our journey continues on, and we find that we've reached additional destinations, some that we hadn't ever planned on visiting.

The third part of this book deals with parenting during life's special circumstances.

Chapter 26 deals with parenting teenagers—an interesting destination we'll all reach sooner or later. As parents to teenagers, our parenting has to handle additional challenges. So much so that we, at times, even need to reinvent ourselves: learn a new language, and handle situations we'd never encountered before. We knew that the journey wouldn't be boring... we didn't know it would be *so* interesting!

The two following chapters deal with destinations that weren't included in our initial planning: Chapter 27 deals with parents who are divorced (it holds some important insights you most definitely would want to implement), and Chapter

28 centers around the matter of parenting children with special needs. These are two very different destinations; both, as stated, were not part of our initial plan when we first became parents and set out on this journey. However, just as with any other trip, not every step is predictable and measured. From the moment of arriving in these areas, it's important for us to equip ourselves with everything we need, so that we can successfully navigate the ways.

Finally, we have Chapter 29, which deals with parenting in "new families" and their many different combinations. While in "regular" families, many parents learn throughout the journey, the parenting path of the "newer" families is well thought out and meticulously planned. The line between "regular" and "special" will accompany us through this chapter.

Parents of teenagers, divorced parents, parents to special children, and parents in "new" families—you're welcome to park alongside the way and choose the chapter that fits your needs; take the path that is relevant for your own unique family.

…And what about all the other parents? As I write in the preface of this book, the chapters in this part may interest you anyway—even if you're not included in these unique groups. Interestingly, it seems that you may find in these chapters too, some elements you may wish to add to your own journey. Let's find out together.

CHAPTER 26

"WE DON'T SLAM DOORS IN THIS HOUSE!"
Parenting teenagers

> *"When I was a boy of 14, my father was so ignorant I could hardly stand to have the old man around. But when I got to be 21, I was astonished at how much the old man had learned in seven years."*
>
> **—Mark Twain**

What hasn't been written about this age? What haven't you heard yet?

On the one hand, you receive a massive amount of scare mongering ("This time is an unmitigated nightmare"), and on the other extreme, are parents who don't know what all the fuss is about ("It's actually a really exciting age, it's a pleasure watching them turn into people"); parents who tell you with certainty that "Nowadays, it starts as early as the age of eight," and others who say, "It doesn't even end when they're thirty..."

And where do you stand in this mess of opinions? What are you worried about? And how are your personal children handling this age? (And if you're not there *yet—how do you imagine it will be?) And also, truthfully: How did your teenage years go? Were they an actual nightmare? Or did they pass easily? Did you "skip over" it and now regret it? Or were you a rebellious teenager who constantly needed to be looked out for? And as parents—should you be worried about your teenagers? And most importantly—how can we stand by them during this meaningful time?*

Adolescence—a relatively new invention

Did you know that adolescence —at least in its current version—hasn't been around for very long? In our society, a child is considered someone who is highly dependent on their parents, while an adult is someone who can stand on their own. Hence adolescence is considered the "in between" time; a bridge of sorts between childhood and maturity. Only, until the end of the 19th century, children were considered a cheap workforce, and their key role was to grow up quickly in order to become functional, helpful adults: girls would marry when they were 14-15 years old, and boys of the same age would leave for work. It so happened that children became adults "right away:" people who are productive for their society. The idea that children should learn, develop, receive an education, build their identity, is a relatively new idea, and it's through that that adolescence—the teenage, in-between years—came to be.

Adolescence—nice to meet you!

Budding breasts that are a little awkward and a little painful; his voice dropping—making it high and low; he lives in the refrigerator—he's always hungry; she asks for a key so she can lock her bedroom door (when, until recently, you hardly noticed the room even *had* a door…); it's impossible to know the mood she'll wake up in today; he suddenly has so much to say about so many different things—where did this opinionated, knowledgeable boy come from? So many changes in such a short time!

Well, as you may have realized, adolescence truly does bring along for our children many different changes in many different areas of life. These changes can be categorized into four different aspects: the physical one, the emotional-behavioral one, the cognitive aspect, and the social one. And since we can literally write entire books on each of these subjects, I'll only mention here the main and most dominant changes that come along during this special time, while focusing on each of the aspects in turn.

The cognitive aspect: shifting proportions and perspectives

One of the main characteristics of adolescence has to do with the changes that happen in the teenager's perspective, regarding both themselves and the world at large. On the one hand, your teenager may develop an interest and opinions regarding a wide array of vital matters; while on the other hand, a tiny pimple that popped out on their forehead might ruin their mood and make them practically dysfunctional for a whole day.

One of the obstacles this age presents has to do with the concept of an "imagined crowd." Teenagers feel as though *everyone* is watching *them*—judging their eyebrows, their eyes, the zit on their forehead. This phenomenon is part of a teenager's natural tendency to think in a highly egocentric manner—as though they are the center of the universe. One of our key roles is to try and pull them out of that thinking course; to shift things so they fit into their proper proportions (> see the latter part of this chapter). At the same time, you most certainly can enjoy the developments in the realm of thoughts: they become conversational partners for meaningful matters, they develop a brilliant sense of humor, they formulate their opinions and values, and it's wondrous.

The social aspect: being "like everyone else" while also being "the most unique"

Another central challenge lies with the teenagers' need to formulate their personal identity, to find out who they "really are." Their social circle—their peers become crucial, and that causes the teenager to judge themselves very harshly in comparison to them. As you may have noticed, this process happens simultaneously to the lessening of the parents' importance in their eyes; up until that point, after all, we've been a vital part of their emotional "refueling."

It's important to know that the first years of adolescence usually include the teenager wishing to be "like everyone else." Sadly and frustratingly, their peers tend to push away any who they perceive as different: those whose interests are different, those who look different, behave differently, have a different sexual identity, and so forth. You should be aware that this time is rough on *all* children-teenagers, but for some of them this can be an actual nightmare. For this reason, you should note your teenager's behavior and emotions, and be vigilant regarding signs of distress (> see latter part of this chapter for more information).

In the second part of adolescence, circa the age of sixteen, the situation usually balances out in a more positive way: the teenager's sense of self is more coherent and stable, and their peers become more open to different kinds of personalities and people. Moreover, during this time, the one who is "different" becomes, in the eyes of society, someone "special." In many cases, this is a highly valued status. Many children who suffered socially in the first years of their adolescence, find their place when they mature a little. This is important to remember. It can be a true consolation for some teenagers.

The physical aspects: growing from a boy to a man, from a girl to a woman

Our children's bodies go through a whole realm of physical changes; changes that allow them to grow from being boys and girls, to adolescents and, finally, men and women. It seems like only yesterday they were still young children, and then, quite suddenly, they are taller than us; and if only recently we were allowed to hug them as much as we liked, an imaginary red line erects around them, as if saying, "Come no farther." The experience of their changing bodies, and their simultaneous changing consciousness—the awakening feelings of sexual attraction, the separation from their childhood and the building of their sense of self as a man or woman—all these aspects oftentimes create vast confusion and embarrassment within our children-adolescents. The additional fact that each child goes through the changes at a different rate creates further worries—both with those who develop early, and those who develop at a relatively slower pace. This makes them feel as though everyone has already "boarded the train" while they alone have been "left behind."

The emotional-behavioral aspect: a window of opportunities

One of the aspects in which our children can show monumental changes is in the emotional-behavioral aspect. Neuroscience research has shown that during adolescence, especially during the first years of this period, teenagers go through massive changes in their brain's shape and functioning—changes that can be aligned only to the changes a baby goes through in their first year of life. This fact creates a "window of opportunities" that is vital for the teenager—it allows for them to "make a change," "reinvent themselves," to be the person they wish to be. Many adolescents can take this opportunity and make the most of it: they can say goodbye to their shyness, adopt certain personality traits, become leaders, put more effort into school or into their social life. It's important you support them in this and help them make the changes they wish for themselves. This is, without a doubt, an exciting and thrilling "window of opportunities."

An exciting and special time

Despite the slander and frightening things you may have heard, adolescence can be a magical time for your child. There's no point in entering it with a bucket-full of worries: "walking on eggshells" or being aggressive or overly strict. Instead, you should go into this time like tourists entering a new, friendly, pleasant country: with lots of curiosity, a willingness to learn and discover, and an expectation of enjoying the journey. There is a good chance of this being a wondrous journey, even if at moments it could be challenging. In the difficult times, it's important to remember that your adolescents have it much harder. As much as possible, try not to let the difficulties set the tone for the entire time.

In the first part of the book, I elaborated upon the "parenting goals" we may have, and above all, the goal of raising "human beings." Adolescence is, without a doubt, an important and meaningful milestone in this process. It's so important to remember that our children aren't meant to be "exactly like us;" they should be "exactly as they are," with all the personality traits, characteristics, and behavioral patterns that come along with that statement. So that our children will be able to finally find their inner voice and build their ultimate, unique self, it's best we not go into a situation that constantly calls for power-plays between you and them. Parental authority is important, but it isn't an actual goal. Not everything has to be an argument, and not every argument has to end with us gaining the upper hand. It's okay (and important) that we exercise some flexibility, that we allow ourselves to be convinced, that we sometimes give in. Our growing children are becoming young adults—let's support them in it and help them get through it.

A possibly dangerous age

It's true that there's no point in needlessly worrying, but we still have to be aware of the dangers this age may present, and I will only mention some of them. Until they entered adolescence, your children were mostly under your supervision. Everything—or at least most of the things—were under our control. One of the basic characteristics of adolescence, is the teenager's wish to be *apart* from you; they wish to experiment with a wide range of experiences in a separate, more independent way. As I've said before, this is an age where your children's friends may hold a huge amount of influence on your children-adolescents. This makes many parents feel as though they are losing control, and thus, makes them fearful of the process.

As you may have realized on your own, teenagers today are exposed to many dangers and temptations—some that weren't even available as options when *we* were their age (at least not with the sheer volume and intensity they are now). These dangers include: alcohol, cigarettes, drugs, electric bikes, scooters, unsafe sexual relations, the variety of dangers embedded in social media, the danger of becoming addicted to screens, and more. This all can reach our doorstep, happen right on the playground downstairs, on the way to their school, at their youth group, and even in your teenager's private bedroom at home.

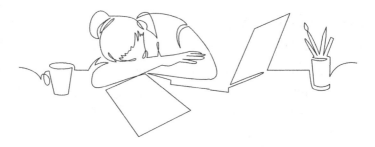

This is also a dangerous age in regard to the mental disorders that can arise during it. First and foremost, I will mention depression, eating disorders, and suicidal tendencies. Though most teenagers won't be exposed to these situations, the danger that they present makes them something we cannot ignore: we must be vigilant and pay attention to signs of distress.

And what are these signs of distress? It's not always easy to tell, and that's because many of the signs are characteristics of "normal" teenagers as well. At the end of the day, it's all about quantities: it depends on the amount of the concerning signs your teenager may exhibit, and their overall health and functioning. Still, it's important to be aware of these signs in particular: extreme shifts in their moods, changes with their appetite and sleeping habits (an excess or lessening of either), a lack of pleasure in things they'd once found enjoyable, social isolation, a pessimistic view of the world and thoughts of death, a tendency to any form of self-harm, behavior that involves risk, and any other worrying sign you're concerned about.

In any case when there's doubt—don't hesitate to ask for counselling. Talk to your children, ask them directly if you have a reason to be concerned, get advice from key people in their educational system and the relevant professionals (➤ see latter part of this chapter for more information).

So, what can we, as parents, do?

Just as our children grow and develop, so should *we* grow along with them. This is, without a doubt, one of the more wondrous aspects of parenting. That said, it is also one of the sources of strife: it's in constant motion, evolving, changing without pause. When our children enter adolescence, we have to change the "operating system," find a style and tone that fit us best, and redefine our priorities.

I'll attempt to sketch out some principles of action that can help you navigate this complex yet beautiful time. Adjust these principles so they align with your individual child: their personalities, characteristics, and age. Parenting a young twelve-year-old is not the same parenting style needed for a seventeen-year-old teenager who'd just begun driving.

Let go, but don't lose control

As I've already mentioned in other contexts, parenting is very much an art of finding the right balances—between closeness and distance, protection and letting them go. In their teenage years—this challenge reaches new heights.

In order to best live through this time, you have to learn how to let go. You have to trust your child to use their judgment; you have to believe that they will be okay, that the values you taught them throughout the years won't be lost the moment you turn away. However, letting go and giving them space does *not* mean losing control or giving up on having boundaries. The boundaries do indeed expand a little, perhaps become a little more flexible, but they are still present. They have to be. Your children need them, even—and especially—in their teenage years.

So, allow them to go out and have fun, but demand to know exactly where they are going; be increasingly impressed by her improving self-expressionism—but don't let her talk back to you; hold back your opinion regarding their individual dress style—but when needed, allow yourselves to interfere with the length of her skirt or his torn jeans.

Don't give up on having open communication with your teenager

Even if your teenager signalizes differently, they wish desperately to have an open line of communication with you and for you to be fully involved in their lives. Many teenagers think that their experiences are singular and rare; that no one had ever been there before them—that there is no one on earth who could ever understand them. It's a balm to the soul to know that that isn't truly the case, and that you can, actually, connect to their experiences and understand their inner world.

When your child decides to share something with you, when they tell you something that you find "horrifying" ("*Many kids in my year smoke;*" "*All my friends are doing this insane diet*"), before you react—make sure you listen closely. Be thankful that they are sharing it with you. It's not something you should take for granted. You should remember that the way you react to that first piece of information will determine if there will be a second or third or fourth time they share something with you. Parents who are too easily "horrified," who react in too strong a way, may possibly become "irrelevant." Your children are older now, they make the choice—over and over—to share with you something, or to keep it from you instead. That said, there will be things you hear that you won't be able to keep silent about. It's here when you have to learn to listen openly and still impart the messages you deem most important at the same time, efficiently and clearly. In many cases you may benefit from holding back and not reacting right away. Let things sink in properly, talk to your partner, friends, or the school counselor—only then give your opinion. By reacting in measured, regulated, and level-headed ways, you may also serve as an excellent role model for your children.

If needed—talk to the parents of your children's friends

Undoubtedly, this is one of the advantages screen technology has provided: allowing us a simple, easy line of communication with groups of people whose name we barely know. When this comes to your children's friends' parents, this can be an actual lifesaver. Communicating with the parents of your children's friends allows for you to coordinate a curfew from a joint meet-up; assure your children aren't putting themselves at risk; share important information regarding your teenagers—both yours and theirs. If you saw one of your son's friends behaving in an extreme way that is possibly also dangerous—don't hesitate to report it to his parents. And if your daughter could be in danger—be open to hearing about it from her friends or their parents. You may find that the information you receive from them could be vital.

Help your teenager keep proper proportions and a wider perspective

As I've stated before, adolescence can be a particularly stormy and turbulent time. Take the fact that sometimes things happen, and they're not always good: your daughter's boyfriend dumped her; he failed his driving test *again*; despite monumental efforts; she wasn't chosen to go on one of the school delegation programs; someone wrote awful things about them on social media. Highly unpleasant business. Yet still, none of this is the "end of the world." It's important that you make sure your children understand this. Show them the bigger picture; explain how the negative events are transitional, that they will pass. Hold onto the optimistic outlook for them and help them keep their proportions in check.

Talk to them about safe sex and healthy sexuality

It's more than likely *your* parents didn't talk with you about this—and you probably think that your teenagers already know all there is to know... only they really don't know everything (and much of what they do "know" is twisted and incorrect), and you have a lot to say about the subject—for boys and girls alike. Moreover, if your children don't get the messages from *you*—you'll never know what they *do* know. And like with every other issue in the matter of education—there is significant value to the *communication* you and your children have over the issues of sexuality, and there is significant value to the mere existence of an "open channel" regarding these subjects. It's something you must maintain continuously.

Here are some of the messages you should pass on:

As parents, you want your children to know that sex is done when there is an emotional attachment, and when both parties are mutually and enthusiastically (!) involved. By the way, in the past we used to talk about "mutual *consent*," but we now realize how elusive the term consent is—so it's best to word it as *enthusiasm*. Furthermore, you'd like for them to know that sex is an intimate and personal matter, and that under no circumstances should it be filmed. It's important to stress that sex is in no way a "status symbol" for either girls or boys. You also want them to be aware that sex has to be done with protection. More information can be found online after searching for things such as "safe sex information."

The older they get, view your role as a "middleman" between them and the world at large

When she was younger, you could tell her *"That's not allowed,"* and that would normally be enough. Sometimes you had to say it twice, or perhaps raise your voice, but it would still do. Now, if you said to your seventeen-year-old *"That's not allowed"* (*"You can't go out with that boy; do get a nose ring; go out with that hideous dress"*), it's more than likely that even if you "win the battle"—you'll lose the war, and if you lose—they lose, too. Everyone loses, and that's a true shame. It's true that in the later stages of adolescence there are situations and subjects where you can and most certainly should be clear and adamant regarding the things you wish to impart (for example: *"You do not ride a bike without a helmet;" "If you drink—you don't drive;" "You never drink alcohol at a party without knowing where it came from,"* and any other "red line" you refuse for them to cross that is relevant). At the same time, there are also many other situations in which you will benefit—and your children will benefit—if you take a stand of "middleman," rather than the final decision-maker. Talk with them, understand their position, explain your own, convince them, allow them to try and convince you, and finally—allow them to make the choice, even if you think it may end up being a mistake (as long as the mistake isn't too costly or dangerous). Lastly, they will very soon reach the age when they don't need to ask permission or your advice, and you might want to be in the position of adviser who mediates between them and the world—even after they're eighteen-and-a-bit.

Keep accurate proportions and view your teenagers beyond the difficulties

As stated in previous chapters, stormy emotions tend to be catching. But the last thing your teenagers need is for you to "catch" their turbulent emotions, and enter the vortex they create with them. Instead, it's important that you keep proper proportions and perspectives; it's important that you remember that the conflicts are temporary, and they *will* pass. Try and hold the image of your teenager as they will be a few years down the line, as young adults. The wider perspective acts as an anchor, and it will help you react to the conflicts in a measured and situational way, rather than get pulled into unwanted realms along with them.

If needed—don't hesitate to ask for advice!

It happens that matters get complicated. You start feeling that you're in over your head, that the situation is dangerous, or that your children aren't at their best; the communication between you is flawed, and you're afraid that your adolescent is on the wrong path, one that does them no good. These are the exact situations when you should ask for help and counsel: with the school counselor, their high school teacher, a psychologist who deals with adolescence matters. Don't be alone with your worries. In many cases, asking for advice from a professional can help improve the given situation, even without involving the adolescent in the actual therapy (▶ see my referencing of the subject of therapy with the parents in Chapter 32).

At this point I have an important message for you: if your child does start psychological therapy—it's vital for you, the parents, to be involved in it, too. Don't get confused by this (and the psychologist shouldn't, either). There are times when we think they're old enough and that they need their privacy and private space; it seems that they need complete confidentiality. We take this from the model we are all familiar with regarding an adult's therapy. However, I believe that adolescents' therapy—done without a certain measure of parental involvement—is therapy that can be more harmful than beneficial. Most of the things your teenager is involved in are things that are in some way also connected to you. If the psychologist-therapist assures your adolescent their private space, a space you will have no part in, the conflicts may deepen, and that is a situation that won't help any of you. Remember that it's easier to be their psychologist than their parents. And, if we look at it for a moment through the point of view of the psychologist—treating a teenager is far from easy when there is an open line of communication with the parents—but whoever promised it would be easy? The complexity is an inseparable part of therapy. So—apart from in extreme and exceptional cases (such as parental neglect or times when parents are incapable of caring for their child), with each psychological therapy in adolescents there should be an open line of communication with the psychologist and the parents (both parents—not only one). You have to make the effort to find the right balance and the correct model for your involvement in psychological therapy for your children.

THE BOTTOM LINE

Adolescence is a time that can be both challenging and frustrating, and also unparallelly beautiful and exciting. It's the time when your children begin to go through massive changes that shape their future image as adults; and even if it sometimes seems as though they wouldn't choose *you*, the parents, to be a part of the journey with them, your children still need your continual presence during this time—more so than ever.

Knowing the many and unique characteristics of this time (that take on different forms with each and every teenager), combining an open line of communication with them and a lot of forgiveness and patience on your end—will all help adolescence pass safely, and hopefully with a lot of satisfaction and joy on all sides.

CHAPTER 27

A BAD PARTNER IS NOT NECESSARILY A BAD PARENT
Being divorced parents

You never pictured it being this way. It was most definitely not what you'd dreamed of. It wasn't part of your life-script as you stood together at your wedding.

In most Western countries (and beyond, too) statistics have shown that between 25 and 50 percent of married couples are expected to separate. Most of them never even considered the possibility of it beforehand. But things turned out differently, and you ultimately chose to separate, and you're quite sure everyone is better off, now. Only... you have children together, and that means that your split can't be complete; sharing children means that you'll never truly be done with each other.

The social view of divorce has changed mightily over the years. If in the past it was considered an utter *taboo* to break up a family, and angry couples stayed together *"for the children's sake,"* the previous years have made divorce much more acceptable, even common. Men and women who refuse to carry on living together in constant strife and struggle, and simultaneously have the growing belief that it's simply "better off" for their mutual children—it's better to live with divorced parents who are happy, than in a family that's under constant stress and conflict.

That said, the fact of it being rather common still does not make it easy to handle. Nowadays we tend to treat divorce as a crisis and possible risk factor for the children. Firstly, I will point out that on the psychological scale of "stressful life events," divorce is rated as the second most severe stressor; second only to losing a loved one. Secondly, research has shown that children to parents who are divorced are in higher risk of having certain symptoms, among which: behavioral problems, a decrease in their studies, damaged self-image, and more.

And why am I writing about all this? This data isn't meant to depress or scare you. Not at all. First and foremost, I'm writing it in order for you to know that the struggles you and your children suffer through around the matter of divorce are expected and natural. Divorce is a complex life event, and it takes time to adjust to it. However—and this is the key message of this chapter: we now know that though divorce may negatively affect the children—the difficulty isn't a fated occurrence. There are many things you can do to better your children's emotional state after the divorce. To succeed with it, we first have to acknowledge the "influence routes" through which divorce can harm children.

How parental divorce can harm the children

Two primary psychological mechanisms explain the negative effect divorce has on children. These mechanisms don't cancel each other out, but explain the influence through different perspectives.

One model is the **Accumulative Stress Model**. As per this model, parental divorce exposes the children to many different stressors that accumulate and build on each other. Some of the stressors begin to affect the children even before the parents separate (an overtly stressful homelife, conflicts, fights and arguments between the parents); the additional stressors are added to the children's lives after the break-up. Besides the actual change in the family unit, parental divorce also puts the family at financial risk, and may also harm the personal functioning of either parent. Additionally, in many cases, divorce also leads to many possible different changes: moving house, changing schools, adjusting to new partners when the parents start going out again, and much more. According to this explanation, the accumulated stressors that build atop each other are what lead to the harming of the children's emotional welfare. So, if we can be aware of this, and minimize as much as possible the stressors to our children, the negative consequences of the divorce are expected to level out.

Another mechanism attributes the negative influence divorce has on the children through the perspective of **Attachment Theory**. Parental divorce can harm the children's "secure base" when regarding their overall sense of safety that is created through the continual, cohesive contact they have with both parents (▶ see also Chapter 3). Divorce exposes the children to the significant fear of loss and separation; this can harm the children's inner model regarding their interpersonal connections and relationships, and to make them worry that they, themselves, are unworthy of love. This situation increases and becomes relevant when one of the parents cuts off contact with the child after the divorce, engages in a "remote" relationship with them, or a non-cohesive relationship. In this context, too, the understanding of the risks and knowing the mechanisms of harm could guide us in better handling the divorce. It's vital to pass along to the children the ongoing, continual relationship they will continue to have with *both* parents after the fact, and give the children clear messages regarding them not being at fault in any way for their parents' ultimate separation.

Two master-principles that are meant to protect the children

Continuing the influence routes through which parental divorce can hurt children, there are two master-principles that may greatly contribute to your children's emotional welfare post-divorce:

1. Lower the levels of hostility between you and your former partner after the divorce.
2. Both of you, continue having an ongoing, successive line of communication with your children.

I'll elaborate on both these principles.

Principle 1: You got divorced? Stop fighting!

As simple as this is, it's even more important. Many divorced couples carry on having incessant battles against each other. This situation causes them (and their children) to lose twice fold: it's not bad enough that you got divorced, you continue to fight and be angry, thus, making it so your children experience both the crisis of your divorce and the continued hostilities. This situation is oftentimes enhanced and worsened by the lawyers and courts that, by nature, perform according to the model of "winner-loser." Only, differently from what happens in court, relationships between people—even couples who've separated—don't have winners or losers. Please note: in relationships between people there is only a situation in which everyone wins, and the opposite, when everyone loses. I believe wholeheartedly for this to be true.

Think about it. You got divorced in order to better your situation; you got divorced to be free of a relationship that was not good for you. When you hold onto your anger, onto your rage, when you continue to feel hostility toward your former partner—you limit yourself from moving forward to a calmer, more relaxed life. Even if this principle is far from easy to assimilate—you should still try and work toward it. We can all only benefit from it.

Remember and remind yourselves of this daily: children, more than anything, need the opportunity to continue loving both their parents—even if their parents have stopped loving each other. The ability to let go of the negative feelings toward your former partner and to have a proper, healthy, respectful relationship with each other, is vital for all of you: for you both and for your children. It's not always possible, but it's definitely something to aspire to.

Principle 2: You divorce each other—not the children!

Alongside the vital importance of lessening the hostilities between you and your former partner, another central aspect comes into play when regarding the continuation of the constant, cohesive communication you both have with your children, after the divorce. Except for the few extreme cases where this is impossible—either due to an abusive parent or a parent with low parental capacity—this principle is central and essential.

Parental divorce undermines the basic foundations upon which the child grew to trust—family, home, mother and father together. So, in order to best assist children with the handling of the given situation and minimizing the damage from the divorce, it's important to do everything possible to keep a consistent line of communication, and a healthy, positive relationship between you *both* and your children. This is an obvious matter to those who are in a "joint custody" arrangement. Otherwise, if you do not have a joint custody arrangement, this message is mostly directed at the parent who sees the child less and does not hold sole custody (usually the father). If you are no longer living at home with the children, you must make every surmountable effort to keep a consistent, meaningful line of communication with your children once the divorce has gone through. The custodian parent, though, may also contribute to the success of this principle. That parent (most often the mother), has to make every effort to allow and encourage the children's continuing communication with the other parent, and never sabotage it.

Furthermore, in order for your children to manage a continuing and meaningful line of communication with you both, you have to establish habits and create a new routine. Sometimes the father moves far away, and coming to see the children isn't an easy matter; in these situations, oftentimes he doesn't have a "natural" place where he can spend time with the children. And if that isn't sufficient, when the children grow up, their extracurriculars have to be considered: their after-school classes, their friends, studying for finals (*"What a shame that your ballet class falls right on Daddy's day..."*). Well, there's no choice—you have to learn to juggle, to find the hidden solutions, and it's also important to be flexible with what's needed to be done. What is ultimately important is the master-principle: the continuation of the communication and relationships the children have with each of their parents, especially after they divorce. After all—you divorce your partner, not your children.

These two principles—the lessening of hostilities and the continuation of the cohesive, meaningful communication with both parents after the fact—are most probably the key aspects of your children's emotional welfare, and their ability to handle the situation. At the same time, there are a few additional guiding points you should take into account and implement. As you'll see, they, too, connect in one way or another to the master-principles.

Got divorced? Here are a few additional principles you should implement

Don't make your children a shared "communication device"

You are co-parents—so there's no way you can completely cut off any communication between the two of you. You have to find effective ways of communicating and cooperating—and it's most certainly not your children's job to pass messages along between you both (*"Tell your father to stop being so cheap and start paying for his daughter's teeth treatment..."*). Additionally, the children shouldn't be your source of information regarding the goings on with your former partner (*"So, huh... your mother has started dating someone, then?"*).

Now more than ever before there are plenty of effective ways of communication. Besides the electronics, it's advised to go sit down for a coffee now and then and communicate face-to-face. If you can't do it by yourselves, do it in joint meetings with a professional every few weeks. The value of your continued, healthy communication regarding your children has no bounds. Either way, remember this: there are many ways and possibilities to share information and transfer messages. Under no circumstances should it be done through the children.

Pass your children the clear message that the divorce wasn't their fault

Even if you try and give your children all the "right" messages, children, by nature, tend to blame themselves and take responsibility for their parents' divorce (*"Mom and Dad fight over me, if I'd have kept my room tidy and behaved better, maybe they wouldn't have split up;" "I remember how they'd always argue about things connected to me. It has to be my fault they decided to separate"*).

And truly, in many cases a large number of spousal arguments, before their ultimate divorce, center around the issues of their children. Additionally, your joint children are the reason for your continued communication—which is also a cause for the children to feel guilty about. In light of these matters, remind yourselves what you already know very well: you did not divorce because of the children, and they are not to blame for your separation. Find ways to get this message through in a clear and concise manner, and do everything in your power to free them from the feelings of guilt.

Do everything possible so that both your core values don't clash

Imagine a situation in which one of the parents expects the children to lead a religious way of living, while the other adamantly refuses, and takes the extreme opposite side. Or, perhaps one of you wishes for your children to be vegan, while the other demands they eat meat every day? Each of you must believe you are "in the right," but your children remain in an impossible and unfair situation.

Well, you did separate because you weren't happy together, you're different people and you disagree strongly regarding many different issues. But still, it's best you don't create a *spilt* between you both, and instead allow for your children to have a comprehensive, and integrative life. It's true you won't always be "on the same line"—children can live with certain different lifestyle choices between Mom's house and Dad's, as long as they're not contradicting at their core. You should all manage to build a set of expectations, values, and demands that will allow you to live one, whole life.

Try and minimize the "loyalty conflict" children feel after divorce

One of the more incessant problems children have after their parents' divorce (no matter their age) has to do with the issue of loyalty conflicts. Each choice they make has a price: "*If I do the holiday with Mom, Dad will be left all alone,*" "*If I go abroad with Dad, Mom will be sad and lonely,*" "*If I have a lot of fun with Dad, I won't tell Mom about it so it doesn't hurt her feelings.*" This creates a situation that is highly complicated for the children, and can vastly harm their happiness levels. It's advised to do all you can to release them from it. Try and communicate to your children that it's not their job to look after you, that you're happy when *they're* happy and having fun, even if that happens with the other parent. Additionally, regarding all the decisions such as who does what holiday with whom, or who goes with whom on vacation—try and make the decisions yourselves for the kids; coordinate between you two, and don't leave the choices up to the children (at least until they reach adolescence).

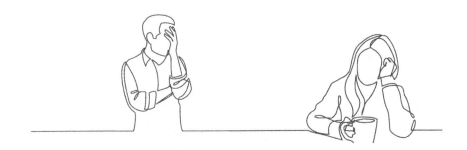

Allow your ex to change for the better

There are times when, after your divorce, the other former partners go through a series of changes you don't truly know how to handle. In this case, I actually mean *positive* changes: a father who'd never been particularly involved in raising the children suddenly picks them up from school twice a week and starts realizing just how rewarding parenting can be; the mother who'd always been short and quick to anger, is suddenly calm and full of patience (she even lets the children get a dog!). *"That's not the person I knew,"* you say to yourself. *"That's not the person I divorced..."*

In these situations, try and surpass the feelings of frustration and confusion, and instead accept the change with open arms: *"How wonderful for the children that they finally got a father who's fully involved,"* *"I'm so glad your mother has become someone so fun to be around (and that you can finally have a dog!")*.

As I've said, the main point is to manage to put aside the anger and stress you shared as a couple, and believe in the possibility of "that person" being a good parent for your shared children after your divorce. And even if he or she are not the *ideal* parent—they're still your children's parents. A meaningful relationship with both of you, and their ability to continue loving you both—that's what truly matters when it comes to your children's happiness and mental health—and that, of course, is what you find most important, too.

THE BOTTOM LINE

You hadn't planned for this situation, and you didn't wish for it; if you could have made plans—you most likely would have chosen for your children to grow up with both parents under the same roof. However, there's still much you can do to contribute to your child's overall welfare after the divorce. Above all else, do everything in your power to lessen the anger and hostility toward your former partner. The better you do so, the better your children are expected to be—and that's also compared to the situation in which you kept living together as one family rife with stress, hostility, and conflicts. Additionally, do everything you can to maintain a cohesive line of communication between both parents and your children. Furthermore, both you and your former partner have to communicate properly, and find it within yourselves to respect and value each other as co-parents. Yes, divorce forces you to deal with conflicts and complex situations, but the effort you put in, pays off. Above all else, remember that even if you have much to say against your former partner—they're still your children's parent. Allow them to be an excellent parent for them—just as you are.

CHAPTER 28

"THIS CHILD MADE MY HEART GROW TWO SIZES"
Being parents to a special needs child

You didn't expect them, nor did you ask for them. The world of "special needs" hardly knocked politely at your door. One day, it simply showed up; it came, and announced it was here to stay. You probably remember the exact moment and exactly how it happened. That point in time when you realized that something was wrong. Who was there with you when they told you the news? Was it right after the birth, or a few weeks later? Maybe only a few years down the line? (You had your doubts before, but you hoped you were wrong and everything would work out; after all, that was what everyone else around you were saying—everything will be fine—and how desperately you wanted to believe that). There are times when the special needs appear slowly, or they arrive after a certain event throughout your lives: a severe accident, a non-successful medical procedure, or an unexpected illness.

Before we dive into the complicated and fascinating world of parenting children with special needs, let's ask first—who precisely is included in this category of "special needs children?"

Is it children with autism? Blind and visually impaired children? Children who suffer from Down Syndrome, or a different physical disability? Well, yes, it seems so.

Deaf children?—some might argue; it depends on whom you ask.

And what about children with attention disorders or the different range of learning disabilities? And children who suffer from a chronic illness—are *they* included in this category? And what about gifted children? Or children with rare and exceptional talents?

It's hard to say definitively. Apparently, the answers to these questions have much to do with your own set of values, and the changings of the social and cultural norms. Did you know, for example, that until 1973, homosexuality was termed as a mental disorder?

This chapter deals with the challenges you—the parents of children with special needs—face, starting with the small (and sometimes invisible) issues, and culminating with the most complex. However, it's difficult to talk simultaneously about parents of children who suffer from physical disabilities, parents of children with Down Syndrome, and parents of children with learning disabilities. In the nature of generalities—they can't accurately depict the complexity of a singular case. So, read this chapter and take what may be relevant to *your* private and unique child and parenting style.

"Why should we diagnose? Who even needs those labels?"

This question may not be relevant to you at all. There are some special needs that there's no doubt regarding the necessity of needing a diagnosis—merely since the facts are clear, visible, and present in your everyday lives (for example, when your child is visually impaired or when your child suffers a physical disability).

But there are also cases where the parents cannot make up their mind, and say to themselves things like, "*Why check? Who said they need to be diagnosed? Why attach a label to them—as though something is wrong with them? We wouldn't love them any less if they* are *autistic, or if their IQ is low.*"

Well, it is *your* child, and you know better than anyone else what's right for them and for yourselves. Moreover, there may be situations—rare though they are—where a specific diagnosis isn't necessary and may instead cause more harm than good. Yet still, professionals tend to be like-minded on this subject, and they do believe that in most cases, a diagnosis that is done as early and most accurately as possible is vital, for two main reasons:

Firstly, we diagnose to evaluate the future, and most importantly, to fit the child with the best possible treatment for their needs. In the vast majority of cases, early diagnosis and proper care improve the special needs children's condition insurmountably. Autism isn't something that can be healed away, but the autistic child who was diagnosed closer to their first birthday or sooner, and started receiving the proper treatments, is expected to do significantly better than if that same child were diagnosed at age five, or later, or never diagnosed at all. That said, it's important to know that the predictions made by the professionals are statistic-based, and do not necessarily describe your own personal child's intended future. Don't allow medical statistics to bring you down or make you want to give up.

Secondly, we diagnose to help the parents and the child themselves understand what "they have." This kind of understanding can allow us to realize the reason for why our wondrous child's behavior is so different from other children their age, and how to react when they behave as they do. In most cases, a deep knowledge of the "disorder" or syndrome—with all its different characteristics—allows us to better understand our child, and may prevent frustrations, misunderstandings, and the incorrect and hurtful labels the child may pick up ("*disturbed child;*" "*Lazy girl;*" "*Self-centered;*" "*Non-empathic;*" and more).

In this context, let's take, for example, children who suffer from ADHD or regulation disorders. As I've mentioned before, these disorders are characterized as "invisible disorders" (► see Chapter 15, page 216). On the outside, everything seems all right; no one can guess what is "wrong" with the child—why they argue about everything, lose their temper so often, or is such a dreamer. However, contrary to what we may believe, these disorders are not limited to academic issues. They may harm the child in any number of settings: after school classes, social connections, familial relationships, and so on. If we are unaware of the disorder, if we don't have it diagnosed and treated correctly, our child may experience the world from a hostile, and unpleasant point of view—and worse, they may view *themselves* as problematic children, as disturbed, or lazy. On the other hand, if we are properly educated on our child's disorder, if the child becomes familiar with it and becomes "friendly" with it, too—we can all understand, guide, mediate, and function in a better way, and ultimately not have our child, ourselves, and all who surround us, suffer through frustration and indignity.

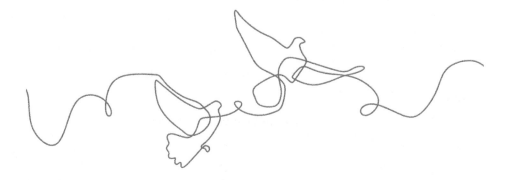

Special needs or special children?

The last few years have shown a growing tendency in the changing of our perspective, so that rather than treating children as *special needs* children, we instead treat them as *special* children.

And indeed, who knows better than you that in many of these cases, these children manifest outstanding qualities: original thinking patterns, exceptional creativity, a fresh outlook on the world, interpersonal sensitivity, unique talents that develop *alongside* their disabilities, and sometimes as a form of *compensating those difficulties.* It's important to note the wide array of these qualities, appreciate them, and nurture them.

Think about it: just how much could our special children—and we, ourselves—gain mentally, if instead of focusing on the disorder and "what doesn't work," instead of trying to constantly "fix" them—we look at them with admiring eyes, that see and emphasize their uniqueness and the wondrous characteristics they carry within themselves.

Disorder or identity?

So where do we draw the line between a disorder and a unique identity? Who, after all, decides what is normal and what is not, and do all "abnormalities" require "fixing?"

An astounding example for this can be found in the deaf community.

Most of us view deafness as a disability. Hearing-parents, whose baby is born deaf, would usually treat the situation as a crisis, and push to do everything in their power to "heal" their child's disability. Wondrously, nowadays there are several effective ways to achieve this. The cochlear implant surgery is a routine operation, which can allow deaf people to bypass their deafness, and hear sounds. Medically, it's advised to do the operation in the baby's first years of life, meaning, before the child can be asked their opinion on the subject.

However, a deeper exploration into the deaf community shows that many of the deaf people don't perceive themselves as disabled in any form. Deaf children born to deaf parents acquire sign language as their mother-tongue: a rich, vast language, that allows for them to fully express themselves. Many of the deaf people live together in communities, and are very proud of their language and the cultural aspects that come along with their unique identity as deaf people. For this reason, many deaf people highly object to the cochlear implant surgery, which threatens to dismiss and eradicate their unique characteristic of being deaf. (If you find this subject interesting, you're welcome to watch the wonderful movie "*La Famille Bélier.*")

The American psychologist **Andrew Solomon** researched the deaf community's wishes to treat deafness as a unique identity—not as a disability. In his book "*Far from the Tree,*" he aligned the issue of deafness to that of his parents' and his own dealings with the fact of him being a homosexual. He states that he believes that if, when he was a young child, his parents would have been offered a procedure that would have made him "straight," then they would have probably agreed for it to have been performed. However, such a treatment would have undoubtedly made the LGBTQ+ culture extinct. Solomon writes that he finds that thought saddening. However, he admits that his parents' approach which he'd viewed as so short-sighted, was akin to the way he himself would probably react if he had a child who was born deaf. His first instinct, he says, would be to do everything in his power to correct the wrong.

There's no question that this is a complex and delicate matter. And in this context, we should ask ourselves: what kind of society do we wish to raise our children in? Should we, as a society, aspire for a certain unity and commonality, or is it preferable to aspire for a society that has room for interpersonal differences and uniqueness—a society that calls for tolerance and openness? And how would you align these thoughts with the previous point of the importance of early diagnosis and care? These are not easy questions to ask, nor are the answers simple. It seems as though reality is, indeed, complex and multidimensional.

The challenges of being parents to special children

"I felt the weight of the world fall on me when I found out..."

And what was it like for you when you found out? You must remember the myriad of emotions that bombarded you throughout those first few days-weeks-months after the initial discovery. How much time has it been since? And how do you feel now?

The psychological theories refer to the several stages parents go through after receiving the first diagnosis of their child as having special needs. These stages are similar to the ones of grief over a loved one, and they usually include, among other things:

- The first stage of shock and denial.
- Later, comes the anger, aggression, and vast emotional confusion.
- With time, the tempestuous emotions make way for additional emotional reactions, that include sorrow, sadness, and depression.
- Only after the fact arrives the stage of accepting the given situation, that includes a "reorganization" of your whole life.

By the way, this wide range of emotions does not contradict the great and endless *love* you feel for your incredible child. Don't feel guilty for the stormy emotions you go through. It's only natural you'll feel deep and vast sadness—for your child who will have to deal with difficulties and challenges most others do not, and for your own life course that has suddenly deviated, too. There was no way you could have prepared yourself for such drastic changes in advance.

Far from the tree: being parents to a child with a "different operating system"

The psychologist **Andrew Solomon** claims that many of the parental troubles with dealing with children with special needs stem from the children forcing the parents to "learn a new language," to enter a realm of unfamiliar terms that they'd previously never encountered. As parents, we have a subconscious wish for our children to be similar to us, for them to "carry on our legacy." In many cases, parenting special children forces the parents to abandon such fantasies, and instead immerse themselves in their child's world, that has that different "operating system." It's far from easy.

Let's assume that you are parents to a visually impaired girl, who suffers greatly from being exposed to sunlight. You get invited to an outdoor family event, and you arrive happy and excited the afternoon of the party—but for your daughter, the blinding sunlight is practically intolerable. If you understand her experience, if you take it into consideration and properly prepared for it beforehand, you may avoid pain—both for you and for her (perhaps make some changes to the area that can ease her being there, or perhaps it's best to even go without her). In order to best do this, you must try and imagine the world through their eyes to the best of your ability. It's not always easy, but it's vital.

Recalculating your route

As parents to children with special needs, you are sometimes required to make vast changes in your own priorities: change careers; look for a more comfortable or less demanding place of work; move to a different city to be closer to the educational system that would best suit your child; abandon hobbies you may have had; and let's not even touch on the financial expenses you weren't prepared for. In addition to all this, your relations with your partner may be challenged, and so may the parenting of your other children (or your plans about possibly having more children one day), all gets viewed through a different perspective. It's not simple at all.

Additionally, there are times when finding out about your child's special needs, reroutes you, the parents, to a new personal-developmental path, and opens you up to a whole, previously unknown world: guiding groups for parents of children with autism, developing applications for children who have trouble being organized, designing accessories for children suffering from diabetes… there are no limits to the possibilities. Well, sometimes the strife leads you toward a wide array of opportunities; you should be open to them.

The meaningful and new outlook you have upon life

Parents to children with special needs have a great and complex weight to carry.

Many of them feel lucky and grateful for life experiences that they never would have chosen otherwise. Most people, after all, wouldn't choose to have a child with special needs. How many medical examinations do we undergo throughout the pregnancy—all so we can up the chances of having a "healthy" child. However, despite the many difficulties and ongoing challenges that come along with raising a special child, many parents report a whole new world opening up to them, and many talk of the wide range of benefits in their lives that are directly correlated to this complex life experience: the broadening of their emotional range, finding previously unknown strengths and fortitude, a new outlook on life.

Above all else, parenting a special needs child is a process that gives life a special meaning. Nothing about it is natural or a given. Each step forward our child takes, every achievement, or milestone—are a victory. Many parents feel an added sense of purpose, one that's bigger than life itself.

Being parents to a special needs child makes you develop some precious qualities: a deep and endless love, true sensitivity, compassion, tolerance and patience, gratitude, optimism. Raising a special needs child can also bring with it a supportive community and brave new friendships. Now, there's no escaping it—we know well who we are, who stands on our side, and who our true friends are.

It's so terribly important to recognize the existence of these attributes: to talk about them and give them space in our lives. The difficulties are there—always present. And exactly for that reason it's so important to widen our perspective, to "dilute" the struggles with the positive aspects and the exciting and emotional moments your parenting supplies. Such a world view can greatly help with coping.

Welcome to Holland

The coming excerpt was written by **Emily Perl Kingsley**, an American mother to a child with Down Syndrome, who wished to describe her parenting experience of a child with special needs. I applied to her and received her consent to publish this wonderful text in this book.

I am often asked to describe the experience of raising a child with a disability—to try and help people who have not shared that unique experience to understand it, to imagine how it would feel. It's like this... When you're going to have a baby, it's like planning a fabulous vacation trip—to Italy. You buy a bunch of guidebooks and make your wonderful plans. The Coliseum. Michelangelo's David. The gondolas in Venice. You may learn some handy phrases in Italian. It's all very exciting. After months of eager anticipation, the day finally arrives. You pack your bags and off you go. Several hours later, the plane lands. The stewardess comes in and says, "Welcome to Holland." "Holland?" you say. "What do you mean, Holland? I signed up for Italy! I'm supposed to be in Italy. All my life I've dreamed of going to Italy." But there's been a change in the flight plan. They've landed in Holland and there you must stay. The important thing is that they haven't taken you to a horrible, disgusting, filthy place, full of pestilence, famine and disease. It's just a different place. So, you must go out and buy new guidebooks. And you must learn a whole new language. And you will meet a whole new group of people you would never have met. It's just a different place. It's slower paced than Italy, less flashy than Italy. But after you've been there for a while and you catch your breath, you look around.... and you begin to notice that Holland has windmills... and Holland has tulips. Holland even has Rembrandts. But everyone you know is busy coming and going from Italy... and they're all bragging about what a wonderful time they had there. And for the rest of your life, you will say, "Yes, that's where I was supposed to go. That's what I had planned." And the pain of that will never, ever, ever, ever go away... because the loss of that dream is a very, very significant loss. But... if you spend your life mourning the fact that you didn't get to Italy, you may never be free to enjoy the very special, the very lovely things... about Holland.

Many parents to special children identify with these wonderful words and find much beauty and truth in them. However, I'll point out as a counter to the text, that another mother to a child suffering from autism wrote an excerpt with a completely different point of view: "*Welcome to Beirut.*" You can probably imagine the message she attempted to pass on, and her vastly differing experience.

Countless aspects to cope with

At the end of the day, life is but a collection of moments—hour after hour, day after day, countless things to cope with: school systems that don't necessarily understand your child's needs (or do, but can't fit themselves completely to their needs); never ending bureaucracy; the countless, complex decisions you have to make on a daily basis (*Is it a good idea to sign my special child to the local sport class?*); the need to divide your time between your special child and your *other* children—who also need your attention (how difficult it is to give more and more of yourself). It seems that the need to balance the needs of your special child and those of their siblings is one of the more complex and delicate missions parents of special needs children have to handle.

And alongside all this, you're endlessly busy with explaining to your surroundings—the differences, the struggles, the needed adjustments. Don't forget to also mention the many strengths and qualities your wonderful child has, and the healthy, functioning aspects of their lives. It's so important to remember— and to remind your surroundings—that the disability does not overtake everything else. It's also important not to be too overprotective of your special child. It's true, in some areas they may find it more difficult than others do, but there are many and vast areas in which they can and should function on their own.

Parenting children with special needs oftentimes brings along existential, complex questions—what will happen when we're not around anymore? Who will look after them? And perhaps you're also concerned about having more children—would you manage to raise another child? And what if you have *another* "special" child? And what if you have to face the impossible decision of terminating the pregnancy to *avoid* such a situation? It's so complex!

Sit for a moment, take a deep breath, and check within yourselves—who helps you handle the wide range of complicated matters? If "regular" parenting is complicated, then parenting special children is doubly and triply so; it's something you cannot do without a proper support system—of family members, good friends, your community, a community of parents to children who have similar special needs as yours (here is another wonderful advantage social media has!), and good professionals. Don't hesitate to ask for help and counsel. At the same time, it's also very important to nurture and strengthen your relationship with your significant other. A strong couple-life is the basis for dealing with the many challenges you will face down the line.

At the end of the day, only you know how much you give of yourselves. Inside you there's an endless spring of energies and coping abilities. In order for you to keep being able to *give*, you have to take care of yourselves, too. Don't stay alone, find the resources that can help you in the best possible way, allow yourselves to be supported, and also let yourselves break every once in a while—it's natural and normal. Find the opportunities to rest during your exhausting daily lives—you truly deserve it! Don't forget that you have to be full so you can help give your children the wide range of support they need. And finally, remember that self-compassion is the key in dealing with this. Be kind to yourselves; smile to that person in the mirror; give yourself a good tap on the back (you incredible parents, you!) and allow others to do the same. Really, you deserve it.

THE BOTTOM LINE

- Special needs—special children.
- An accurate diagnosis and a proper treatment—a wide acceptance of their unique identity and differences.
- So difficult and painful—expands the heart and gives life a new meaning.

It seems as though this chapter is full of contradictions. In actual fact, you know this better than anyone: it's the reality which is complex; it's the reality that holds so many different aspects regarding being parents to special needs children; being parents to special children.

CHAPTER 29

SO MANY POSSIBILITIES
On parenting in "new families"

When will we be able to drop the word "new" from this chapter's title? When will we be able to drop it from our family's title? When can we simply be: family—a regular family: a family with a mother and a mother, or a father and a father, or only a mother (or father)? A family with a mother and father and father's partner, or a family where the mother and father came together not as romantic partners, but as co-parents, instead, or... there are so, so many possibilities!

Look for a moment at the wondrous family unit you built for yourselves—it was such an effort to bring your children into this world; the emotional energies, the bureaucracy, the financial aspect... and that's not even mentioning the curious-nosy looks from the people around you, and the endless efforts to explain. Would it ever be easier, more available, more natural? And on the other hand, you must tell yourselves, in the future we can hope everything will get simpler—but we're so lucky we managed to do it. We're so lucky to be alive today, and not twenty or thirty years ago—then we might not have managed to build a family at all.

The far-reaching advancements that happened in the last decades in the realm of fertility, and the social and legal developments, as well—are what allowed the creation of new families in their wide variety of compilations: families created by only one parent, families with single-sex parents (either two mothers or two fathers), families where a man and a woman bring a child into this world as co-parents, without them being in a romantic relationship, and more. "Sperm donation," "egg donations," "in vitro fertilization (IVF)," "surrogacy," "adoption," "parenting order"—all these are only a short list of all the possible relevant terms one would need to build a "new family;" you would know them and all their different combinations better than anyone; combinations that allowed you to create a family.

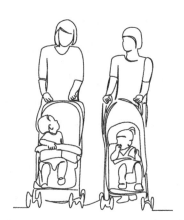

On the line between normal and special

This line between a normal, regular family, to a special one, is probably one you're well familiar with already. After all, most of the parents in "new families" grew up in "standard families:" families with a mother-father-children unit, and perhaps a dog, too. It's no wonder, then, that we all—yes, even the parents of the "new" families themselves—are so busy with comparing the *new* families to the "regular" ones, that are based on heterosexual couples. You may look at your roles as two mothers within your family unit, in comparison to the parental roles in families that have both a mother and father; single parents tend to examine their parental functioning in comparison to families with *two* parents; and if you're a family of two fathers, you may find yourselves wondering who among you gives your children those "motherly qualities." It seems that, at least as of today, we're still very set on this way of thinking.

INTERESTING TO NOTE

A mother's brain, a father's brain, and the brains of homosexual fathers

In a research conducted in Israel by Professor **Ruth Feldman** and her colleagues, the researchers followed the brain activity of parents while they were interacting with their babies. The parents who participated in this study were composed of heterosexual families (mothers compared to fathers), and homosexual males, who were the primary caregivers of their babies. Apparently, *mothers* in the *heterosexual* families (who acted as the babies' *primary* caregivers) had more activity in the areas of the brain responsible for emotions and survival mechanisms (vigilance, awareness, attentiveness to the baby's distress). However, the *fathers* in those families (who all acted as *secondary* caregivers), had increased activity in the areas of the brain that are attributed to understanding the baby: areas connected to empathy and "higher" thinking. And yet, one of the most interesting findings of this study occurred when looking at the brain activity in the *homosexual males* who were the *primary* caregivers of their babies. These men had increased activity in *both* the aforementioned areas at once: the emotional-based and survival areas (that are usually attributed to the mothers), and the "higher" brain areas (that are usually attributed to the fathers). These findings prove the wondrous flexibility of the human brain, and its ability to adjust itself and its function to the reality-based given situation.

An additional study showed that same-sex families are attributed with a higher level of partnership and equality between the parents, and the flexibility regarding the parental roles. We know now that women and men can both adopt characteristics considered to be either "feminine" or "masculine." This flexibility comes into play in the routinely-daily functioning (for example, expressions of warmth and love, that coincide with setting boundaries, order, and discipline), and as I stated above, this flexibility receives evidence-based affirmation through brain studies.

The challenges you face

As I've previously stated, the "new family" units can be very different from each other, so there is no way to truly generalize the parenting in them. Each family has its own unique matters it needs to cope with. Yet still, there are certain subjects that are alike and shared. While reading the following, try and make the adjustments needed so that it fits your own private family unit.

Creating the story and telling it

Your family was created in a special way; it's important for your children to know how it happened. Don't assume they'll "figure it out on their own," or that "it's so natural for them that they don't even notice the differences between our family and others." It's important to remember that children can accept any situation as natural and acceptable, as long as it's explained to them in a clear and simple manner.

In order for you to tell your children your story, you first have to make it clear to yourselves; gather the facts and make them into a coherent narrative. Tell your children how desperately you wanted them, share the journey you had to take in order to bring them into this world, and how the whole marvelous thing happened. If you'd like, you can also *write* the story: create a kind of book for your children, and add in some pictures from your family album.

The story you create should be a "good story," one that, naturally, fits the needs of your children's age group, and their ability to process and contain the given facts. During the process of creating the story, remember the rule—it's vital to tell the children the truth, but that doesn't necessarily mean the *whole* truth. Additionally, there's a great importance to the mere existence of an open line of communication between you and your children regarding the creation of your family. The older your children get, the more details you can add, deepening and expanding on the narrative, while being open and willing to answer any of the many questions that will most likely arise.

In this same context, if your children came into this world through the use of sperm or egg donation, you should be aware of the growing calls from professionals to share this information with your children starting at a young age. Research has shown that the children's early exposure to this fact of life—before they reach the age of seven—helps them accept it more easily, and naturally incorporate it into their life story.

Keeping an open line of communication with the people who surround you

In the last few years, there's been a growing acceptance of there not truly being any such thing as "normal;" each and every one (every child, every family) is different and unique in their own special way. Yet still, as a "new family," you (and your children) oftentimes need to deal with being "exceptional," while simultaneously being exposed to questions, queries, curiosity, and perhaps even some criticism. It seems that the key to properly dealing with this is to openly communicate with your surroundings. The more comfortable and natural you feel regarding the uniqueness of your family, the more you'll help others treat your family similarly.

Further on this matter, it's important to avoid secrets and lies; secret and lies are, after all, a gateway for unneeded complications. So, if your son makes up a story about his father "living abroad," or if your daughter tells her friends that her mother is living with a "roommate," you shouldn't play along, and instead always encourage your children to tell the truth. The more simply and openly you treat the reality of your lives, the people around you will see it in the same way, too. Simultaneously, you should also engage the educators and have them help you with these processes. For example, before Mother's or Father's Day, ask the teacher to talk to the class about there being different family formulations, and how each family is unique in its own special way.

Help extended family members fit into their roles

Another complication may arise from your original families—first and foremost, from your parents, whom you'd wholeheartedly waited to be able to call grandparents. There are some families where this is a nonissue—some of the grandparents jump into their new roles naturally and with honest joy and excitement. However, there are also situations in which the extended family members have trouble accepting the new family dynamic, and rather than pull their weight and help, rather than enjoy the wondrous role of grandparents, they make it harder on you, forcing you to engage and confront them over the issue.

When regarding same-sex couples, this can more often occur with the set of grandparents from the side of the parent who is not genetically related to the child. So, in other words: there are people who find it difficult to step into the role of grandparents to children who are not their biological grandchildren.

These situations call for an understanding of the different perspectives, and call for an open line of communication between you and your parents. It also requires a great amount of patience. You can assume and hope that with time, once your parents see the honest joy your children bring you, and your true devotion to them in return—then they'd manage to cut themselves free of their defensiveness and instead understand that they can only benefit from having a warm and close relationship with their grandchildren. This relationship holds significant meaning to you, the parents, as well, and you should do everything in your power not to give up on it.

Getting advice and support

Parenting is a complicated life mission. This has been reiterated throughout this whole book numerous times. "New" parenting can be at times (though not always…) especially complicated. On the one hand, the "new" parenting brings with it a powerful sense of will, choice and gratitude—nothing is taken for granted. On the other hand, "new parenting" holds elements that do not necessarily exist in "regular families," elements that can sometimes make your lives harder.

For example, in single parenting, the single parent has to deal with raising a child alone, without the natural balancing system between two parents, and without another person to take advice from. The issues of "what will happen in the future," and "what will happen if something happens to me" suddenly sharpen and get moved to the forefront.

In same-sex parenting, there sometimes occurs an asymmetry based on one of the parents not being the child's biological parent. There are certain same-sex partners where one of the couple doesn't participate in the parental role at all, and does not hold any legal standing as the child's parent. They remain in a role as "the parent's partner" and at times even have other children of their own. Each of these situations holds different meanings, of course.

If you're in a co-parenting relationship, it's possible that you have to handle differences of opinions that arise regarding your children's education and the way you both wish to raise them, issues that hadn't popped into your mind at the beginning of the line—issues you were unprepared for. These families also sometimes have to deal with the entrance of additional new partners into the family unit.

Each of these issues and many others, too (such as: sibling matters or separation), are viewed differently through your simply being a "new" family, and they may involve certain sensitive matters.

Alongside this complexity, it's vital to say—don't stay alone with your troubles and deliberations. In order to best handle the complex situations that arise due to your special parenting circumstances and the additional, daily parental tasks, it's important to get help, to be supported, and to be in contact with families similar to your own, and, of course, receive professional help when needed.

INTERESTING TO NOTE

Research findings regarding children who grew up in same-sex families

Same-sex families are relatively new, and research regarding them is still only at its infancy. Beyond that fact, there are so many variables that affect parenting and child development, that same-sex parenting is but a part of a wide array of variables and characteristics. That said, research so far has shown that child development in these families continues on a steady, positive, and healthy course. For example, an American study, which was published in 2019, showed that children who grew up with homosexual parents developed well, and in some areas performed even better than children in heterosexual families. The children in same-sex families were found to be better socially adjusted, have a higher level of rule adherence, and suffered relatively low levels of depression and anxiety—all this when compared to children of heterosexual families. Similar findings were received in other studies, as well.

The research additionally shows that children who grew up in same-sex families tend to develop a stable, fully-fledged sexual identity, and that their sexual preferences are affected through genetic aspects they were born with, making the process no different than what occurs in heterosexual households.

THE BOTTOM LINE

New families, with their wide variety and compilations, are each unique and all encompassing. They constantly change and develop, and hold within them many challenges and emotional wonders. Parents in new families usually feel a deep sense of gratitude for their parenting. No part of their experience is taken for granted.

In many ways, you may also feel as though you're innovative. These feelings can be the "fuel" you need to deal with the curious environment, and the efforts to properly explain what's needed to the people around you. Your ability to tell the story of your special family—to yourselves, your children, and surroundings, and your willingness to treat the reality of your lives with openness, are qualities that are greatly important for you and for your wonderful children. There will always be struggles, and there will always be things that you have to deal with, but the most important thing of all is that *you did it*—you created a truly special-regular family.

4

PART IV
GO SLOW
ADDITIONAL THOUGHTS ON PARENTS & PARENTING

GO SLOW
A PREFACE TO PART IV

We've reached the fourth and final part of this book.

And what have we had so far? First, we set out our goals as parents and the ways to reach them; later, we put ourselves and our parenting in the center; in the third part of the book we focused on the wide array of special parenting circumstances—every one of you could choose the path most right for yourselves. And now, we can slow down a little, open the car window, look out toward the horizon, breathe in the clean air, and think... think additional thoughts on parenting and parents.

For example, have you ever asked yourselves what kind of parenting occurs in the animal kingdom? Does parenting in nature only happen with cats, dogs, and other mammals, or does it also occur with birds, fish, and other species? You can read more on these subjects in Chapter 30; you may also be surprised to find that a deep introspection of the parenting in nature could provide us with some interesting insights regarding our own parenting.

And while broadening our horizons—I invite you all to look at our own not-so-distant past. Did you know that only decades ago, parenting wasn't considered a particularly important or monumental task? Could you believe that in the beginning of the 20th century, doctors would tell parents to raise their children "with no human touch," and psychologists believed that parental love was actually a dangerous business? These subjects and others will be explored in Chapter 31. Once you finish reading this chapter, you'll breathe easily knowing that you are raising your children in today's reality, and not those not-so-distant pasts.

Finally, I will share my own personal-professional thoughts regarding the world of child psychotherapy, and the centrality I view in working in therapy alongside and through the parents. My beliefs, which have been built throughout the many years I've worked therapeutically with parents, were in fact what led me to writing this book. I'll conclude this book with my views on the wondrous role we fulfil as parents. Are you ready? Let's carry on. But this time, let's go slow…

CHAPTER 30

IN NATURE, TOO—IT'S IMPOSSIBLE TO DO WITHOUT LOVE
On the commonalities between human parenting, and parenting in the wild

Parenting... what hasn't yet been written about this special and vital role. Count-less book, articles, blogs, personal columns. And with all the words floating around, it almost seems as though we invented it—parenting itself. It seems as though it's unique to us, humans—who think, talk, and record our feelings. It seems as though there's no way to have parenting without thinking of it first—without the pondering of boundaries and quality time shared, without expectations and disappointments and insights regarding the parent we wish to become.

However, if we widen our perspective, we'll find that parenting isn't something that is solely human-centered. The wonderful characteristics of parenting happen in the wild, too, in many different species.

We all know that animals in the wild procreate and have offspring. However, sel-domly do we actually pause and ask ourselves: "What kind of parents are they? Is the parental role in nature solely attributed to that of the mother-females, or is there room for fathers, as well? What does parenting in the animal kingdom include? Does it conclude with feeding the pups? Protecting them? Or, perhaps the wild also holds space for an actual true mother's love?"

And if you're wondering "Why should parenting in the wild interest or concern us," I believe the answer is tied to the fact that we are also irrefutably connected to it: a part of a long line of evolutionary growth. Looking at this chain of evolution can teach as much about ourselves, and about our parenting; after all, we weren't the first to invent parenting.

Sea-turtles, fish, and penguins: the wonders of parenting in nature

If you were asked, *"What makes you your children's parents?*

What are the essential components of your parenting?"—one can assume you'd answer along the lines of: it starts by us merely giving birth to them (though, nowadays we also have additional options, such as adoption, parenting order, and so forth); and above all, we *care* for them, *nurture* them, *educate* them, and *love* them boundlessly.

Could it be possible that animals in the wild have similar parenting characteristics to ours? Let's see, then.

Before we start, it's important to understand that parenting in the wild holds one central goal: the continuation and survival of the species. There are animals whose "parenting" role concludes with simply birthing the next generation. Sea turtles, for example, do not take care of their offspring. In order for their species to survive, the female sea-turtles act on the principle of the more the better; they lay a large number of eggs. In actual fact, most of the eggs are either infertile, dry out, or get eaten by predators, but it is enough if a mere few of them survive, bringing life to a new generation of sea turtles and ensuring the continuation of their species.

However, if we look instead at the fish world, we find that their parenting is more developed, and includes not only having the offspring, but also *protecting* them. The tilapia fish, for example, lay their eggs and keep them and the little fish that hatch from them—inside the mother's mouth, and sometimes even in the father's mouth, too. By so doing, they protect the baby tilapia fish form predators.

Moreover, you'll certainly agree that human parenting requires us to give up our comforts, and in many cases put our children's needs before our own. Well, the same is seen with fish: when the baby fish find refuge in their parents' mouths, the parent-fish stop eating for a while, to avoid harming their babies. This incredible mechanism also occurs in some species of frogs.

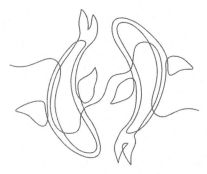

And what happens with birds?

Birds, as we know, build nests for their chicks, where they incubate the eggs until their hatch. However, their parental role does not end there. Birds continue taking care of their offspring long after they hatch. Throughout the day, the baby chicks remain in the nest, while one of the parents goes to hunt for food for them. When the parent-bird returns to the nest, they place the food straight into their chicks' opened mouths. The young birds are featherless and weak, and lack the ability to fly or even walk—which means that without that parental effort, they would not survive.

By the way, throughout the book I mentioned the human fathers who do not give up on the right and privilege of being fully and actively involved in raising their children. This situation has been termed "the New Father model." Well, it's fascinating to find that with birds, this model is not new in the least. Apparently, in over 90 percent of bird species, the parental tasks are divided and performed by both parents together: mothers and fathers. And it's not simply about how the parent-birds share their parental roles; there are even bird species that demonstrate actual "feminist" traits. With the emperor penguin, for example, the male parent is the one to incubate the eggs and watch over the baby chicks, while the female mother penguin goes out to hunt for food for their offspring. It seems we have much to learn from the emperor penguins regarding freeing ourselves from the set, fixed gender-based roles (Mom at home—Dad at work).

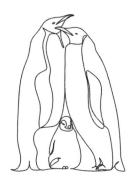

Breastfeeding—far beyond mere sustenance

Moving on from the fish, frogs, and birds—straight to the mammals.

The mammalian offspring develop as fetuses in their mothers' bodies, and they are the ones who benefit from the most long-lasting, continual, and dedicated devotion in nature. All mammals, without exception, are fed from their mothers, and so need to be close to the mother throughout their first weeks of life. And yet, if you thought that breastfeeding was merely about *feeding* the young cubs and fulfilling their dietary needs—it's apparent that breastfeeding holds a much broader and more significant weight.

Through breastfeeding and the additional behaviors that come along with it— such as licking the cubs—the female mammals in nature nurture and care for their offspring. Amazingly, nurturing offspring is what gives them the basis for continuing their adult functioning, and even allows the young cubs to one day become parents themselves. And how do we know this?

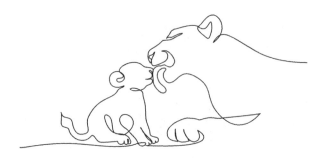

A series of fascinating studies examined the functioning of rat pups who were separated from their mother only hours after their birth. The rat pups were fed artificially, so that their physical needs were met. Despite this, however, the rats' development was severely harmed: they did not properly react to stressful situations, their social functioning was dramatically decreased, and there was a slowing of their growth rate. In certain cases, the lack of a mother's presence in their early lives even led to death—despite having had their physical, base needs met (these findings echo the jarring study Spitz conducted regarding orphans which was mentioned in the first chapter of this book).

So, what did those rats actually miss out on having? Well, it's apparent that the lack of a maternal presence in their early lives caused a hormonal imbalance in their bodies, and led to some irreversible damage in the development of their brains. One of the most severe consequences of this situation was observed in female rats who had been separated from their mothers when they were young. As these female pups grew up, they were incapable of becoming mothers themselves; they simply did not know how to adequately care for their offspring. The lack of maternal care essentially memorialized itself, harming the adult rats throughout the rest of their lives—so much so that they could not raise the next generation (▶ see too Chapter 24, regarding intergenerational transmissions).

By the way, if you ask why psychology was even interested in studying rats, the not exactly flattering answer is that though we are vastly different on the outside, there are significant genetic similarities between the DNA sequences of rats, and our own. So we can reach conclusions regarding humans through rat studies.

A feeding mother, or a mother who is soft and comfortable?

Another series of fascinating studies that further cemented the necessity of parental love in animals, came from an American researcher named **Harry Harlow**. The research was conducted in the mid-twentieth century. At the time, when Harlow wished to research "love" scientifically, most of his colleagues thought him insane. Now, his research is viewed as a classic work in the realm of psychological studies, and they mark a significant milestone for understanding the parental biological mechanisms.

Harlow researched a particular species of monkeys. He separated the monkey infants from their mothers right after their birth, and transferred them into a lab where they were presented with two alternative mother figures: one "mother" made out of barbed wire but equipped with a milk bottle, which the infant could latch onto; and a second alternative "mother"—who could not feed them, but was made out of soft fabric. Until that time, the researchers tended to believe that the relationship between animal infants and their mothers was based on the fact that the mothers fed them and lessened their hunger. Harlow's study proved different. Harlow found that the monkey infants all preferred to cuddle up in the soft "mother's" lap—despite her not having the ability to feed them. The monkeys would lay for hours with the soft "mother," while only going to the "barbed wire mother" for a few moments when they had to feed (▶ search on YouTube for Harlow's monkeys). And what do we learn from this?

A limited amount of love—mothers who eat their offspring

Love does not always win. Those who ever raised hamsters or rabbits as pets, perhaps may be familiar with this distressing phenomenon where females, at times, eat some of their offspring mere hours after giving birth to them. How is this possible? Well, among the possible explanations for this "parental cannibalism," arise the mother's need to lessen the number of her offspring so that she can adequately feed the remaining ones; the fear of predators harming their children; and the mother's understanding of there being a certain defect with the given offspring, leaving it unable to survive regardless. Another explanation attributes the mother's need to return the energy she lost throughout the pregnancy and birth to her body.

However, it's fascinating to see how some animals manage to bypass this cruel phenomenon. Gerbils, for example, have a hormonal mechanism that overrides the mother's need to hunt during the days after the birth (fascinatingly, this impulse is mirrored in the male parent, too!). This mechanism enables the parents to recognize the specific smell of their own babies. After this short time, the gerbils will return to preying on unfamiliar gerbil pups, if the opportunity for that arises, but will avoid harming their own private pups. The wonderful (and often cruel and odd) ways of nature.

Harlow's research findings teach us that an animal's need for maternal care, for warmth and love, is a need unto itself, and poses a central foundation for the relationships forged between mothers and their offspring. And indeed, today we no longer have any doubt in this regard: every offspring—be they monkey infants or human ones—hold a massive *existential* need for parental love and care.

We were born to be parents

So, if we thought, for a moment, that parenting is a "human invention," then the rats, Halow's monkeys, the stray cats who tirelessly care for their kittens—and so many other animals—all prove that parenting is a genetically predisposed function. Humans and all sorts of other mammals in the wild—we are all born with a predisposed system: the caregiving system, that aims to help us care for our offspring, protect them, feed them, and also nurture and love them, and become emotionally tied to them. We were born to become parents.

Moreover, since at its core, our parenting is simply a part of nature, we also have much to learn from other animals' parenting. Let's examine some key aspects.

It's no coincidence that breastfeeding is so demanding: it shouldn't be avoided

In the initial stages of a baby's life, parental presence holds a vast significance. A mere few decades ago, scientists believed they could surpass nature: the food companies developed infant formula, that promised a scientifically based, perfect way to feed our baby. Many parents rushed to follow the science's promises, and stopped breastfeeding, which was then viewed as primitive. Nowadays, we well know how the scientists' illusions fell through. We now know that there is no better way to feed a child than through breastfeeding. And beyond the health benefits it provides, both to the baby and the mother, breastfeeding also forces the mother to stay close to the newborn. This situation—though far from convenient, makes more sense from an evolutionary point of view. Our babies need us—not merely for sustenance, but for—and mainly due to—our consistent presence in their early lives.

In September 2018, the world stirred when Jacinda Ardern, the prime minister of New Zealand, came to the UN convention with her three-month-old baby. Ardern is the second woman in history to have given birth while being prime minister (the first was Benazir Bhutto, who served as the prime minister of Pakistan). When faced with the countless raised eyebrows—male eyebrows, that is—the New Zealand Prime Minister simply said: "*I'm breastfeeding, and my baby needs me. I can't part from her.*"

At this point it's important to stress that consistent parental presence can also be achieved if the baby isn't breastfeeding (if breastfeeding didn't work, if you decided to not try in the first place, if you're two men raising a child together, and many more reasons). At the end of the day, mother's milk does have alternatives. However, what can't be exchanged, is the consistent parental presence (or that of other permanent caretakers). Babies in their first stage of life need stable adult presences to care for them with dedication and love.

Our children's needs change fast as they grow

Parenting in the wild happens for a set time. When the offspring grow, they part from their parents and go out to follow their independent paths—their parents' presence is no longer needed. With us, things differ, and it's not inconceivable or rare to hear complaints from parents of twenty-plus-year-olds who won't leave the nest, as it were (*"Get out of the house already.... and stop using us as a laundry service!"*). Yet still, it's important to remember that parenting a fourteen-year-old is different to parenting a ten-year-old, and that further differs from parenting a two-year-old. Our children grow up so fast, and their needs change constantly. Every parental attempt to preserve their children's needing them, as if they were infants or young children—can ultimately harm the children, their developing independence, and their sense of security and self-worth (▶ see too Chapter 3, in regard to helicopter parenting).

Care for your children today, and accept the fruits of your labor in the future

In nature, as mentioned, the goal of all living creatures is to ensure their species' continued survival. When mammals nurture their young, they invest energy that contributes to their offspring's eventual ability to become parents themselves. We, too—the human parents—tend to benefit from seeing our children grow into independent adults, and one day, become parents themselves—parents who are loving, dedicated, and caring. Remember, the effort you put in today is what builds and creates the future "parenting resources" of your own children. The love you give them today will one day teach them to love their own children similarly, to nurture and care for them properly. And it seems to be our way of ensuring the survival of the human race; to assist with transferring our legacy to the next generation—and not only the genetic legacy, but the one based on values, emotions, and social and cultural matters.

THE BOTTOM LINE

Parenting isn't the sole attribute of humans. In many animal species, there are wondrous parenting examples that include different elements: from birthing offspring, to protecting them, feeding them, caring and nurturing them. In a general sense, we can say that the more evolutionarily developed the animal, the more parental aspects are included in their parenting. It's apparent that the need to care for our offspring is genetically imbedded in us, and now we know that love and parental care are not a mere triviality. When we care for our children with love, dedication, and devotion, we answer their basic needs that are essential for their continued, healthy development, and will even affect their own parenting when the time comes.

CHAPTER 31

RAISING CHILDREN "WITHOUT A HUMAN TOUCH"
On the historical changes in parenting

Many of us tend to think that parenting and parental love are one of the most basic human traits and characteristics. Well, apparently, that's not exactly the case; parental love has not always been a natural and given fact. Moreover, in the not-so-distant past, parenting itself wasn't fully formulated, and most certainly wasn't a central part of peoples' identities, as it is today. And, not only were people less preoccupied with the question of parenting, but the children themselves weren't considered so vitally important. It's a hard concept to grasp, but until about one-hundred years ago, the childhood years were perceived as "the preparation years for adulthood," and children were considered to be "underdeveloped creatures"—ones that had to grow up in order to be productive for society, and for them to hold value.

Fortunately, these concepts are a thing of the past. Nowadays, there's no doubt regarding the massive importance of parental love and the centrality of the childhood years. Yet still, a glance at the history of parenting, beyond being fascinating, may also teach us quite a bit about our functioning as parents in our day and age, and sharpen some of the points and principles that are most important and central to our parenting.

Allow me to start with the surprising fact that "parenting" is a relatively new concept. The term itself was first introduced to the Oxford dictionary in 1918, and before that, was simply nonexistent. The parental guidance books that started showing up in the early twentieth century, referenced "child raising and rearing," but did not specifically target the issue of parenting. It was only in 1975 (!) that a turn occurred, and the term "parenting" started working itself into the modern spoken and written lexicon. Now, today, it's rare to find parents who don't occupy themselves with issues regarding their parenting. So, how could it be that during such a short amount of time we underwent such a fundamental change?

Babies as transitional creatures

Until the mid-1800s, the survival rate of babies and young children was very low, so they were considered naught but "transitional creatures," and held no status within their families. In the mid-eighteenth century, philosophers and religious leaders began working the concept of the babies' and children's importance into their communities' consciousness: the importance of paying them apt attention and putting effort into educating them. These ideas were utterly new for the given time. As a result, parents started "finding the space" for their children to be an inseparable part of their family. It was also when they started planning out the family unit. That said, however, the nuclear family never functioned as a separate unit, the way it does today. Babies and young children were cared for by the multitude of the village women: mothers, aunts, grandmothers, and young women without children of their own. This allowed those young women to gain experience with caring for children, well before they became mothers themselves; while the new mothers had full support and the help they needed, sharing the burden of raising their children with other women. It turns out that parenting, as an exclusive, intense bond between parents and their children—held no foundation.

Raising children in a sterile environment, and from a distance

Although the nineteenth century presented a positive status raise for the human baby, infant mortality throughout the world still remained high. In the latter half of the nineteenth century, about a quarter of the babies in the United States passed away before reaching their first birthday: one in five of the white-Caucasian babies, and one of every three in the black communities. Just imagine such a bleak reality; no wonder the parents feared getting too attached to their children. And it wasn't only the babies who died. Many women died during labor. In light of these harsh statistics, it's truly unsurprising that *parenting* remained unfounded and unestablished.

In the early twentieth century, doctors in the United States and Europe started realizing that there was a serious problem of contaminations and infectious

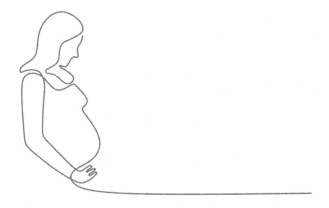

diseases, which led to the high number of deaths. Reports at the time showed horrifying data regarding the goings on in orphanages. Apparently, in almost all the orphanages checked across the United States, not one child lived over the age of two. They all passed away from infections and diseases.

These insights led the doctors to call for distancing one's self from others (isn't it incredible how COVID-19 "refreshed" our outlook on these sorts of guidelines…?). The doctors advised keeping a safe distance from the children, putting them to bed in separate rooms, and to try and raise them in an absolutely sterile environment—"without a human touch."

So, for example, a doctor named **Arthur Albutt** wrote in his book "*The Wife's Handbook*" published in 1888:

> *If you really love the baby, you should maintain a cautious distance:*
> *it is born to live and not to die, and so always wash your hands before*
> *touching, and don't indulge the baby with too much contact, so that it*
> *may grow up to fill a useful place in society.*

While another pediatrician named **Luther Holt** called for parents to avoid kissing and hugging their children:

> *Good childcare means good hygiene, clean hands, a light touch, air*
> *and sun and space, including space from you, Mom and Dad. And*
> *that means avoiding even affectionate physical contact. What can be*
> *worse than kissing your child? Did parents really wish to touch their*
> *babies with lips, a known source for transmitting infection?*

In the mid-nineteenth century, a German doctor named Martin Couney first invented the incubator—a wondrous machine that allowed for premature babies to stay alive as long as they stayed in a "glass cage," that remained in total sterility. It was no wonder that science became so vastly admired. Everyone wanted to raise their children in the pure-scientific method. Governments gave out massive budgets to share with the public the principles of keeping the parents' distance from their children and keeping a sterile environment in order to avoid getting diseases.

"A mother's love is a dangerous instrument"

Aside from the medical doctors, the realm of psychology, which, at the time, was a young science working to establish its "scientific base," started calling for parents to pull away from their children, and to keep their relationships with them cold and practical.

Thus, for example, **John B. Watson**, a young and charismatic psychologist, acting as the president of the American Psychological Association (APA), spread to the public at large, in any way conceivable, his strict and harsh views regarding child rearing:

> *Nothing could be worse for a child than being mothered, and being mothered means being cradled, cuddled, cosseted. It is a recipe for softness, a strategy for undermining strong character. Doting parents endows their children with weakness, reserves, fears, cautions, and inferiorities.*

In the popular magazine "*Infant and Child*" published in the year 1928, under the chilling title: "*Too Much Mother Love*," Watson expanded his views with:

> *Never hug and kiss them, never let them sit on your lap. If you must, kiss them once on the forehead when they say goodnight. Shake hands with them in the morning. Give them a pat on the head if they have made an extraordinarily good job of a difficult task. Try it out, in a week's time you will find how easy it is to be perfectly objective with your child and at the same time kindly. You will be utterly ashamed of the mawkish, sentimental way you have been handling it.*

The goal: to raise children who are productive to society

It's truly no wonder, then, that the early twentieth century made so many parents believe that indulging children, giving them physical affection, and answering to their needs was a dangerous business. In a rather paradoxical manner, it was actually the more educated parents, the upper-middle class, that tended to follow the scientists' instructions, thus, avoiding the possibility of "spoiling" their children, so that they won't be spoiled in the future. A further point that is important to understand: at the time, the prevailing perception was that childhood years were naught but the preparation for adult life. Children were seen as a cheap workforce, there to help the adults around them. *"One must train and beat discipline into children, so that they may take on a productive role in society once they've reached maturity,"* the American Dr. Holt said.

Freud: changing the way of the world

The massive changes in the perceptions regarding the importance of children are vastly attributed to the work of **Sigmund Freud** and the psychoanalytical theory he developed. There's no doubt that Freud changed the world order regarding the way we think both about ourselves and about our children. His revolutionary ideas that were first introduced in the mid-twentieth century, clarified to everyone just how vital the early childhood years were to the shaping of the future adult we become. These ideas were expanded and developed through the works of many other psychoanalysts who came after him: D. W. Winnicott, Anna Freud (Freud's own daughter, the sixth and youngest child of his), Margaret Mahler, Melanie Klein, Heinz Kohut, Sándor Ferenczi, and many others.

Simultaneously to the new theories regarding the importance of the early childhood years, many studies done from the mid-twentieth century left no room for doubt: babies need their parents' love. They need it for their literal survival. Babies need human touch, and much of it, and need adults to be astounded by them, and mediate between them and the world at large. By the way, almost unbelievably, the Convention on the Rights of the Child, which regards the basic set of rights children possess in the matters of education, the receiving of medical treatment, the protection from harm, and more—was first approved by the UN only in 1989 (!) and not beforehand.

Nowadays, there is no doubt: Watson and his generation that warned so adamantly on the dangers of parental love were fundamentally wrong. As I've mentioned time and again throughout this book, without parental love, our children will not manage to develop into healthy, functioning human beings. In addition, there's a wide consensus regarding the massive importance of the childhood formative years, that act as a base for the adult the child will soon become. It seems, then, that we and our children are lucky—lucky to be raising children in this era, and not one-hundred years previous.

INTERESTING TO NOTE

Even in the incubator—it's best not to give up on human touch

A fascinating research series done by **Ruth Feldman** and her associates in 2018, examined the effectiveness of the *"Kangaroo Care method"* ("skin to skin") in regard to treating premature babies. Seventy-three preemies who were born at an average week 30, and weighed an average of less than 3 pounds, received one hour of physical touch from their mothers throughout a two-week period. The preemies were taken out of the incubator and put on the mother's chest, between her breasts. The control group included an identical number of preemies who had not received the "Kangaroo Care" treatment, and instead only received touches through the incubator walls. The researchers kept following these children until they were ten years old. Apparently, the short treatment given to the preemies in their first days of life made a dramatic impact on their future: throughout their whole development, they had better relationships with their mothers, better emotional regulation abilities, lower levels of the stress hormone cortisol, and a lower rate of attention disorders.

In a similar study, the researchers followed a group of premature babies who received the "skin to skin" treatment during their first weeks of life, but this time they followed them until they reached the age of twenty. They then asked the twenty-year-olds to perform an empathy-necessitating action, while going through a brain fMRI. The same people, treated with the "skin to skin" treatment when they were born prematurely, showed activity 1.5 times higher in areas of the brain responsible for regulating emotions, and had many more neuro-connections between these brain areas; this is in comparison to a similar group of young adults who were born as premature babies but hadn't received "skin to skin" treatment at the beginning of their life. These findings show that even for preemies growing in an incubator—there is no substitute for human touch. Sterility is important, but human touch does *not* fall short of it.

And what can we, as parents, learn from this?

We've seen that the view of parenting has gone through dramatic changes in a relatively short period of time. This situation can affect and have actual, practical consequences on our own parenting. I will attribute a few of them.

Differences in parenting styles between ourselves and our parents

The perceptions regarding parenting have changed fast in the last couple of decades, so much so that many of the parents currently raising their children, were raised themselves in households where their parents believed that indulging the children and showing parental love and affection were a dangerous matter. This situation can cause confusion and tension, and it makes the previous generation one we wouldn't necessarily want to lean on, as a source of knowledge and authority. Let's take for example the treatment of a crying baby. If you're parents to a young baby, and one of your parents advised you to ignore their crying (*"You shouldn't jump at every noise she makes... she'll become spoiled if you do..."*), you most likely won't listen to them. That can cause tensions to arise between you and your parents (the grandparents), and you might find it difficult to consult with them regarding other matters centered around raising your children.

A gap in the parental approach among partners

Continuing from the previous section, in certain cases there may be gaps in the parental perceptions between the two partners: one of you aiming toward a more attentive style of parenting, while the other worries about overindulgence and spoiling. These gaps in parental approaches can be a central conflict matter, especially being as the subjects tied to educating your children only become more complicated and complex the older they get.

Choosing the other extreme: over-parenting

The lack of stability when it comes to parenting perceptions throughout the previous decades can sometimes cause a kind of pendulum swing, leading to a too-extreme parenting style; and yes, there is such a thing as *over*-parenting. Infants indeed need parents who are well-attuned to their needs, but the older the children get, being *overly* attuned can instead cause them damage and harm their developing sense of self. When a nine-year-old grows up feeling that the world revolves around them—around their every need and want—they lose out on countless opportunities to handle the different situations life sets out before them. They cannot develop resiliency and coping mechanisms (▶ see too Chapter 3, regarding "helicopter parenting," and Chapter 16, regarding boundaries). It's important to be aware of such situations, and to find the best balance between properly and sensitively answering the children's needs, but still not being overly involved and overly tuned to them, leaving them weak and lacking the ability to handle themselves.

And still, above all, we cannot forget: there is nothing more important to children than having loving parents—and that is true no matter the child's age. These words are not a general social convention or intuition—they are research-proven, leaving no doubt to their accuracy.

THE BOTTOM LINE

Good parenting, which we now see as self-evident, was not so formulized—not even so long ago. This is due to a combination between high rates of infant mortality and women mortality during labor, and the medical and psychological perceptions which emphasized the negative effects physical displays of affection and love from parents to their children could create.

The sharp change in this matter happened in the mid-twentieth century, both due to Freud's revolutionary theories regarding the importance of the childhood formative years, and the slow gathering of research findings that grew during that time. The research proved, beyond all shadow of a doubt, the importance of love and the emotional connection between parents and their children. Nowadays there's a consensus regarding the importance of these elements for both the physical and emotional welfare of the children, and the adults they will grow to be. We are incredibly lucky to be raising our children now, in this time and age, and not during that confusing time when parents worried about loving their children, touching and hugging them.

CHAPTER 32

"TAKE THIS CHILD AND FIX HIM"
Thoughts on psychotherapy in children, and the therapeutic work done with parents

"Choose a job you love, and you will never have to work a day in your life."

—Confucius

For many years, I had no idea what I wanted to be when I grew up. Even when I was quite-old-enough, I still had no idea. I started my academic journey studying law. A year into it, I realized I was not in the right place for me, and from the law school, I transferred to that of psychology.

I started my master's degree in "The Child's Clinical Psychology" at Tel Aviv University full of doubts. Unlike my fellow students, who'd all dreamed about one day being a clinical child psychologist, I mainly chose this path for having been told it was interesting and would later "open doors" for me—no matter the direction I chose.

Throughout my studies I became exposed to the world of child therapy, a world

I found fascinating and magical. Yet, something still bugged me deep down. At the time, I couldn't name it, but now I can put it into words: the fact that a child came into the treatment room while their parents stayed outside disturbed me more than anything.

When I graduated, I had my firstborn, Noam. It was a perfect reason for me to take a step back, to dive into this delicate, complex parental role, and to think. A year later, intuition led me to start a residency in school psychology. A short time after starting the residency, I finally knew what I wanted to be when I grew up.

School psychology doesn't stand in contradiction to clinical child psychology, but its emphases are a little different. While clinical psychology—at least in its traditional sense—puts much weight to the child's own inner world, school psychology emphasizes the importance of treating the child through the wide lens of their life connections. It emphasizes the fact that child will forever be a part of a wide tapestry of social aspects: one that includes the parents, the family, the school, the community, and so forth. The psychanalysist D. W. Winnicott claims that *"there is no such a thing as a baby, there is a baby and someone,"* meaning, babies never stand on their own merit; they're always a part of a relationship that occurs between them and those who care for them. And if we borrow that train of thought: there are no children without parents; there is no child without a family, a school, a community; there is no child without a wide system that surrounds them.

This difference in perspective sharpened the understanding I had about just how deeply parents affect their children. This perception, which centralizes the parents, is becoming more and more prevalent throughout the world of psychology, and many different professionals aspire to it. This point of view will affect the way we choose to handle situations in which children experience difficulties: tantrums, excessive shyness, anxieties, social problems, regulation issues, a low self-esteem, and many more. Should we send our children to therapy when encountered with one of these problems? Or would it be better if we went ourselves? And perhaps there are certain issues we can simply "live with" and learn to get around?

I'll share a few of my insights regarding psychological therapy with children, and the therapeutic work done with parents. These insights guide my professional life on a daily basis, and they are also what led me to writing this book.

The "garage fantasy" (the parents' version)

Once every few days I receive a phone call such as this: *"Hello, you're a child psychologist, right? Can you accept my child for therapy sessions? He's six and he's got emotional difficulties, I believe he needs emotional-based therapy."*

Such calls are humorously referred to, among the experienced professionals, as the "Garage fantasy" calls. They reflect a situation in which the child's parents—full of good intentions as they may be—wish to send their child to receive emotional therapy, just as we expect when we leave our car at the garage—*"Take him, check what's wrong, and give him back fixed."* Only, *unfortunately*—and more so, *luckily*—it simply doesn't work that way. There's no way to treat a child's emotional issues "at a psychologist" (or with any other kind of emotional therapist), the way you would treat a broken car at the garage. Children's emotional difficulties—no matter their kind—always show up as a part of a wider context. This context includes, first and foremost, the child's parents.

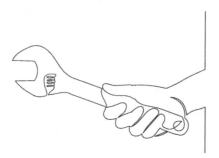

Although the parents may not be the direct *cause* for the child's difficulties and are surely not to "blame" for their appearance, I believe that the parents are the main *key* to better deal with the child's problems; they are the key to successfully cope with these issues. Without the parents being fully involved in the therapy, the child isn't expected to get much better. And even if that one symptom lessens, the process itself may have some very steep prices; for example, it may weaken the parents, make them feel guilty, and may even make them feel a hidden form of jealousy toward the therapist. I'll delve deeper into this matter later on.

The savior fantasy (the therapists' version)

The complementing fantasy to the parents' "garage fantasy" is the "savior fantasy" of the therapists. It's true that most professionals avoid entering this trap, but it's still important to know of its existence and be aware and weary of it. It concerns a situation in which the psychologists find themselves worried about the depicted struggles the child shows, and in response—they rush to help the child and feel as though they need to "save" them from their parents. In these situations, the therapists, deep down, blame the parents for the creation of the difficulties, and feel as though it's up to them to "fix the wrongs and damages" done by the parents. This approach is incredibly dangerous and destructive. It's important to remember that the parents are the most important people in the child's life. There is no one who wishes for the child's ultimate benefit more than the parents. A therapeutic approach that blames the parents and aims to "save" the child from them, is expected to do more damage than good.

Additionally, when one of our children suffers through a form of strife (an emotional difficulty, a social one, and so forth), we tend to blame ourselves for the problems regardless. So, when a child goes to therapy, and the psychologist tends to blame the parents for the difficulties—it can cause a deepening of the feelings of frustration and helplessness in the parents. There's no worse outcome for the child and their family. (This is, of course, assuming that the given situation isn't that of extreme cases of parents who lack parental abilities—parents who abused their children, neglected them, or treated them in a harmful manner.)

It's easier to be the child's therapist than to be their parent

It's important to remember that in many of the cases, it's much easier to be the child's therapist-psychologist, than their parent. The therapist sees the child for one hour a week, and they come to that hour with a wealth of patience, perfectly attuned to the child, and in many of the cases, they are also receiving monetary rewards for their precious time. However, the parent lives the actual *life*, a life filled with disturbances, commitments, additional occupations, more children, work, romance, and stressors. At times, the child comes in with a smile and excitement to the psychologist's clinic, believing in their heart or perhaps even saying out loud: *"This is the only place I'm understood,"* their anger toward their parents grows, and at the same time, the feelings of guilt and helplessness of the parents grow, too. Thus, you receive a script where, in the long-term, everyone loses.

What, then, can we do to get out of such a mess?

Placing the parents in the center

In my opinion, there *are* certain situations when psychological therapy for children can actually help. For example, in regard to specific symptoms children may suffer from (anxiety, for one), and in children who've reached a certain age—their teenage years. If you choose to send your child to psychotherapy, the therapy *has to* directly include a significant weight in regard to the child's parents, treating the parents as an inseparable and vital part of the therapy process (▶ see too Chapter 26, page 373, regarding therapy in adolescents).

However, as per my professional world view, in many cases it's not the correct call to "send your child to therapy." Instead, you can and definitely should deal with the child's problems, through working therapeutically with the parents, and without directly involving the child in the process. I believe that meeting the parents for therapy sessions, where both the parents and the psychologist have only the child's best interests at heart, when they all talk about the child's issues (and no less importantly: the child's strengths!), and look for a way to help them—it's these kinds of meetings that can be the main key in successfully handling the struggles.

Think about it: we, the parents, want our child's benefit more than any other person on earth. We also influence our children more than any other person—we are those who are with them 24/7, 365 days a year. Why shouldn't we confer with others, think and learn the different ways we ourselves can help our children?

Working therapeutically with parents also holds countless benefits. When the psychologist-therapist meets the parents for therapy sessions, they have the opportunity to be empathetic toward them, to empower them, and help them be the ones who ultimately help their child successfully manage their difficulties. Additionally, when we ourselves go in for advice, we see in our mind's eye our whole family—and so we may end up helping our other children, too (meaning, not only the child exhibiting issues). This form of advice taking can also help us preserve the benefits of therapy for a long period of time. It further allows us to look at our different life contexts—for example, the childhood experiences we ourselves underwent—that may be relevant for handling our child's current problems.

The bottom line is, that thanks to the myriad of attributes I've mentioned, working directly with parents supports our emotional welfare, and by so doing, further allows us to successfully help our children. As I've mentioned before, the situation is akin to emergency protocols while landing a plane: first the parent-adult has to put their own oxygen mask on, and only then can they properly help the child next to them.

Not every problem demands a solution

And yet, as we all know, our parental daily lives are filled with issues, struggles, and tensions. Sometimes it feels as though we don't have even a minute of quiet; there's always *something* to keep us from fully resting. So, what do we do with the wide range of stressors and problems?

One of the central answers to this matter is that not every problem demands a solution. It sounds surprising, doesn't it? Perhaps even wrong? Well, it's not a mistake, and I stand behind these words. Western culture has cemented the perception of constantly having to *fix* the problems or struggles we encounter—and quickly. "The most important thing is to be happy" (and healthy, and rich, and worry-free).

As opposed to this perception, in the last few years the western psychology began to adopt some ideas and principles from East-Asian perspective, such as the Buddhist one (► see too Chapters 19 and 20, regarding Mindfulness and self-compassion). At the basis of these theories lies the belief that struggles and challenges are an inseparable part of life. There's no life without suffering, there's no life without problems; *to live* means to deal with different types of issues. These ideas are relevant also for our parental lives.

The parental role, by nature, creates a space—space between two different people: between a child and a parent. By the way, with each of our children we create a different kind of space, or, as Winnicott put it, "*A mother of eight is, in fact, eight different mothers simultaneously.*" In this space, many different occurrences happen: emotions, thoughts, conflicting needs, different points of view and perspectives, disagreements. One of our goals as parents is to learn how to *deal* with our children, within the given space, openly, with endless love, out of genuine curiosity, and without pulling back in fear when stressors and disagreements occur. Our ability to handle the different problems that arise between us and our children, and to still function beside them—that ability allows for growth and development: both for the children, and ours, the parents (!). From this vantage, our children will be able to go out into the world, capable of dealing with the many life challenges ahead; it's also where we ourselves will grow and develop. After all, life is full of different challenges, and we can only benefit if we look at these situations as inseparable parts of our daily lives, and not as obstacles we have to remove.

And in the meantime… it's been over twenty years since that time when I was unsure what I wanted to be "when I grew up;" twenty years of my daily working therapeutically with parents, parenting, and parental processes. This work is full of wonder, beauty, magic, and more than anything—it's vitally meaningful. In my mind, that long stretch of time when I was so unsure of my future, definitely paid off. I believe wholeheartedly in parents and parenting. I believe in our good intentions, in our influence, and our daily work toward the ultimate benefit of our children. These ideas are also what led me to writing this book.

THE BOTTOM LINE

When our children suffer through difficulties, we are the ones who can help them—more so than any therapist. Parents who confer with a psychologist can find great emotional benefits, for both of the parents, and for the children.

If our children still go through direct therapy sessions—it's important that we remain fully involved in the process, and that there not be a divide between us and the therapist. There are also a myriad of challenges that there is simply no point in trying to erase; instead, it's best we learn to function alongside them. This process can be a significant gift we give both ourselves and our children; a life lesson for the road ahead.

FINAL WORDS
ON A PERSONAL NOTE

"Successful parenting is a principle key to the mental health of the next generation."

I opened the book with this **John Bowlby** quote, and I will end with it, too. After all, we are the most significant and important people in our children's lives. We are the ones who create their emotional climate through which they grow and develop; we are the ones who influence their thoughts about themselves more than any other (*"What am I worth?"*); we create their safe base through which the children go out and deal with the challenges the world cooks up for them, and we're also their safe harbor they return to. The relationships we build with our children will be the model on which they build their relationships with people they meet throughout their lives, and most likely, with their own children, too.

These insights are what led me to write this book, and they are interwoven in each of the chapters. Through this book, I wished to put light on and name certain principles and thought processes that can help support our good parenting. These principles are meant to strengthen your own natural parental intuitions and help guide them accurately. I hope I succeeded in doing so. You didn't find a certain "manual" within this book on how to raise children—mainly because, in most cases, there are no such instructions.

I further wished to emphasize the complexity of the parental role, and besides that—our right to enjoy our parenting. In this context, it is important for me to reiterate: the words in this book were not meant to cause you further guilt or to weigh you down. Not at all. Quite the opposite, in fact: they were meant to help us look at our parenting with kind and benefiting eyes; it seems that it's from that place of calm and self-compassion that our parental resources will grow and flourish, something which everyone benefits from.

I wrote this book out of my great love to parents and the parental role they have; I wrote it with the belief that we have the power to help our children to become wonderful human beings; I wrote it with the firm and true belief that parenting is one of the most wondrous gifts life can give us; it's exhausting, anxiety-inducing, it makes us endlessly busy and preoccupied with countless big and small tasks... but let's be honest: it holds the greatest meaning of all, and we're so lucky to have it. We're so lucky to have them, these wonderful children of ours. I hope—and am certain—you feel just as I do.

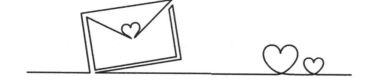

ACKNOWLEDGEMENTS

It takes a village to write a book.

I would first like to thank the wonderful professionals who read, pondered, and contributed from their vast experience to my ultimate enlightenment regarding several matters discussed in this book. Your contribution has significantly elevated the professional level of this book, and for that I am eternally thankful.

- **Professor Yoram Yovell**, a psychiatrist, brain researcher, and psychoanalyst from the Hebrew University in Jerusalem. Thank you for your vital contributions to the many parts of this book that deal with the question of brain function in parenting.
- **Professor Amiram Raviv**, a school and clinical psychologist, the Dean of the department of psychology at the Collage of Law and Business, formerly the head of the department of psychology in Tel Aviv University. Thank you for your comments and insights that contributed to the chapter regarding parenting and romantic relationships.
- **Professor Malka Margalit**, a senior psychologist in educational psychology

and rehabilitative psychology, winner of the Israel Prize for education, and the Dean of the School of Behavioral Sciences at the Peres Academic Center. Thank you for your comments and insights regarding the chapter centered around motivation and the theory of hope.

- **Doctor Nava Levit-Binnun**, the director of the Sagol Center for Brain and Mind, and the founder of the Muda Institute for Mindfulness, Science and Society in The Interdisciplinary Center, Herzliya. Thank you for the sharing of your knowledge, the effort and important insights you gave that contributed to the chapter regarding Mindfulness.
- **Doctor Ilan Diamant**, a senior clinical psychologist, head of the Israeli Center for Mentalization. Thank you for your thoughts and insights that so vastly enriched the chapter regarding mentalization.
- **Doctor Tami Gavron**, a psychotherapist and art therapist at the Academic and Technology College of Tel-Hai, and of Haifa University. Thank you for your sensitive and vital comments that contributed to the chapter regarding mentalization.

Thank you to the many parents who read the book's different chapters in their various written stages; you commented, perfected, and helped me believe in the necessity of this book. A special thank you to Daphna Olmer, Yaeli Chapsky-Shenhar, Efrat Idud, and Liat Gindi-Bar. Your enlightening, intelligent words greatly contributed to the book.

Thank you to all who set my way to the academic path. Thank you to my students throughout the years. It was your curiosity and willingness to know more and learn that so enriched my knowledge and helped me put it all into words. Without you, this wouldn't have happened.

Thank you to the colleagues in Kinneret-Zmora: to Eran Zmora and Yoram Roz, who said, "Yes!" even before I fully knew what I was offering; to Shmuel

Rosner, the non-fiction editor, who helped me find my way, lit the road ahead, and helped me know where I wanted to go with this (and where not…); to Yael Yanai, who joined this journey toward its end, yet still gave of her special, unique qualities; a huge and distinct thank you to Rona Muzikant-Shtibel, who edited this book with much love, delicacy, sensitivity, and wisdom, who helped me turn the countless uncertainties and questions into clear-cut, decisive sentences; a huge thank you to the exceptionally talented Imri Zertal and Adam Guri, who managed to turn written words into art—your contribution here is immeasurable. Thank you to Adi Kafri, for the supreme effort of translating this book into English—professionally, talentedly, and with lots of patience. It's no simple task to keep my voice when using a different language, yet you doubtlessly managed to do so. I am truly appreciative of it.

And on a personal note:

This book is, by and large, a mark of the person I am. And I—similarly—am a product of all the wonderful people who surround me and are close to my heart. I hold a piece of each and every one of you; thank you for being a part of me and my life.

Thank you to my close friends—those in my personal life and in my professional sphere, and to those who fit somewhere in between. Thank you for being the people you are and the small and large gifts you give me by your simple nearness.

Thank you to Amiram Raviv, the best professional father-figure I could have ever wished for myself. Thank you for opening that door to the realms of psychological writing, and thank you for the model you give for managing to do "this, and this, and this, and that." Just like any good father, you always want the best for me, and allow me to grow.

Thank you to my mom and dad, Ruthi and Kobi Gindi, the best parents, who also happen to be the best readers, and many other "bests," too. Since this book is about parenting, it seems that you hold a part in its making—in deeper and more meaningful ways than you could ever appreciate or imagine. I have no words to truly thank you for that, and all the many other things, too.

Thank you to my wonderful children, Noam, Nitzan, Neta, and Gali. For the exceptional, marvelous, individual worlds you are, that broaden my heart, enrich my life, and cement boundless meaning into it. You inspire within me depths of love I never knew beforehand. I am so incredibly lucky to be your mother.

And one last, special thank you—to Arye, my wonderful husband, my person, and the man who forever supports, believes, encourages, and appreciates me. You know that none of this could have been possible without you. And you know that "this" attributes so many other things in my life. You are one of a kind. Simply so.

Throughout the book, numerous additional works and excerpts are mentioned:

References:

Mama's Best Boy, by Zeruya Shalev; Secure Base, by John Bowlby; Reset your Child's Brain, by Victoria L. Dunckley; The Drama of the Gifted Child by Alice Miller; The Prophet, by Gibran Kahlil Gibran; Outliers, by Malcolm Gladwell; Motivation by Daniel Pink; Payoff—The Hidden Logic that Shapes our Motivations, by Dan Ariely; The Art of Loving, by Erich Fromm; The Seven Principles for Making Marriage Work, by John Gottman; 21 Lessons for the 21st Century, by Yuval Noah Harari; Far from the Tree, by Andrew Solomon; Welcome to Holland, by Emily Perl Kingsley

Made in the USA
Monee, IL
12 November 2022

17560483R00254